Women in the Superintendency

Discarded Leadership

Joyce A. Dana
Diana M. Bourisaw

Published in partnership with the
American Association of School Administrators

Rowman & Littlefield Education
Lanham, Maryland • Toronto • Oxford
2006

Published in partnership with the
American Association of School Administrators

Published in the United States of America
by Rowman & Littlefield Education
A Division of Rowman & Littlefield Publishers, Inc.
A wholly owned subsidiary of The Rowman & Littlefield Publishing Group, Inc.
4501 Forbes Boulevard, Suite 200, Lanham, Maryland 20706
www.rowmaneducation.com

PO Box 317
Oxford
OX2 9RU, UK

British Library Cataloguing in Publication Information Available

Library of Congress Cataloging-in-Publication Data

Dana, Joyce A., 1940–
  Women in the superintendency : discarded leadership / Joyce A. Dana, Diana M.
Bourisaw.
    p. cm.
  "Published in partnership with the American Association of School Administrators."
  Includes bibliographical references.
  ISBN-13: 978-1-57886-374-7 (hardcover : alk. paper)
  ISBN-10: 1-57886-374-0 (hardcover : alk. paper)
  ISBN-13: 978-1-57886-375-4 (pbk. : alk. paper)
  ISBN-10: 1-57886-375-9 (pbk. : alk. paper)
  1. Women school superintendents—United States. 2. School management and
organization—United States. 3. Sex discrimination in education—United States. I.
Bourisaw, Diana, 1956– II. Title.
  LB2831.72.D36 2006
  371.2'011—dc22   2005023530

To Duke and Steve, who understand,
support, and cheer us on!

Kept Women

Baby girl,
childhood treated you to childish delights
that ignored difference.
Running
   Leaping
      Shouting
         Laughing
   Fighting
      Crying
         Cursing
      were gender-neutral
                     gerunds
that wound their way easily
around school yard games.
      So when was it,
         girl child,
you first discovered—
      or was it forced on you—
      that you were kept?

            . . .

Rich man, poor man, beggar-man,
   thief, doctor, lawyer, indian chief.
Was it glimpsed while your muscled
   legs tapped out to a peppered
      chant choices kept for you?

No son ever dared enter those
   entwining ropes where futures
   were decided by a faltering foot.
      Oh, no! their play toughened
them to become the prize sought
by you, while your training had
you jumping madly
            feverishly in one spot.
And your body? Was it for you that
   you let your hair grow? the bother.
   or snipped it off?
            Was it for you that

brows were plucked from
unwanted follicles and arms
and legs denied their heritage?

Woman-child, mourn.
Beat your breasts for time
wasted.
And with it all—
were you kept?

Sister, this is where the ancient chant
begins. You'll know it even
though you've never heard it.
Yes, you were kept.
kept down
kept ignorant
kept poor
kept shackled
kept naked
kept broken, kept quiet
kept sorry, kept abused
kept thwarted, kept tired
kept threatened, kept hungry
kept tainted, kept angry
kept spiteful, kept used
kept unused, kept crying
kept unconnected, kept washing
kept ironing, kept cleaning
kept cooking, kept second
kept broken, kept around

You have it now, don't you?
I know you do.
I see it in your tapping
fingers
your clever eyes—
Your clever eyes which
have kept the secret of
your misery for so long
they stare past the

sound of words at the
   burden of memories.

Oh, I know you know.
      keep it going . . .
Listen to the beat of
            words
whose cruel rhythm
   was set by the
   inspiration of your
   broken lives.
         For you were:
      kept by mothers who knew
      and wanted sons.
      kept by fathers who didn't want to know
      but knew—
      and wanted sons.
 kept for amusement
 kept for pleasure
 kept for barter
 kept for booty
   appearance   others
   submission   rejection
   convenience   spite

      Enough, you cry out,
Enough of chanting.
Stop the sounds that stir the beat
   that forces the tears to fall
in a rhythm all their own.

But it's
      too late.
The belly of your mind quivers with the sounds
      of plucked memories reverberating such
            sour tunes that haunt you.
And where are you going to hide
                  when closing your eyes
                  and holding your ears
         don't do it any more?

How are you going to shut out this chant
that's measured by the beat of your
very own heart?
Where are you going to go to hide
from so much keeping,
old woman-child?

Hush!
Here It comes again.
kept from righteousness, kept from history
kept from accusing, kept from position
kept from power, kept from speaking
kept from owning
kept from being
kept from justice
kept from respite
kept from ritual
kept from place
keep it going
kept in ignorance
kept in torment
kept in tow
kept in chains
kept in fashion
kept in need
kept in darkness

Kept til the end.

STOP.
There's where hope lies,
Dying woman-child.
Death's rattle will block
your ears
and
quiet memory.
And in the silence that surrounds your going—
its beat will sound your
freedom.

—Julia Galligan Breslin

CONTENTS

CONTENTS

CONTENTS

PREFACE

L ong ago in the Land of Make Believe, little girls and boys were taught that they could "become" anything they wanted to become if they worked hard enough and developed the essential skills. They could become doctors, lawyers, firefighters, police officers, cowboys or cowgirls, teachers, researchers, etc. If a child wanted to become a superintendent of public schools, she could. To do so would simply mean acquiring the required degrees and certifications and moving up the steps: teacher, assistant principal, principal, assistant superintendent, superintendent. This is the career path generally followed by those who become public school superintendents. The job requires great knowledge and skill, and adults will tell children, "You *can* do it!" So goes the dream.

Although there are many ways to describe the nature of the American Dream, becoming what or who you want to become is the primary descriptor. Fortunately, in the United States of America, the dream is frequently realized by individuals who develop their competencies, meet the requirements for job entry and advancement, and work hard. However, if the dream is becoming a successful public school superintendent—the CEO of a school district—it is achieved far more often by men than by women. That is, for women with this dream, the barriers and challenges are such that meeting all of the requirements, gaining competency, and demonstrating good interpersonal skill and a strong work ethic are *not all* that is needed to reach their dreams of serving as superintendents of schools. A small number of women who do acquire a public school superintendent position continue to face barriers and challenges during their work that no longer exist for men. Their gender often raises doubt about their capacity to accomplish difficult tasks and demonstrate the "right" relational skills to work with both the internal and external school district community. Gender-related challenges will continue to confound women's successes in acquiring superintendent positions.

This book presents a research- and experiential-based understanding of what the following experiences are for women: working in the "trenches" to acquire a superintendency, providing leadership as a superintendent, and being dismissed from that position as the superintendent. The narratives that illustrate chapter concepts are real; however, pseudonyms are used and some contextual details have been changed to provide confidential treatment of information collected from the experiences of the authors and their many friends, acquaintances who have been colleagues with similar dreams, and subjects of current research.

We need fully to understand the differences between women's and men's experiences in leading school districts as superintendents. We need to act on and change the lack of equity in acquiring superintendent positions and serving in school districts (and in other organization CEO positions). We *must* address these issues, acknowledging that gender prejudice and gender structuring *are* the problems, cultural problems. For a nation that values justice, we have a long way to go.

ACKNOWLEDGMENTS

Much like the birth of our daughters, we birthed this book with care, commitment, and passion for excellence, but excellence cannot be reached alone. Many joined us in our efforts. As female leaders, it is our nature to collaborate and develop products that are evidence of contributions from many. We salute Julia (Judy) G. Breslin, a woman of quality, an author and artist who shared her poetry with us so we could share it with you; Judy Dixon, a passionate editorial cartoonist who will continue to contribute her work until her last breath; D. K. Hirner, who reviewed, edited, and provided insight to womanizing our writing; Christy Checkett, who provided a mirror for us as we sharpened our voices; Alana Cooke and Rachel Schwartz, who conducted some of the research and read and critiqued our work; Cindy Tursman, our managing editor who consistently provided clear and helpful guidance; and all the women and men in our lives who have assisted us with shaping our thinking, expectations, and forthright and courageous voices that helped us speak to the rich and personal experiences combining leadership and gender.

We pay tribute to every woman, young and old and all those yet to be born. We do this for you. We are the women of yesterday, today, and tomorrow.

CHAPTER I

SOCIAL JUSTICE: 100-PLUS YEARS OF EFFORT

⌐⌐

Improvement is so minimal that working toward future opportunities seems futile.

The life span of the U.S. Constitution is remarkable, particularly for a society that has experienced and continues to experience significant differentiation and diversity among its residents. Our carefully constructed U.S. Constitution can be credited for what has resulted in the longest-existing democratic society. However, the development and implementation of policy and governance related to constitutional rights does not assure equitable freedoms, rights, and responsibilities for women. Social justice does not exist for women. The causes are rooted in cultural norms and values coupled with systemic overlays of policy and governance that are most difficult to change. What women want is equity of opportunity, equity of access, and equity of treatment; what they don't want is to be "kept women."

To more deeply understand the sense of social injustice felt by women in our culture, it is helpful to briefly consider the history of achieving voting equity; equity in workplace conditions, salary, and benefits; and the glass ceiling that prevents women's equitable access to leadership positions.

Voter Equity

Until the Nineteenth Amendment was ratified, political, social, and cultural prejudice supported the rights of only men to vote, albeit initially voter eligibility for men depended upon their status. Since the passing of the Nineteenth Amendment, there continue to be some structural problems that exist between women's right to fully participate in voting and the actuality of their voting.

It was during the latter part of the nineteenth century and into the twentieth century that strong women activists worked diligently and continuously to influence political support of women's right to vote. Their work was not easy, by any means. It called for political and cultural change. Because there was such strong resistance to supporting women's right to vote, their access to voting equity did not occur without four decades of persistent lobbying and persuasive efforts by dedicated women. They achieved their goal with the Nineteenth Amendment. Achieving the right to vote was anything but easy. The efforts of these strong women continue to guide our twenty-first-century efforts to insist that all citizens have equal rights and experience social justice in our pluralistic culture.

There are still noticeable barriers for women (and minorities) who want to vote. For example, difficulties exist for poor women living in rural areas without transportation, without access to voter registration, or without access to reaching the precinct polls on election day; difficulties exist for women working twelve-hour shifts during hours when voting is allowed by state law; women with children at home, including infants, more often than not have no one to assist with child care while they vote. Those who are poor, disenfranchised, of a minority race, or disabled are those most vulnerable to not voting.

Many stories told by women tell about restrictions on their voting opportunities. Jane Oldfield is just one example. She works in a factory and has for just over four years. She worked her way into a line supervision position and was beginning to make progress in covering the costs of housing, food, and school needs for her three children.

Jane's husband had disappeared with their only vehicle just about two years after Jane began working at the factory and just after Jane discovered that she was pregnant with their third child. Jane found herself without any resources except her own job and salary. When Jane's husband disappeared, her church accepted donations to help pay the cost of delivery and medical help for the third child.

Also, a neighbor who was a member of the church that Jane attended volunteered to care for her baby and preschool-aged child while Jane was at work. Her neighbor also was willing to care for the school-aged child when he was dismissed from school on school days and during the summer months.

Jane's work schedule was a forty-hour week divided into four workdays of ten hours in length. She felt fortunate to be earning $8 an hour; it seemed considerably higher than the $6.25 minimum wage that was then paid. Wal-Mart would not provide that amount. McDonald's required considerably more hours late in the day than she felt she could manage with three young children at home. Nonetheless, her salary produced just under $17,000 a year. Jane's budget was as follows: rent, $450 a month; utilities, $200 a month; telephone, $35 a month; groceries, $400; clothing, school supplies, health needs, dental costs, and other needs for the four family members were covered with what remained after taxes were deducted from her paycheck.

Jane walked nearly two miles to work and did not purchase much beyond the basic needs. Two of her children were asthmatic and required medication and medical care. Jane needed funds to take care of those medical needs and, she reasoned, to spend unnecessarily was to risk the welfare of her children. Consequently, when a child was quite ill on the only day Jane had to vote an absentee ballot—the Friday before Election Day—she was not able to vote. She was at work (walking to work, working ten hours, walking home) on Election Day. Jane reports that she was more fortunate than many who worked on the line under her supervision. According to Jane, "her line people's income" did not allow as much—and they were so disenfranchised that they had long since lost their interest in voting.

Of course, Jane's experience could be the same for poor men or for other women, although their circumstances may differ. Specific to Jane was that she was the caregiver for her children—and the only family income earner. An increasing number of women in our country would identify with this.

On an annual basis, those who are responsible for operating the system for all eligible citizens to exercise their voting rights should evaluate their efforts in every detail. It is critical that they review their policies and practices to identify any potential unintended (or intended) biases in the operations that might be prohibitive for some of the voting population. For example, if registration can occur only at county court offices or city offices and only during designated hours, the system is structured against many: poor women, single mothers, single fathers, those who do not receive information about voter registration or deadlines for registering or transportation to places where they can register to vote and can arrive at the polls for voting, and other potential voters—in other words, those who already are disenfranchised. Strong efforts need to be made in order to open up opportunities to vote. It is easy enough to have a well-trained person available to register folks on site at their workplaces.

Other strategies need to be pursued as well. If support strategies for those who are poor or disenfranchised in other ways are not developed, they experience a de facto denial of their voting rights. Those empowered to vote should step forward to provide support for voting to those who seem to have a number of roadblocks between them and the ballot box.

Likewise, knowing what the issues are in an election, knowing how to vote, knowing how to use the ballot correctly to match their intended vote, and knowing where and during what times voting can take place is essential for all eligible voters. Without that information being distributed effectively and successfully—meaning that the information does, indeed, reach all of the potentially qualified voters—there can be a perceived structured, systemic bias to voting. Simply completing a ballot accurately can become confounding—not only for those who are disenfranchised and do not understand the process completely but also for those who are educated and experienced with the voting process.

Those who are poor, disenfranchised, of a minority race, or disabled are those most vulnerable to denial or loss of their rights to vote. A significant number of those poor, disenfranchised, or of a minority are poor women and children. Laurinda Logan, who moved from an urban area to a farm outside a small, rural community, reported that when her neighbor took her and her children in to register the children for school, she expected to be able to register to vote, as she had done in her previous urban community when she had to change apartments. The school secretary reported that she would have to register at the county clerk's office. When she arrived at the county clerk's office and inquired about the places where she could have registered, she expressed surprise that school secretaries did not automatically register adult residents; the county clerk explained that only county personnel registered voters, and the county clerk's office was the only location. The rationale was that there will not be as many voter registration errors. The inherent bias was clear. The same county clerk had informed the school principal that people who move around a lot and who don't even know how to vote don't deserve to vote.

However, today women *do* have the right to vote and women *do* go to the ballot box to have their voices heard. They have done so for eighty-five years. It's certainly a beginning.

Workplace Equity

By 1960 the roles women and minorities filled in the workplace became recognizable and predictable; women's roles were not equitable with white men's roles. Two workplace issues were and still are (1) access to equity of conditions, salary, and benefits in the workplace and (2) access to the strongest leadership positions in organizations and in government. Regardless of the right to vote, conditions in these two areas have not changed measurably for women.

Efforts to achieve equity and social justice in the workplace existed throughout the twentieth century. In 1938, "the Fair Labor Standards Act establishe[d] minimum wage without regard to sex" (National Women's History Project, 1997–2002, 3). In 1961, President John F. Kennedy created the Committee on Equal Employment, requiring that projects financed with federal dollars "take affirmative action" to "ensure that employment practices are free of racial bias" (Brunner, 2004, 1). The Equal Pay Act was passed by Congress in 1963 promising "equitable wages for the same work, regardless of the race, color, religion, national origin or sex of the worker" (National Women's History Project, 1997–2002, 3). Then in 1964, the Civil Rights Act was signed by President Lyndon B. Johnson, and Title VII of this Act prohibited discrimination of all kinds toward race, color, religion, national origin, or sex.

The following year, on June 4, 1965, in a commencement speech, President Johnson helped establish the concept of "affirmative action" by stating, in part: "This is the next and more profound stage of the battle for civil rights. We seek not just freedom but opportunity—not just legal equity but human ability—not just equality as a right and a theory, but equality as a fact and as a result" (Brunner, 2004, 1).

For the first time, affirmative action enforcement became policy with Executive Order 11246 issued on September 24, 1965, by President Johnson. The executive order requires "government contractors to 'take affirmative action' toward prospective minority employees in all aspects of hiring and employment," and "on October 13, 1967, the order was amended to cover discrimination on the basis of gender" (Brunner, 2004, 2). The "Nixon Tapes" reveal the great hesitancy President Nixon experienced in providing support to this initiative. In fact, in his one-on-one discussions with his advisers, his discomfort was clear, as was his strong prejudice against women. With pointed pressure from his wife and daughters, President Nixon reluctantly moved forward in supporting discussion of an amendment. Regardless of how the initiative evolved, the resulting legislative and policy language could be seen as promoting equity of opportunity for women in their efforts to access a school superintendent position. The increase in the percentage of superintendencies held by women between 1970 and 1990 was 4.11 percent. However, when the increase moved from 0.55 percent to 4.66 percent of the superintendencies held by women in that twenty-year period, it was hardly remarkable.

Given the legislative and policy effort to "level the playing field" for women, has it resulted in equity of conditions, benefits, and salary for women in the workplace? The answer is a definitive "No!" and the effect of the policy and legislative efforts is visible in the examples throughout the remainder of this book.

The Glass Ceiling

For many women, experiencing equity and social justice in the workplace is simply a dream and an illusion. Glass walls and ceilings have been systematically constructed as a consequence of our cultural attitudes, behaviors, and practices. Awareness of this fact is witnessed in the passing of the 1991 Civil Rights Act, which created the Federal Glass Ceiling Commission to conduct a study and prepare recommendations concerning "(1) identifying artificial barriers blocking the advancement of minorities and women; and (2) increasing the opportunities and development experiences of women and minorities to foster advancement of women and minorities to management and decision making positions in business" (Federal Glass Ceiling Commission, 1991).

Among the findings of the commission were the following:

- Prejudice against minorities and white women is the single greatest barrier to their advancement into the executive ranks.

- Glass ceilings exclude able people of diverse backgrounds that businesses need to compete successfully from top leadership of corporations.

- Three levels of barriers do exist: societal barriers which may be outside the direct control of business, internal structural barriers, and governmental barriers.

The recognition that societal barriers may be outside the control of business is worthy of analysis. Chapter 2 discusses the relationship between prejudice and cultural norms and expectations, both of which exist not only in the nation's businesses but also in government, local cultures, subcultures, politics, and so on.

Given the social, political, and ideological movements that have occurred for the past 125 years, we have to ask, what is it about human beings in our culture that allows them to miss a deep, implicit, emotional, and intellectual understanding and value for equity for all human beings? We seem to find so many reasons for blocking equitable opportunities for achievement and acquisition of a quality life for everyone. Color, gender, religion, nationality, differing beliefs—you name it—an increasingly vocal number of citizens in the United States will speak out defending opportunity for some but will oppose that same opportunity for all. Over the one hundred years of the twentieth century, women and minorities experienced again and again the lack of opportunity—and equity, with the exception of voting rights.

U.S. citizens either have forgotten or they choose to discard the intentions for the glass-ceiling study. The Federal Glass Ceiling Commission's report notes: "During the last 15 years, virtually all of this nation's economic growth went to the wealthiest fifth of American households. The United States is now the most stratified major society in the industrial world, as incomes have fallen for the poor and stagnated for the middle class" (1995, 5). The report reminds us that the economy has undergone significant change, that education has becoming a function that divides winners from losers, and that "discrimination—the glass ceiling in particular—remains another deep line of demarcation between those who prosper and those left behind" (4–5)

The Civil Rights Act of 1991 also reversed a number of Supreme Court rulings and raised the ceiling for discrimination claim damages.

Then, in 1994, Congress adopted the Gender Equity in Education Act to "train teachers in gender equity, promote math and science learning by girls, counsel pregnant teens, and prevent sexual harassment" and the "Violence Against Women Act[, which] funds services for victims of rape and domestic violence, allowing women to seek civil rights remedies for gender-related crimes" (National Women's History Project, 1997–2002, 5).

The "glass ceiling" is an apt metaphor for the levels of leadership beyond which women have not been admitted, and it is just the beginning of the complete metaphor. Meyerson (2004) pointed out, "It's not [just] the ceiling that's holding women back; it's the whole structure of the organizations in which we work: the foundation, the beams, the walls, the very air."

Social Justice

Efforts of our strong women forebears who led the voter equity effort continue to guide our twenty-first-century efforts to insist that all citizens have equal rights and experience social justice in our pluralistic culture. Although there clearly is some progress toward equity between 1880 and 2000 in the United States, there continue to be strong cultural constraints on achieving equity and social justice for women.

Even more worrisome is that since 2000, ultraconservative, "political right" federal and state congressmen and congresswomen, with support from the ideological religious "right wing," have been amending and developing policy that limits selected practices that, until now, have provided some opportunity for increasing equity in the workplace and in society in general. For example, affirmative action policy is under attack; legislative opportunities to discontinue parts of affirmative action policy are frequent behind the closed doors of congressmen and leaders in the executive offices. It's difficult to locate anything on record from our state and national leaders that gives attention to implementing recommendations from the Glass Ceiling Act or even collecting data that identifies if there even is any movement toward meeting those recommendations.

We believe in justice. Our judicial system is founded on efforts to serve justice. However, we are quite successful as a citizenry at "talking the talk" and not successful at all at "walking the walk." In the twenty-first century, our emergent leaders should be following leadership paths that result in equity for all citizens! Doing so is essential if, indeed, we must build a stronger, more educated, more successful, economically stable social order. Over the long term, all citizens would have greater benefits—even those who hoard their wealth and who close doors to others so that their wealth can be magnified rather than contributed through taxation to the fiscal support of those in need. We are all judged by how we serve the least of us.

We do not live in a country founded upon the principles of opportunity for some but not for all, of discriminating against those who are unlike us so we can be the only determiners of what policies are adopted, what outcomes achieved. Indeed, we value a capitalistic society—but certainly not at the misfortune of others. Increasingly more frequently, citizens are asking, "Just how much wealth does a person need?" Truly, this is a new day and age for our social order.

How does all of this fit together? Voter equity, workplace equity, and the glass ceiling are all ways in which to view the efforts of women to achieve equity of opportunity and access. There is progress with voter equity, yet much remains to be done. There is limited progress with workplace equity, and again much remains to be done. The glass ceiling certainly continues to exist in nearly all major institutions, agencies, corporations, and public services. The result of the glass ceiling effect is not only women experiencing difficulty in acquiring CEO positions—a "discarding" effect on qualified and competent leaders—but also women experiencing a shorter longevity of service in CEO positions—another "discarding" effect.

So whose social justice are we talking about? Obviously the concern of the authors is justice for all. We are a society of "different folks with different strokes," yet we refuse to accept others with "differences" and refuse to live peaceably without punitive actions toward those who are different from us.

Case Study: Delayed Gratification

Elaine Swenson referred to herself as a "late bloomer" in terms of her career. She and Bill were married right after college. Bill began his career in the insurance industry, and Elaine stayed home to rear their two children. Elaine had earned a bachelor's degree in elementary education and decided she would begin her career once the children were in school full time.

When Elaine was ready to return to work, supply exceeded the demand in the elementary schools in and near her community. She decided to substitute teach in her local schools and placed her application at each elementary school. Shortly thereafter, she was called to substitute and she quickly demonstrated her ability to teach quite effectively—a nice feat for a substitute teacher who does not plan the lessons.

The following spring, Elaine was interviewed for an elementary position and was soon hired for her first teaching job. The following fall, Elaine and her two children left together "for school" each morning.

Elaine's principal quickly recognized not only her excellent teaching skills but also her seemingly innate leadership skills. He encouraged her to think about taking some time within the next few years to return to school and earn an administrative credential. She was excited about this new potential venture, but she delayed her planning of more formal study until her children had "developed some independence." When Elaine and Bill thought that the children could manage if Elaine were to enter a master's program that would prepare her to become an elementary principal, Elaine was in her late thirties. With children's activities, her teaching career, and her husband's busy career, there was little time for more than one course each fall and spring and two courses in the summer.

Consequently, Elaine completed her master's degree and her principal certification at the age of forty-two. Even in that time, however, Elaine had served as copresident of the local PTA chapter, had chaired two school district committees (teacher performance evaluation and public relations), and had influenced the consideration and adoption of the Accelerated Schools program at her school.

By the time Elaine was credentialed, her previous principal was no longer the principal at the elementary school where she taught. The new principal, Mr. Brian Stone, had been promoted from within the school. Brian had taught sixth grade at the school. In fact, he and Elaine began their administrative course work at the same time. Brian finished two years earlier than Elaine and applied for the vacancy of the retiring principal. He had been in the position for two years.

Elaine was ready to enter administration and was fully prepared for the principalship. She had completed more than ten years of teaching experience in the classroom and had earned her administrative credentials. She also had demonstrated her leadership as a teacher, chaired school committees, and actively participated in school district curriculum audits.

Elaine applied for the next several vacancies in the school district. Her credential licensed her to serve as an assistant principal and a principal in early childhood education through grade eight. She was a finalist for every position she applied for over the next three years, but she was never offered a position. Each position was offered to a man in the school district who also was credentialed but who was younger than Elaine and without the breadth of teacher leadership experiences Elaine had demonstrated.

While Elaine continued to apply for positions, she was visibly frustrated with the process and her lack of success in acquiring a position. Elaine decided to contact her now-retired former principal. After all, he was the one who encouraged her to seek administrative certification.

His comments were less than encouraging. Principalships always had been awarded to men in the school district. He had hoped that things would change by the time Elaine sought an administrative position, but they had not. Did she want him to speak to the superintendent about this? he asked.

Chapter Questions

1. What points in chapter 1 relate to Elaine's experience?

2. Should Elaine have pursued her interests differently?

3. What would you advise Elaine to do at this point and what would be your rationale?

4. Based on the limited information in the case study, how would you describe the culture in Elaine's school district?

5. Do you think that it would help Elaine if her former principal spoke with the superintendent of schools? Why or why not?

6. Summarize the key problems in this case study.

CHALLENGES FACED BY
WOMEN SUPERINTENDENTS

"This community doesn't want a woman superintendent!"

—M. W., board member, 1997

E ducational professionals who are or have been public school superintendents will confirm that there are barriers to accessing and
entering the position of school superintendent and, for women,
they are likely to be ever present. They also will confirm that the superintendent's job is very complex and continuously requires facing and addressing ever-present challenges. Successful superintendents effectively
meet whatever challenges occur. The voices of current or former women
school superintendents confirm what a number of research studies in the
past two decades have found: being female increases the difficulty of successfully overcoming barriers and of successfully meeting challenges
(Shakeshaft, 1989; Grogan, 1996; Blount, 1998; Brunner, 1999a).

Similar observations are made by women who begin their journey to acquire other school or school district leadership positions, including school
principal, assistant principal, or school district assistant, associate, or deputy
superintendent. Similar challenges have been faced by women who sought
leadership positions in highly varied and differentially structured organizations that provide public service throughout all parts of the United States.
Regardless of structure, location, or discipline, the common factor is gender.

It is the gender factor for women—gender prejudice, gender
structuring—that influences what the national profile is for women in
the school superintendency and that motivates the writers to address the

following questions. What are the barriers that are difficult for women to overcome? What are the challenges that aspiring and practicing women leaders face in school district leadership? How can barriers be removed and challenges be diminished? Why is "discarded" appropriate for the title of this book? What are the lessons learned and what can be done? Answers to these questions will unfold throughout the following chapters.

Gender

Gender is the inherent and ever-present barrier. Whether it is extending efforts to acquire quality preparation, gain experience, enter into administration, move up the hierarchy, or serve as a school superintendent, the barrier for women *is* gender. The research on women's leadership of school districts during the past two decades provides testimony to the male-dominated profession and to the differential treatment of women who occupy the CEO's chair in a school district. In U.S. public schools, women are the teacher workforce; men occupy nearly all leadership positions.

Regardless of the efforts of women, legislative and statutory developments, governmental or institutional acts and affirmative action, the increase in the representation of women at the CEO level in schools continues to be minimal. Jackie Blount (1998) provides the following data reporting the number of women in local school district superintendencies and the total number of local school district superintendencies by state and regions in the United States for the years 1910, 1930, 1950, 1970, and 1990. Table 2.1 converts Blount's numbers into percentages of women in local school district superintendencies in each state during each time period.

Table 2.1. Percent of Local Superintendents in the United States Who Are Women.

Region	State	1910	1930	1950	1970	1990
Northern	Connecticut	0.0	2.9	2.0	0.0	7.9
	Delaware	0.0	0.0	0.0	0.0	0.0
	D.C.	0.0	0.0	0.0	0.0	40.0
	Maine	8.8	4.8	1.8	0.8	0.0
	Maryland	n/a	0.0	0.0	0.0	4.2
	Massachusetts	1.6	0.8	1.7	1.3	7.7
	New Hampshire	0.0	0.0	0.0	0.0	3.3

	New Jersey	0.0	1.3	0.0	0.3	4.5
	New York	1.1	5.1	3.3	0.4	4.7
	Pennsylvania	1.0	0.4	0.0	0.7	6.4
	Rhode Island	2.6	0.0	6.3	0.0	6.1
	Vermont	4.9	11.8	2.9	8.5	3.7
Southern	Alabama	14.2	7.1	2.7	0.0	7.3
	Arkansas	1.2	3.2	2.1	0.6	2.4
	Florida	0.0	5.0	4.2	0.0	9.0
	Georgia	2.5	1.1	3.1	0.0	6.3
	Kentucky	0.0	2.0	6.1	3.6	2.9
	Louisiana	n/a	0.0	0.0	0.0	4.7
	Mississippi	6.3	0.0	3.6	1.4	2.6
	North Carolina	1.2	0.0	0.9	0.0	4.3
	South Carolina	0.8	0.0	1.9	0.0	9.4
	Tennessee	0.0	2.8	2.5	2.3	6.3
	Virginia	4.8	0.0	1.8	2.9	2.3
	West Virginia	5.2	3.1	0.0	n/a	7.7
Midwestern	Illinois	2.2	3.9	0.7	0.6	2.1
	Indiana	2.3	0.6	0.6	0.0	2.1
	Iowa	0.0	1.6	1.1	1.1	3.3
	Kansas	2.4	1.9	2.7	0.6	1.7
	Michigan	0.0	0.9	1.3	0.2	1.7
	Minnesota	1.5	0.0	0.0	0.2	3.2
	Missouri	2.1	1.0	0.0	0.0	2.2
	Nebraska	18.6	2.4	1.2	2.1	2.0
	North Dakota	0.0	0.0	0.0	1.5	0.9
	Ohio	0.3	0.6	0.9	0.3	5.2
	South Dakota	0.0	1.7	0.0	1.0	0.0
	Wisconsin	1.5	2.1	0.7	1.0	2.9
Western	Alaska	n/a	n/a	n/a	0.0	11.5
	Arizona	26.7	0.0	0.0	0.0	9.2
	California	0.0	3.2	3.1	0.6	8.8
	Colorado	4.7	1.5	3.0	1.7	2.3
	Hawaii	n/a	n/a	n/a	0.0	28.6
	Idaho	0.0	0.0	3.4	1.0	1.9
	Montana	3.5	0.0	3.0	0.0	5.9
	Nevada	28.6	8.3	0.0	n/a	0.0
	New Mexico	0.0	0.0	4.3	0.0	8.0
	Oklahoma	1.4	0.9	0.9	1.2	2.0
	Oregon	22.4	0.0	1.6	0.0	4.6
	Texas	5.1	0.7	0.7	0.5	2.7
	Utah	0.0	0.0	5.4	0.0	0.0
	Washington	10.1	0.6	0.0	0.0	4.7
	Wyoming	17.9	2.4	2.3	0.0	4.3
Total Percentages		9.83	0.96	1.64	0.55	4.66

Excerpted and adapted from Blount (1998), 185–196.
The number of women computed as a percent of the total superintendencies during a given year at the local level did not include those superintendents whose names were not clearly feminine.

Blount (1998) notes: "Women have not enjoyed easy access to the local district superintendency. . . . In 1910, women served in 327 out of 5,284 local school districts. By 1970, women superintended only 73 out of 10,431 local districts, producing a steady decline in representation from 6.19 percent to only .70 percent" (183).

Women also have not enjoyed easy access to the school principalship. Lunenburg and Ornstein (2004) reported, "At present, women constitute 72 percent of the nation's teachers and 43 percent of the principals" (637).

Lynch (1990) noted, "It is an interesting commentary on the American workforce that in education, one of the few professions where women have historically dominated the numbers, women are outnumbered by men four to one at the administrative level" (2). The ratio is smaller for women in the CEO position in public schools. Shakeshaft (1989) reports that 3 percent of the nation's superintendents in 1984–1985 were women (20). Just over ten years later, Shakeshaft (2000) reported even more specific data regarding the disproportionate representation of gender in the educational workforce: 52 percent of the elementary principals were women and 83 percent of the elementary teachers were women; 26 percent of the secondary principals were women while 54 percent of the secondary teachers were women; and 12 percent of the superintendents were women while 65 percent of the school districts' employee workforce were women.

The barrier is even more prohibitive for African American women. Their barriers are both ethnicity *and* gender. Table 2.2 reports the number

Table 2.2. Number of Women Superintendents and African American Women Superintendents Based on Research Studies.

Year	# Districts	# Women Superintendents	Percent*	# Black Women Superintendents
1910	5,254	329	6.26	n/a
1970	10,380	71	0.28	3
1982	13,715	241	—	11 (Arnez)
1983	n/a	n/a	—	15 (Ebony)
1985	16,000	—	—	29 (Revere)
1989	11,007+	284	6.00	14 (Bell and Chase)
1991	10,683+	424	5.60	19 (Bell and Chase)
1993	14,000~	800	7.10	32 (Jackson)
1995	14,000~	800	7.10	45 (Alston)
1996	14,000~	800	7.10	33 (Jackson)

* Percent of all superintendents
+ Bell and Chase (1993) used only K–12 districts in their studies
~ Approximate figures from AASA
Source: Brunner (1999b), 146.

of superintendencies in the United States at designated years, the percent of women in a superintendent position, and the number of those women who are African Americans. The total number of superintendent positions is an estimated number provided to Brunner (1999b) by the American Association of School Administrators.

Women employed as school leaders are primarily serving as elementary school principals and curriculum and instruction assistants or coordinators. Although the data since 1950 show some slight growth in the number of women serving across the positions in school and school district leadership, the overall profile for women superintendents during the past century reports very little growth (Blount, 1998; Shakeshaft, 2000).

Sexism

Sexism supports gender barriers and pervades the various cultures within the United States. Sexism is recognizable in the attitudes and behaviors developed from sex-role expectations within different cultures and subcultures and in the ensuing stereotypes that develop into descriptors of and expectations for the behaviors of men and women are one result of sexism. Sexism is a barrier for women who aspire to become CEOs of school districts because people respond to women on the basis of sex-role stereotypes. Social and organizational policy does not seem to prevent sexism, use of sex-role stereotypes, or gender discrimination from occurring regularly. The review of literature completed by Lips (2003) found:

> Modern sexism is manifested in underlying negative attitudes about women and in resentment of and lack of support for social policies aimed at reducing gender inequalities. Scales measuring such subtle forms of sexism ask respondents to indicate their level of agreement with items such as "Women shouldn't push themselves where they are not wanted" (Tougas, Brown, Beaton & Joly, 1995) and "It is rare to see women treated in a sexist manner on television" (Swim, Aikin, Hall, & Hunter, 1995). In general, North American studies using these scales show that men hold more of these attitudes than women do, and that modern sexism is associated with negative attitudes toward women, feminists, and affirmative action and a lower tendency to define a situation as sexual harassment. (23)

Measures of predispositions, such as the above scales, provide insightful inferential data that create a portrait of the extent to which sexism exists for women.

One of the many consequences of sexism for women is that "women more than men must walk a tightrope of conflicting expectations" (Bolman and Deal, 2003, 347). For example, leaders are expected to build power and use it, but women should not be powerful. Leaders are expected to be authoritarians; women are expected to nurture others. Leaders are expected to aggressively pursue interests that improve the education of children, but women are criticized if they are aggressive in their pursuit. Models of leadership frequently employed by men develop skills to establish "power over" others; women work differently, establishing "power with" others (Brunner, 2000b).

Cultural expectations, norms, and mental models condition the development, education, and interaction of children as they grow into adulthood. That conditioning, then, is reinforced throughout adulthood in the form of sexism and sexist practices. Fairy tales portray women as witches or as extremely naïve and unknowing. Powerful women are associated with evil in literary classics. Archetypes persist throughout cultures providing associations and descriptions for women that are less than desirable for the gender (Estes, 1992). Historically, for the most part, women have been denied freedom of choice and men have made the cultural, social, economic, and legal choices. Western cultural expectations for boys and girls, men and women are prejudiced on behalf of male leaders. Gender structuring is designed and controlled by those who have tightly conditioned prejudices—many of those prejudices are evidenced in the leadership of those who have been superintendents of schools and their predominantly male school board governance team.

Research conducted by Dore Butler and Florence Geis (1990) illustrates one visible result of sexism—gender prejudice regarding leadership. Butler and Geis conducted a research project involving a leadership simulation with men and women as participants.

The simulation involved women and men who had received training and a leadership script. The prepared men and women were assigned the responsibility of participating in a mixed-gendered group activity, demonstrating leadership by following directions specified for leaders in the script. The goal was that the rest of the group members would follow or agree with the ideas and suggestions of the women and men who had experienced some brief training. Findings included group members reacting with disapproval toward the women and approval toward the men. Body language toward the men and women "leaders" differed considerably; women "leaders" experienced frowns and nonverbal communication associated with discomfort, possibly rejection, of what the women "leaders" said. Men "leaders" experienced more favorable body language from the group in response to their use of the same script. The findings jibe with the statements made by women who describe their experiences with participating in decision making, presenting ideas, and making suggestions around an administrative council table. The body language is referred to as "loud," and there is clearly a differentiated response to the gender of the participants.

The twenty-first century continues to witness and experience sexism and discriminatory practices toward women. One example is the lack of adequate representation of women in U.S. military key positions. Women are denied positions on the battlefront, and women experience a "glass ceiling" effect in their efforts to move into CEO positions in the military. As it is for the superintendent of schools, so it is for top-level positions in the military—the scarcity of women in those leadership positions is notable. Representation of congresswomen in state and federal legislatures also is minimal. The small minority of congresswomen in both the Senate and House of Representatives leaves congressmen in the driver's seat when making the key decisions regarding women's issues.

In 2000, the 107th Congress was served by seventy-five women. Sixty (13.6 percent) of 440 representatives were women in the U.S. House of Representatives; two women (0.45 percent) served the House of Representatives as delegates. In the U.S. Senate, thirteen (13 percent) of one hundred senators were women. In 2005, the 109th Congress was served by eighty-three women. Sixty-five (15.8 percent) of 440 representatives were women; three women (0.68 percent) served the House of Representatives as delegates, and one (0.23 percent) served at large. In the U.S. Senate, fourteen (14 percent) of the one hundred senators were women (Office of the Clerk, 2005; U.S. Senate, 2005). It is likely that state legislatures have similar gender demographics. Women do take strong interest in their issues and do work diligently to influence objective policy treatment. They are quick to recognize and resist gender-structured systems being established in ways that will negatively affect their own and other women's lives.

Internationally, the systems in which women exist are considerably more closed than they are in the United States. In fact, policies in many countries place women in subhuman conditions. Afghanistan provides a startling example. By supporting the rule of the Taliban to the tune of billions of dollars, the U.S. male president and congressmen contributed to one of the most punitive and increasingly inhumane international policies regarding the women in Afghanistan's culture. Under Taliban rule, women in Afghanistan were expected to be completely covered when they left their homes to worship or shop for household needs. They were denied education, punished for meeting a member of the opposite sex without having a family member present, given designated times when they could be outside of their homes, and so on. Even in Saudi Arabia, a country with similar Arab roots and with ties to leadership in the United States, many women are not permitted to drive cars (Lips, 2003). Policy can quickly become punitive without equity of representation at the decision-making tables of policy and practice. And it does not just occur outside the United States; it occurs within our country.

Both nationally and internationally, powerful people fail to take powerful steps to move those without power into decision-making positions. Only when women have equitable roles and responsibilities in policy decision making will they have a meaningful voice regarding their own destinies.

Most women educators understand that the road to economic independence and away from welfare dependency begins with education—education coupled with health care, social development, and emotional development. It is this understanding and drive to improve the future for all children that strongly interests women in becoming major decision makers and acquiring leadership positions where they can make a difference for children. Women who have strong interests in leadership are well aware of the demographics that currently exist for women and children. For example, the U.S. Census Bureau reported that the percentage of Americans living in poverty increased from 12.1 percent of the population in 2002 to 12.5 percent in 2003, and to 12.7 percent in 2004. In excess of thirty-six million people lived in poverty by the end of 2004 (Public Agenda, 2004). There is purpose to taking on policy issues, including those that result in a prejudicial overlay of systemic structures for the education of children that prevent equity of results.

Discrimination

Gender structuring, sex-role stereotypes, sociocultural conditioning, religious and political ideologies, and power and control issues contribute to gender discrimination. Gender structuring and sex-role stereotypes are analyzed in the following pages of this chapter. Sociocultural conditioning and ideologies are presented in chapter 3, and issues relating to power and control are addressed in chapter 4.

Gender Structuring

Gender structuring is evident in commonly accepted cultural practices involving sex-role conditioning, extent of access to opportunity for socialization to leadership in organizations, and practices employed in the preparation, mentoring, recruitment, and selection of women for school and school district leadership positions. Legal efforts to achieve equity can be witnessed in some major legislation during the twentieth century. With the passing of the Civil Rights Act of 1964 and Title VII and Title IX of 1972, minorities and women gained employment rights and equal opportunity rights in the workplace and in other organizational operations. The Women's Educational Equity Act of 1974 provided federal funds to support dismantling of sex-based inequities in a number of areas, including education.

Affirmative action is a phrase first used by President Lyndon B. Johnson to assert that civil rights laws alone were not enough to "remedy discrimination." Regulations followed, diligently guiding organizational and institutional movements toward equity for minority races and women. Administration of the equal employment opportunity regulations was carefully watched by womanist standard-bearers, minorities, and those seeking employment. One of the more visible changes was the addition of women's sports at most colleges, universities, and public schools. Equity in the sports world meant, in part, that women had an opportunity to participate in the same number of sports as did men. One superintendent, Dr. Martin, stated,

> I'm convinced that the affirmative action regulations that were guiding public school decisions are the reasons for the major successes women's teams have had over the past two decades. Conferences, divisions, even the Olympics have experienced some remarkable women athletes competing at amazingly high and difficult levels.

While women were gaining equal footing in the field of athletics, women aspiring to acquire and work successfully in public school superintendencies experienced troubling times, despite more than three decades of civil rights, equal employment opportunity, and affirmative action regulation. As one of many examples, in 1997, Louis Walter, a school board member, explained to the school district's woman superintendent, Dr. Devonshire, that her "challenges are going to be constant because the community does not want a woman superintendent." When Dr. Devonshire explained to Mr. Walter that what he had just said represented discrimination based on gender, which was illegal at both the state and federal levels, Mr. Walter responded, "Well, I'm trying to help you understand. I just thought you'd want to know." This exchange illustrates what Skrla (2000b) stated: "The U.S. public school superintendency is understood to be a man's role, and women who inhabit this role will necessarily have difficulties caused by their femaleness" (293).

Beginning in the late 1970s, legal decisions from state supreme courts and the U.S. Supreme Court began to clarify and/or impose limitations to affirmative action. Two cases clarified that use of inflexible quotas was not acceptable (*Regents of the University of California v. Bakke*, June 28, 1978; *City of Richmond v. Croson*, January 23, 1989). On November 3, 1997, a state ban on all forms of affirmative action (Proposition 209) was passed in California. In February 2000, the Florida legislature approved Governor Jeb Bush's "On Florida" initiative, which aimed at ending affirmative action in the state. On June 23, 2003, the U.S. Supreme Court upheld the University of Michigan Law School's policy, making clear that race can be one of many factors considered when selecting students for entry into the program; however, the point system that was the formula used to rank students for selection purposes was found to be unacceptable and needed to be modified (National Women's History Project, 1997–2002).

President George W. Bush and the Republican Congress continue to place policies on the legislative agenda that have the effect of dismantling affirmative action. Affirmative action policies remain vulnerable to being weakened, "watered down," or eliminated by near-future U.S. Congress members.

Active sex-role stereotypes become barriers to equity because they reinforce discriminatory practices (Bolman and Deal, 2003). One of the most traditional sex-role stereotypes is the woman as family and home caregiver. Because women are the childbearers, they also are expected to be the primary family caregivers, which traditionally has meant that women stay home to rear the children, fix the meals, maintain the house and all family operations, and, since they are at home, take care of secretarial, organizational, and social duties for the family. Men are expected to be the financial providers for their families. Although some of that cultural expectation has weakened over the past three decades in the United States, the expectation still is culturally strong. Along with these two persistent expectations come a host of related sex-role expectations that are potent stereotypes when women have interest in working and in moving into leadership positions, particularly CEOs in the workforce.

At the same time, women's caregiving responsibilities for maintaining family life and rearing children becomes problematic if the men in the marriages do not share the responsibilities of caregivers. It is particularly problematic if women with children aspire to enter increasingly powerful professions and increasingly powerful leadership positions, which require additional training, longer hours, and more responsibility.

Women are viewed by men supervisors as employees who frequently leave work to tend to children when they are ill, frequently arrive at work late because of an emergency or semi-emergency with one or more children, frequently need to leave school right after classes are over because their children will be arriving home from school, and so forth. Most women can resolve these problems, work in challenging and complex positions, have necessary emergency provisions arranged for children, and provide high-quality time with children. However, some strong, sex-role stereotypes come from the experiences of women whose spouses do not share responsibility for caregiving. Stereotypes also become well developed around perceived behaviors of single women who have no options that include another caregiver for children.

Lunenburg and Ornstein (2004) explain another troubling aspect of equity issues for women school administrators:

> Several studies have suggested that there are career differences between male and female school administrators. Women have more years of teaching experience than men (fifteen years versus five years) and are older when appointed to administrative positions (median age forty for women, thirty-two for men). . . . Discrimination continues to plague women, not only in terms of salary but also in terms of access into administrative positions and sexual harassment once they make their way into the administrative hierarchy. (637)

The caregiving responsibilities are culturally supported, and because women and men are conditioned to believe that women have the caregiving responsibilities, their ability to enter administrative or leadership work is delayed until the children in the family can take care of themselves. The reason that this is considered a lack of equity is that the delay of entry to school leadership means that there will be less time to work "up the ladder" to the superintendency and less time to serve as a school superintendent. Kamler and Shakeshaft (1999) quote a "well-established regional consultant" from a search firm who raised the following issue:

> Many of the females had been teaching fifteen, twenty, twenty-five years, so they were very experienced teachers—senior-type persons. At fifty-five or sixty, they're out looking for a superintendency when the males were retiring at fifty-five, and so it was difficult for them to get jobs. The board's looking [to replace] somebody who is retiring at fifty-five and the women who were applying for the job were fifty-eight and had never been a superintendent. Board members were saying, "Well, wait a minute." (57)

Sex roles are powerful discriminators, and they are established, taught, and reinforced within a culture. That is not to say that those expected sex roles have no implicit value. They do. The very traditional sex role of caregiving homemaker who is at home for the children and who spends her time on the duties of providing excellent care for and teaching the children has great value. Likewise, serving as the family "social secretary" has value. The equity issue is that allowing these and other sex-role stereotypes to influence decisions for employing women is discriminatory. When women and their families can develop a plan of action so that the women in the families can pursue a job or a profession, there should not be an opinion or judgment made by screeners or employers that women do not "belong" in the workplace or in a specific position or that men are more qualified by virtue of their gender to perform organizational leadership responsibilities effectively.

Sex-role stereotyping is evident when the interview questions posed to a woman candidate about a position include those about spouse, children, or family role of applicant. At times women candidates for leadership positions as school superintendents will be asked if their spouses will be moving to the school district with them. What the employing agent should want to learn about is the knowledge, competencies, disposition, and performance that the woman candidate can bring to the position. Decisions on employment should be based on those qualities, thereby removing the vulnerability of the employment agent to charges of discrimination.

Another factor that establishes a structure for covert or implicit discrimination is the dominance of men in school leadership and in the key decision-making roles. Their dominance provides fairly open opportunity for the development of systemic overlays and gender structuring of policies and processes that become barriers for women who want to enter school leadership. Recruitment and selection practices, advancement opportunities, power in making decisions, and other norms and expectations of the school district can be—and frequently are—covertly discriminatory (Lunenburg and Ornstein, 2004). Because people are accustomed to seeing men as school superintendents, they tend to prefer what they are accustomed to seeing.

Sex-role stereotypes, which are learned from the culture and subcultures, have existed for generations and are accepted and used by many for a number of purposes. Certainly one of those purposes is intentional discrimination for power and control. As men in leadership positions influence the structural development and operations of organizations and institutions, they often establish a number of structural overlays that prevent the entry or promotion of women within the organizations or institutions. Bolman and Deal (2003) note that stereotypes associate leadership with maleness, women more than men must walk a tightrope of conflicting expectations, women encounter discrimination, and women pay a higher price (347). It now is commonly understood that there are some special problems that women face that confound their aspirations and work. Women usually must be better than their male competitors to be considered for administrative appointment. For years it has been customary to see an intermittent bumper sticker or window sticker or sign that reads, "Women leaders have to be smarter and work wiser than men; fortunately that's not difficult." Renditions of this saying can be found in places where people gather to dine or socialize and even in truck stops.

Aggressiveness usually is viewed as a negative trait in women. The term is strictly accepted and understood where educated men of some stature demonstrate aggressive behavior to get what they want for their organization. Such is not true for women. Even in some contexts, assertiveness on the part of women conflicts with what women are hoping to achieve. Women frequently do not receive salary, title, and status to match their responsibilities. A look at census data reporting wages earned over a period of fifty years clearly illustrates the lower pay women receive for the same job. Women usually are not expected to compete for top-level jobs and are often conditioned to not even think about going after a CEO position, and consequently, some women do not demonstrate willingness to pursue that dream. Other women have conflicting experiences with the culture overlaying its expectations and sex-role stereotypes on them and attempt to dismiss the cultural overlay and pursue their CEO dream. Sex-role stereotypes and the nature of organizational structures have contributed heavily to controlling the gains in the numbers of women superintendents in this country.

Not only are the roles of wife and mother sex-role stereotypes that become overtly or covertly discriminatory in women's attempts to access leadership positions, but there are also other stereotypes that emerge from the culture and that have become customary. For example, on income tax forms, the "taxpayer" is listed on the first line and "spouse" is listed on the second line. The unspoken implication is that the "taxpayer" is the husband, who has a higher income than does his wife, the "spouse." Even when the wife/spouse has a higher income, it is the practice of accountants to place the husband's name and income on the first line and the wife's name and income on the "spouse" line—because it is customary (translate: cultural norm).

Jeanette Randall, a retired public school superintendent, told about her experience with banks. When she was a high school teacher, she and her husband, Sam, needed to purchase a car. An affordable car was located, and Jeanette made an appointment with the bank loan officer. At her appointment, she explained that she and her spouse wanted to purchase a car to replace her family's old and beginning-to-be-unreliable car. There was no question about the loan. The form was provided, and the bank officer indicated that the loan would be approved after all of the required paperwork was submitted. Jeannette listed only herself as the loan recipient and provided all data about her salary and the value of the family's assets. Her spouse was a full-time student and was not employed. When the loan officer explained that she would need to place her husband's name on the loan and acquire his signature, she stated that her spouse fully approved of what she was doing and that he would not be the person making loan payments. Nonetheless, Jeanette had to drive home and wait for her spouse to arrive home from classes so she could acquire his signature—and on the first line! She was demeaned, angry, and justified!

Superintendent Lois Graves reported her experience with her bank. When she was employed as superintendent of schools, she and her husband shopped for and purchased a home and established two bank accounts (hers and his, placing both names on each account), and her husband opened a computer consultant business. Each monthly bank statement for each account arrived addressed to Joseph Graves and Lois Graves. Because Joseph Graves was the first name on each account, whoever collected and opened the mail first would open both reports. After several months of this, Lois telephoned the bank and requested that her name be listed first and her husband's name second on the account with the number that she used. The clerk informed Lois that it is customary for the husband's name to be listed first because the computer system automatically places all items in the proper account number under the husband's name. That was the way it was going to be printed on all paperwork. Lois again requested that on the account she used the names be reversed. The clerk replied, "I'll have to check with my supervisor to see if that can be done." Irritated by then, Lois said, "Don't bother doing that. Just transfer me to Mr. Brendt" (the bank president). When Mr. Brendt answered the telephone, he listened, and then he said, "We can do that, Lois. I'm glad you called." Changes can be made to these kinds of practices now, but because of "custom," both husband and wife usually have to request that the names be reversed. This is built-in gender structuring that influences the categorizing of citizens and that comes from decades-old cultural practices. It becomes ingrained in the fabric of organizational and institutional operations throughout the culture and within the context of communities.

When descriptors surface for men and women, the result reflects another clear, gender-structuring effect. For example, women are considered to be primarily emotional. Men are considered to be rational. Women are considered to be "soft" leaders; men are considered to be "strong" leaders. Women gossip; men talk. Women suggest; men direct. Women nurture; men conquer. Women who exercise their authority are seen as micromanagers; men are seen as strong leaders. Internalization of these descriptors can result in gender structuring that feeds into decision making in educational leadership and puts women at a distinct disadvantage. Research conducted by Skrla (2000b) noted the following:

> In the same way that U.S. society has constructed the superintendency as male, it has created a package of norms about femininity and female behaviour. Bardwick and Douvan (1971: 147) described that package as consisting of "dependence, passivity, fragility, low pain tolerance, nonaggression, noncompetitiveness, inner orientation, interpersonal orientation, empathy, sensitivity, nurturance, subjectivity, yieldingness, receptivity, inability to risk emotional liability, and supportiveness." These same societal norms for femininity were more succinctly summarized by Tavris (1992: 20): "Females [are] the repository of nature, intuition, and weakness." (297)

Research completed by Lips (2003) brings together evidence of the effects of sex-role stereotypes. She identifies the following descriptors from the research: "Competent women may be viewed as unfeminine (Lips, 2000; Lott, 1985)"; "women who have a no-nonsense, autocratic, directive leadership style are judged more harshly than men with a similar style (Eagly, Makhijani, & Klonsky, 1992)"; "when women *do* exercise authority or behave in competent or directive ways, they may receive negative evaluations because they have violated the feminine stereotype (Lips, 2000; Lott, 1985)"; "women who promote their own competence are judged less likable than men who do the same (Rudman, 1998)"; "women who act in such highly assertive, confident, or competent ways sometimes find that their ability to influence others, particularly males, is reduced (Carli, 2001)"; "in many work environments, women are viewed with less respect than their male co-workers (Reskin, 1998; Zafarullah, 2000)" (22–23). Brunner's research (2000b) supports Lips's findings.

Biases toward women also include a few descriptors that relate directly to the structuring of the public school superintendent. Superintendents must work directly with boards of education, the "trustees" or "directors" of the school district. School board members are not appointed by the superintendent; instead, they are elected by the community's registered voters or appointed by a mayor. A majority of the board members have been men (Hess, 2002), and the board members usually represent the culture and subcultures' ideologies, values, and politics of the communities from which they come.

Developing strong, interpersonal relations with board members such as the CEO is fraught with challenges for both men and women, but the gender challenge for women tends to bring some discomfort to how school board members talk with the superintendent and vice versa. Dr. Roberta Reams described her board (all male) as being accustomed to telling jokes and, sometimes, "dirty" stories. She said that when board members were casually together at places like their retreats, study session "recesses," or state board training for board members, they would tell the latest jokes and preface them with "No offense, Dr. Reams" or "Pardon me, Dr. Reams" or "Roberta, I shouldn't be telling this joke in front of you." She would respond, "Tell a clean story." The board members would laugh and then the joke-/storyteller would tell the story. Dr. Reams finally requested that they not tell jokes that involved gender, disability, or making the disadvantaged the "butt" of the joke and explained that she was offended by that. From then on, their behavior toward her was reserved. Additionally, they would arrive at a meeting that she attended with them and the first one to the door opened it and all men waited until she passed through the door first. Customary.

The sex-role stereotype of women being unable to properly balance their checkbooks surfaces subtly and insidiously at times when women school district CEOs are leading discussions about major or potentially controversial financial and budgeting decisions. Often because of the stereotypes, women are operating in a "Catch 22" as a school district CEO. They are expected to fit some of the stereotypical context (nurturer, listener, kind, considerate) so others can "predict" their "womanly" behavior; yet when they behave stereotypically, they are not viewed as having the strength, financial knowledge, and competencies that men have.

A startling story was told by a woman superintendent in Missouri. During a board meeting when the public had an opportunity to address the school board, a local minister came forward and said that he had a suggestion to make that he thought would help the school board in getting the next bond referendum passed. He complemented Dr. Arlen, the current woman superintendent, claiming that she was "one of the strongest and best educational leaders he knew," and he went on to say, "What the schools need is a man to be the superintendent with Dr. Arlen serving as the educational leader so that there can be some credibility in the financial operations of the schools." He earnestly placed that proposal before the school board. Of course, Dr. Arlen was incensed. The school board members said nothing, which bothered her immensely, particularly since they each knew that through Dr. Arlen's individual efforts alone, the school district revenue had increased by approximately one million dollars each year. This was a relatively small, rural school district with a budget of approximately $13,000,000.

Quality Preparation

Gender structuring, identified earlier in this text, plays a role in determining whether or not women have access to quality preparation for the job. The lack of mobility and role of wife and mother continue to be bigger barriers for women than for men: "Women often lack equal access to training programs, and discussions of bureaucracy frequently overlook the interdependence of job and family responsibilities, treating work as public and masculine and family as private and feminine" (Hoy and Miskel, 2005, 96).

Certainly, accessing a quality higher education preparatory program for educational leadership can be achieved if a woman lives in the proximity of an institution that offers the needed preparatory program in educational leadership, if she can organize her life so that multiple demands upon her time can be managed, and if she has the support (emotional/physical/fiscal) from significant others (parents, spouse) in her family. As one of the women in a current doctoral program in educational leadership said, "As I was driving to the university this afternoon [approximately a one and one-half hour drive one way], I seriously thought about dropping out of class. Doing well in a doctoral-level class is hard enough, but when you have two preschool children as I do and a full-time elementary principal job, it's nearly impossible. And it's *so* expensive!"

Good job performance in professional positions does not come easy. It begins with an individual's drive, positive attitude, desire to learn and practice, hard work, and persistence. It also requires full development of a strong background of knowledge, skills, competencies, and dispositions and diligent work on establishing good interpersonal relationships and other performance factors that will help the individual provide successful leadership.

A quality preparatory program individualizes the development of each student, meaning that in a quality program, each student has unique strengths that are developed more extensively and applied to performance tasks in a clinical manner. A quality preparatory program also assures frequent encounters with diversity and with diverse perspectives. The future professional school district leader is reliant on the quality of the educational preparatory program. For women in educational leadership, opportunities to practice what is taught—a clinical approach—is very important, simply because women's leadership is different from men's leadership. There needs to be ample opportunity to study what is working for men *and* for women who are school leaders. Furthermore, it means learning how to use one's strengths to advantage in developing effective and successful leadership for public schools.

Access to a quality preservice educational program is essential. To be a quality program, the program must include the following: well-designed syllabi containing intellectually challenging issues and materials; curricula that provide current, practitioner-oriented learning; and alignment with state and national standards. Additionally, a quality preparatory program offers substantive fieldwork at school or school district sites. It further demands course work that requires the graduate student to apply theory to practice and textbooks and other materials that are supported by good research and are general-neutral rather than gender-structured (Skrla, 2000b).

There is an abundance of insightful research on effective leadership in general and school and school district leadership in particular. However, the majority of the research emanates from male-dominated leadership in organizations and male-dominated studies. The CEOs for public school districts are almost entirely men (Glass, 2000).

Learning about leadership from textbooks and the study of research in leadership programs does not fully prepare women for what effective leadership is for women CEOs—a gender-structured disadvantage. Without the incorporation of the research regarding women CEOs in public schools, the preparatory program is "gender-structured"—and intentionally so.

Professors in colleges and universities determine the selection of textbooks and materials, and interestingly enough, educational leadership programs in higher education are delivered predominantly by men. Bjork (2000a) reports: "Books on the superintendency published during the 1990–2000 period were surveyed. Of the 19 books released during the past decade, 8 were classified as textbooks and all but 1 were authored or coauthored by men" (6).

Many leadership books have published findings and illustrations about school superintendents. However, the norms represented in the books do not reflect the different career paths followed and the different experiences that women have when they enter administration and move to the position of school superintendent. Because women—and persons of color—do not recognize themselves in the books that are used in graduate preparatory programs that prepare school leaders, the transition into leadership is more difficult than it is for white men.

There are a few, solid, scholarly texts on the market now that present the research and analysis around women's leadership—either at the school, the school district, or CEO level. The texts are supported by research on women superintendents and school principals; however, those texts are rarely selected for reading, discussion, and study for either the master's or doctoral programs in educational leadership. What is studied is leadership knowledge, disposition, and performance in school districts from a male perspective, since most superintendencies are filled predominantly by men. The message to women who are studying school and school district leadership in graduate school is: "This is what men do to succeed. If you will learn and practice this, behave the way that men who want to be successful behave, you might succeed in the leadership position—if you can acquire it."

Becoming a high-quality leader at the CEO level in public schools requires extensive knowledge, skill development, disposition development, performance, insight—and a license awarded by the state, indicating that the educational program has been completed successfully as have all other requirements identified by the state. Educational preparatory programs should be designed to provide graduate students in the program an opportunity to develop themselves in ways that not only help them qualify for a license as a school principal or school district superintendent but also have the essential skills to provide leadership effectively and successfully. The preparatory programs that offer this differentiation are structured so that students must demonstrate in their own performance the knowledge, skill, and disposition required to be successful school and school district leaders. That means the program must be strongly participatory and clinical. Additionally, that educational program must provide effective mentoring and oversight to be sure the student develops a functional toolbox of knowledge and skills and a strong value for diversity and service to all students. The toolbox is constructed by first identifying each student's strengths and growth needs and, from there, structuring the opportunities to grow class by class. Coaching behavior development is also useful. Not all preservice preparatory programs meet these needs.

Ph.D. and Ed.D. programs in educational leadership are accredited based on their ability to meet Standards for School Leaders (Interstate School Leaders Licensure Consortium, 1996). To remain accredited, preparatory programs must have evidence of their students' knowledge, disposition, and performance in meeting those standards, including their value for and use of practices that include diversity in meaningful ways. Also, to be and to remain accredited, graduate programs must offer course work that states require for graduates of the program to be certificated to work in school leadership positions and school district leadership positions.

Preparatory programs routinely provide research "mentors" at the graduate level to guide the development of dissertations, but they seldom offer mentoring services outside of program advisement by designated faculty. Formalized postgraduate mentoring is virtually nonexistent. Male principals and superintendents often conduct mentoring experiences on the golf course. Because they become "golf buddies," they find mentoring an easily accessible practice. Women are excluded from those experiences and generally do not have women CEOs available to them for mentoring. Being excluded is discriminatory; not having women CEOs as mentors is misfortune. Mentoring is probably one of the most important aspects of socialization and may be particularly relevant in helping women move into higher levels of school leadership (Dunlap and Schmuck, 1995).

Access to Leadership Positions

Another factor that becomes a barrier for women is gaining the necessary experience at entry levels of leadership in public schools and then moving up the hierarchy into school district leadership. Gaining experience is sometimes difficult for men as well, but it's particularly tough for women. Issues for women are career path, location of job, nature of the job, lack of mobility, interviewing and selection, and gender-structured systems.

Brunner, Grogan, and Prince (2003b) discuss the data collected and reported by Glass, Bjork, and Brunner in *Contrasting Years of Teaching Service: Women, Men, Full Sample* and *Persons of Color* (2000). In their early findings they note:

After examining the disaggregated data by ethnicity and gender, it can be seen that some of the responses from the full sample of superintendents are significantly different than the responses of women and persons of color. The responses from the full sample shape the discourse to include at least two strong messages for aspiring superintendents. First, if one wishes to be a superintendent, one must identify aspirations early and move into administration with the first five years of teaching. Second, if one plans to be a superintendent, one should have more administrative experience than teaching experience. Both of these messages generate discourse that does not support access for women or persons of color to the superintendent, because most often they do not follow what is considered the *normative* or *natural* path. (8)

The candidates for superintendent are most often those who follow a common career path. That path involves five to six years of teaching, assistant principal, principal, assistant superintendent, and superintendent. Leadership positions (director, coordinator, etc.) may exist between the school principal position and assistant superintendent position, particularly in a large school district. And, of course, the career path can be abbreviated—principal, assistant superintendent, superintendent—and sometimes can be an alternative path. Commonly, though, the path is a five-step process.

Location of opportunities and lack of mobility pose dilemmas for women seeking admission to school leadership. If mobility is a problem, the opportunities are fewer and become increasingly more important to the applicant. In a school district with approximately 4,000 students, there will be only six or seven assistant principal positions in the school district. Only when elementary schools are large, generally around 500 students, will there be an assistant principal position at the elementary level. Unless there is frequent turnover in those positions, the opportunities are quite limited for those who lack mobility. Men do not experience lack of mobility to the extent that women do. It is rare for a man to say that he cannot move to work at a better-paying job. Married women, on the other hand, experience lack of mobility as a product of their marriage and their spouse's job and their desire to keep the family together. Commuter marriages have become more common for women whose children are reared and who wish to pursue their professional opportunities (Harris, Lowery, and Arnold, 2002).

The nature of the job at the entry level, the assistant principalship, also is problematic for women. Even when women have strong teacher leadership, have chaired task forces and committees for their schools, have served on districtwide councils, have solid reputations as effective and successful educators, and have secured the necessary credentials, acquiring an assistant principal position remains challenging. Increasingly, school principals interview, select, and recommend the candidate for assistant principal. Periodically, observers note that the employment recommendation is made without evidence of a "competent and qualified" candidate; the "chemistry" that passes between the candidate and the interviewing principal will influence the appointment, as will previously established friendships.

Typically, at high schools and middle schools, one or more of the assistant principals will be assigned student discipline as his or her primary assignment. More men serve as assistant principals than do women. Male principals tend to prefer placing a man rather than a woman in a position where handling student discipline is the primary job assignment. Of course, that provides a predominantly male job pool for promotion from assistant principal to principal and provides men assistant principals with leadership experience at the entry level and denies women equity of entry and access.

Superintendent Alice Ford tells her story of acquiring a high school principal position in a school district new to her. She had served as an assistant high school principal for four years in another state, moved with her spouse to help establish his business in a new state, drove 400 miles round trip each week to complete her Ph.D. at a state university, and then applied at age forty-three for the principal position. She was interviewed and called later by the superintendent to be informed that she was the candidate that he would be recommending to the school board to be appointed as the high school principal. A date was made for her to arrive at a school board meeting for introduction to the public after the board took action on her contract. She was encouraged by the superintendent to bring her husband, if she would like to do so. Believing that it was good public relations to be present, Alice and her husband arrived while the superintendent and school board were in executive session prior to the public school board meeting. Shortly, the superintendent came to the door of the room where the public meeting would be held, beckoned Alice to the door, and explained that the school board wanted to interview her. It was not a "done deal," after all. Alice agreed, entered for the interview, and answered three questions: (1) How do you feel about athletics? (2) How will you discipline a 235-pound football player who initiates a fight with another student? and (3) Will your husband be living in the school district with you? Alice reported that her inclinations were to announce the discriminatory nature of the questions, but she agreed to answer the questions. Evidently, her responses were acceptable because she was hired. At that time, she was one of approximately twenty-five (of 600-plus) high school principals who were women in the state. She also added, "To fairly represent the school board, I must add that two years later, this very same school board approved my appointment as superintendent of schools."

Entering the superintendency also requires some experience that is related to the work of a public school superintendent. In fact, a strong majority of superintendent vacancy notices in *Education Week* state that superintendent experience is required or preferred. Even now, as higher education preparatory programs in educational leadership become more practitioner-oriented, advertisements in the *Chronicle of Higher Education* advertise college and university faculty vacancies in educational leadership preparatory programs with a requirement of experience as a school superintendent. To have access to the public school superintendency, a candidate generally needs to have worked in the central office as an instructional, human resources, or financial resources leader; otherwise, mid- to large-sized school districts will seldom consider the appointment of an otherwise qualified woman to the CEO position for the school district. Lack of adequate experience will be the rationale. Sometimes, the reason is worded as "missing some of the required competencies." The specific reference will be to having never developed a budget or negotiated the resolution to a strike or led the community through establishing and accomplishing a vision, mission, and objectives for school improvement.

Consequently, many women begin their CEO experience in small, rural school districts where there is no other central office leader to meet all of the responsibilities of a public school superintendent, and where applications for the position as school district superintendent are small in number. Eakle (1995) noted, "Research on women currently employed as superintendents found they are usually 'from rural areas and small towns that have allowed them to build power bases and overcome stereotypes'" (17). Growe and Montgomery (2002) found, "Proportionately more women tend to occupy superintendencies in the smallest and least cosmopolitan districts, with the fewest central office administrators, declining student enrollments, more reported stress on the job, less satisfaction, and the greatest vulnerability lethal to school board conflict" (2).

Although women are the majority gender now entering preparatory programs, there still is very limited growth in the numbers of women in school district superintendent positions (Bjork, 2000a). Keller (1999) confirms that

> women now make up around half the ranks from which the vast majority of superintendents are drawn: central-office administrators and principals, according to the "Invisible CEO" report from Superintendents Prepared, a group formed nine years ago in Washington to help create a larger and more diverse pool of superintendents. (1)

Keep in mind that images, expectations, and qualifications for school superintendents are developed from the experiences of men: "Superintendents usually have less than ten years of classroom service and almost half of them have less than five years of service" (Brunner, Grogan, and Prince, 2003b, 7). Women teach ten years longer than men before entering administration and are vying for superintendencies when they are considerably older than men.

Also, more men are elected or appointed to school board positions than are women (Hess, 2002). Glass (2000) reports,

> Women superintendents perceive some restrictive forces working against them being hired by boards. Nearly 82 percent of women superintendents in the AASA study indicated school board members do not see them as strong managers and 76 percent felt school boards did not view them as capable of handling district finances. . . . Sixty-one percent felt that a glass ceiling existed in school management, which lessened their chances of being selected. . . . Interestingly, about 43 percent of the male superintendents agreed that school boards tend to view women as incapable of managing a school district. (5–6)

Superintendent search firms, along with the boards of education with whom they work, serve as the gatekeepers to many superintendent positions.

When superintendent search firms commence their work, there appears to be an implicit structuring of the "kind" of candidates they will recruit. Tallerico (2000) reports that a search consultant for twenty-six years described the "best" superintendency candidate as:

> My model is [a man who] was a teacher for 3 to 5 years. . . . Many [others] of them teach too long. When you teach 10, 15, 20 years, you get socialized into the norms of teaching. Now, in my book, administrators *are* teachers. But teach 5 to 8 years, then move on. . . . Now if you've taught for 15 years and haven't even gotten into a principalship yet, or some other central office position, when you finally get to that superintendency position, you're 50 years old. (73–74)

The challenges are numerous and, at times, overwhelming. However, knowing and recognizing gender structuring and discrimination, refusing to fit sex-role stereotypes that are degrading or that prevent access to a superintendency, and continuing to develop understanding and competency in leadership will arm a woman leader well.

Case Study: She May Be Smart, But Can She Balance a Budget?

Dr. Billie Vallo had been superintendent in the Lone Elk School District for two years. Lone Elk was a small, suburban school district. The school district was going through economic changes, and it was becoming increasingly difficult to attract businesses to the community.

When Dr. Billie Vallo arrived, school district finances were strong, with fund balances exceeding 40 percent. Dr. Vallo's predecessor, Dr. Howard Sweeney, received accolades for his financial expertise. He ran the school district like a strong father runs the home—with an iron fist. Dr. Sweeney kept tight control on school district funds and nearly all expenditures were approved by him, as well as officially by the school board. State revenue was strong during Dr. Sweeney's tenure, and large school district fund balances were not uncommon throughout the region. Billie Vallo had strong financial skills as well. During the past two years, state revenue experienced a serious decline, but Billie developed a budget that provided adequate instructional resources, maintained school district facilities, and provided a minimal raise for hardworking school district employees. The school board, employees, and community seemed satisfied with Dr. Vallo's budgetary expertise, and all was well in the school district.

Soon things began to change for the worse. The school district was home to a large automobile manufacturing plant that provided employment for a significant number of school district patrons and that provided a large part of the tax base. Automobile sales were in decline, and the company had already shut down one shift. Another shift was in danger of closing. The company was seeking tax relief from the state and local government, and current tax payments from the company were behind schedule.

Billie Vallo needed to revise the school district budget to address current and future revenue reductions. Employee salaries and benefits constituted 85 percent of the operational budget, so her recommendations included freezing employee salaries. Additionally, she recommended deferring facility maintenance projects. The school board received these recommendations and reacted unfavorably. "We can't freeze our employees' salaries," argued the school board vice president. "We have an excellent staff. A lot of their spouses work at the plant, and some are already laid off. We can't treat our folks the same way the plant treats their employees."

Later that evening and behind closed doors, school board members chastised the superintendent for making these recommendations in the first place and making them publicly, which they considered "opening a can of worms" that they wouldn't be able to survive. Billie was told to "find the money" to pay the staff, several of whom were married to school board members. They said that Dr. Sweeney had done well with the finances and asked why she couldn't. "Who pays the bills at home, your husband?" a veteran school board member asked. Perhaps, they said, they should have hired someone who could better manage the money. Billie knew that meant they should have hired a man instead of her.

Dr. Vallo left the meeting filled with anger and doubts, specifically angry about the school board's blatant display of sexism and some doubt about her ability to accomplish the task the school board had given her. Would Dr. Sweeney's recommendations have been under question? Would the next set of recommendations be questioned? Would the school board second-guess all future budgetary recommendations?

Chapter Questions

1. What are the specific issues facing Dr. Vallo and the school board?

2. Describe the culture of the school board.

3. What have you learned from chapter 2 that would apply to this case?

4. How has this situation affected Dr. Vallo's credibility?

5. If you had been Dr. Vallo, what would you have done differently?

6. What is Dr. Vallo's future with this school board?

7. If you were Dr. Vallo, what would you do now?

CHAPTER 3
SOCIOCULTURAL, POLITICAL, AND RELIGIOUS IDEOLOGIES

"From early childhood on, boys and girls play with different sets of rules."

—Gail Evans (2000)

Leaders at all levels of public service are faced with ideological challenges, which have become more pronounced, more absolutely expressed by ideologues, and increasingly controversial. Public organizations, institutions, agencies, and legislatures often find themselves embroiled in controversy that is rooted in ideological differences within a culture, and their leaders have become targets for removal if their positions differ from those of ideologues. Ideological controversies have touched public schools and their leaders more frequently in the past three decades. It is anticipated by school leaders that controversies will develop around selection of school library books, curriculum content, and textbook selection because those are areas where community members have commonly created issues for public schools. School reform to improve the educational performance of students has introduced considerable controversy for school leaders and for classroom teachers. When cultural norms and values are touched by decisions made by schools, the potential for controversy exists. For example, if the CEO of a school district has not set up processes for gaining consensus for school improvement, school reform efforts can be the context leading to the leader's replacement. Overt and covert negative influences and campaigns in school communities, like those in the United States, have become routine and they do create damage—even when they make statements that are not true and establish inaccurate contexts. People

41

believe what they want to believe—accurate or not—and will make decisions to support the dismissal of a CEO. It will be helpful to the potential or actual CEO to know how to recognize ideologies at work.

An ideology is:

> 1. the body of doctrine, myth, belief, etc. that guides an individual, social movement, institution, class, or large group. 2. such a body of doctrine, myth, etc. with reference to some political and social plan such as fascism, along with the devices for putting it into operation. 3. *Philos.* A. the study of the nature and origin of ideas. B. a system that derives ideas exclusively from sensation. 4. theorizing of a visionary or impractical nature. (*Webster's New Universal Unabridged Dictionary,* 1996, 950)

The basic doctrine on which ideologies are constructed may not be readily apparent, but positions that ideologues take will reveal the general nature of their doctrine. For example, given the fact that citizens are taxed for purposes of supporting the operation of public schools, some people believe that if the law requires taxes to be collected to fund public schooling for children, the funds should be distributed to all schools that teach children, public and private. Others believe that funding all schools would be a violation of constitutional language regarding the separation of church and state. Some people believe that those who have children in any kind of school should provide full support of that schooling and those who do not have children attending a formalized school should not have to be taxed to support the existence of public schools.

The three ideological areas that have had a strong effect on schools and women aspiring to acquire or to maintain school and school district leadership positions are sociocultural, political, and religious.

Sociocultural Ideology

The culture of a school district can make or break a woman's successful superintendency. Both social and cultural ideologies are being discussed together; where there is a culture, there are accompanying sociological expectations (fundamental laws or strong expectations of social behaviors) that emanate from well-formed and reinforced characteristics of the culture. For example, social and cultural ideologies promote teaching children how to behave. Social and cultural ideologies promote specific lifestyles.

Social and cultural ideologies promote accepted ways of establishing and maintaining relationships.

Because "culture" is often used so broadly, a definition is helpful. Its primary characteristic is "certain things in groups are shared or held in common" (Schein, 1992, 8). The plethora of research that addresses studies of culture does so within defined categories, and Schein (1992) provides an overview of those categories, which are: (1) observed behavioral regularities when people interact; (2) group norms, (3) espoused values; (4) formal philosophy; (5) rules of the game; (6) climate; (7) embedded skills; (8) habits of thinking, mental models, and/or linguistic paradigms; (9) shared meanings; and (10) "root metaphors" or integrating symbols (8–10).

Developing skill in recognizing the sociocultural ideologies at work in school communities is helpful to school leaders. School district leadership can be planned and implemented within the context of those ideologies, and a school district leader can expect greater success in leading if she acquires essential information. The following provide examples within each cultural category to assist the reader with differentiating how each category might be observed within a school community's culture or subcultures.

Observed Behavioral Regularities

Behavioral regularities when people interact can be observed in the routine nature of the conversation in beauty parlors, barbershops, and local coffee shops or cafés. Factual reports, rumors, and hearsay "of the day" surface at those locations and can provide very good insight into the attitudes, behaviors, language, and traditions that exist and that are valued in the culture.

Observing the behavior of citizens toward new residents in a small, somewhat isolated community gave a woman superintendent helpful insight into the culture. Long-time residents made a strong effort at being hospitable toward new residents, and new residents would respond by returning the hospitality. Over time, local residents would encourage the newcomers to invest in their new community—acquire debt through land purchases (land was inexpensive), acquire a business (cattle herd, failing hardware store), or purchase good, used equipment at higher costs than the value in that area but lesser costs than where the new residents previously lived. The local residents would finance purchases. Then, over time, the no longer "new" residents would learn that what had been purchased was not helping to increase their financial stability and assets; instead, it was a liability. In this community, it was common to take advantage of new residents and that behavior was accepted by the culture. Some new residents made good investments; most did not—and moved soon, selling the same property for less than its purchase price. One female superintendent commented, "After three years, when my husband and I knew it was time to move on, we were grateful that we had only rented a home when we arrived in this community."

Recognizing Group Norms

Recognizing what the group norms are also is essential. It can be expected that there may be some bias against employing a woman for high school principal when the history of the position has been entirely male. However, for Jan Smithers, who had served several years as a very successful teacher in a large high school and had just completed her doctorate, applying for the high school principal position in the small school district community where she and her husband recently had moved did not seem daunting. She had received her license from the state to serve as a secondary principal. Her family had opened a business practice in the community and thought that they were successful in stabilizing good relationships and "fitting in" to the community. She applied for the open high school principal position. After the closing date, she hoped to have an invitation to interview.

Several weeks later, Jan telephoned the superintendent's office and asked about the interviews. When she was informed that the interviews had ended, she inquired about the qualifications of those interviewed. The superintendent's secretary told her that she would have to check with the superintendent who would get back with her. Within a couple of hours, the superintendent telephoned and set up an appointment the next day for an interview. When Jan arrived, four school board members were present, along with the superintendent. She knew all of them.

The superintendent began the interview with, "I'm sure you all know Max's wife. She submitted an application for the high school principal position and is here to tell us about her interest today." From then on, Jan felt like she conducted the interview. There were no structured questions from any of the interviewers and no specific interests expressed about hearing from her about her background of professional experience, and she led the interview. She was not hired. The "norm" was to have men in the superintendent and high school principal positions.

The first evidence of the customary socialization of women in that community that became personally and professionally meaningful to Jan surfaced two days later when she was playing tennis on Saturday morning at the tennis courts with seven local women in the community. The banker's wife said, "We were shocked and then really excited to learn that you had applied for the high school principal opening, and we were really cheering for you. The report we received was that hospitality was properly extended to you and that you had to conduct the interview! Darn! Wish they would have hired you!" The spouses of the community's men leaders had accepted their status as "spouse" and had no ambition beyond that status. They were successful as wives of local community leaders, and they were comfortable within the established culture.

To the credit of these women, they became campaign "managers"— that's what they called themselves—for Jan Smithers when she filed for a school board position and her name was placed on the ballot. Jan won one of the school board seats in a landslide. A comment at the local café was that every woman in the county must have turned out to vote for this new woman school board member. Shortly thereafter, the school superintendent resigned. Additionally, over fifteen years have passed now and a woman still does not hold any employed administrative position in the school district.

Identifying Espoused Values

Espoused values of a community can be identified from the following case. Sandra Lefton had been employed as a new superintendent in a community not far from the city where she had worked previously. As she waited for her home to be constructed (she was asked to live in the community where she was employed), she commuted to work. One Sunday after early church services, she drove to her office in the neighboring community to get some paperwork from her desk. At 10:45 A.M. the streets were empty. At first, she felt an eeriness about being the only car on the road. Then, as she passed several churches and noticed that large numbers of vehicles were parked around the churches and filling the parking lots, it occurred to her that she was witnessing one of the primary espoused values of this community—their churches and faith. It was apparent that she would need to transfer church membership soon and that she would need to move quickly to establish agreement with the local ministerial council to meet with her on a regular basis. It would be important to establish a collaborative discussion on a regular basis with the folks who were talking with the citizenry every Sunday morning.

Formal Philosophy

School board policies reflect the underlying philosophies of the school district—provided the policies are, indeed, followed. Sometimes the policies are "on record" to meet legal requirements but not enforced. Reading school board policies and studying the school district budgets will be steps that provide insight to the formal philosophies at work in the school district community. For example, how are textbooks to be selected, who makes decisions about curriculum, to what extent may the community use its school facilities, and what decisions will be made at what level of school district governance? There are many other questions, and sometimes what is not stated in policy is as informative as what is stated in policy. Policy represents what the school board has read and approved, and the budget represents the priorities of the district; both provide insight into the community's philosophy. It is always wise to discuss school board policy with the school board. The members will be able to offer explanations of the extent to which the policies should be enforced. They might also be able to describe any history of the school district that is wrapped around one or more of the school board policies.

Dr. Lorraine Torante tells of an issue that arose, representing a contradiction between policy and approved practice. A contingent of parents made an appointment with her to discuss use of school facilities. At their meeting, Lorraine provided copies of all school board policies that related to public use of school facilities. Shortly what she learned was that from the parents' perspectives, school teachers were being allowed priority in scheduling the elementary gymnasiums in the evening and on weekends for their community youth teams' basketball practice, leaving very little time for teams not coached or administered by school district teachers to use school facilities. The parents' request was that the use be equitable or that some formula be developed so that they could have equity of access, based on the language of school board policy.

Lorraine began the discussion at the administrative team table. She provided a brief summary of the parents' interest and asked for discussion of how to resolve this issue successfully. The principals asked that they have an opportunity to review the schedules and report back the next week. The intent was to determine the validity of the parents' observations.

At the administrative team meeting the following week, the data clearly supported parents' observations. The high school and middle school gymnasiums were fully scheduled during all of the approved pre-, during, and postseason times for student athletics. Elementary gymnasiums served the needs of elementary students and were available for community "teams" to schedule for games and practices whenever the gymnasiums were not needed for school activities. High school principals brought the sports schedule for the current school year, and it reflected no available time except the last two weeks in May and first two weeks in June. The elementary principals also brought their schedules, plus the rationale they used for scheduling first those teams coached by employees. Dr. Torante asked that the principals pull together those employees who had a stake in this decision (teachers who were coaching or administering community teams, employees who coached, and some representatives from the parent group), use the guided questions that the administrative team would develop shortly, and conduct a discussion about how to establish equity of usage. Then the administrative team went to work on the questions.

Following one month of work on this issue, the result was the development of a draft plan for equity of usage to present to the school board—and the anger of two teachers toward the administration. One teacher was married to a school board member, and the other was married to a community business leader. Both coached youth teams and were usually first in line for reserving all practices in one or the other of the gymnasiums. Formal policies do guide groups' actions, yet there are times when implementation of the policy or implementation of policy change—for example, school board policy and the issue of equity of usage—can make enemies out of friends.

Identifying the "Rules of the Game"

Learning the "rules of the game" very early in one's leadership experience is critical. Dr. Deanne Judet tells of her efforts as a superintendent to recognize employees. When Teacher of the Year nomination forms came across her desk during her first year, she sent an e-mail to school board members inquiring of their interest in participating in nominating a Teacher of the Year candidate from the school district and she initiated a discussion with school principals about participation. She believed that celebrating the successes of others was good practice and a way to highlight for the community the excellent performance and achievement of one or more teachers each year.

The all-male principal group was reticent about moving forward and encouraging participation. The school board was encouraging and thanked Deanne for "grabbing" this opportunity. Deanne spoke with her teacher advisory council and was informed, "*All* teachers should be recognized as teachers of the year because of their hard work and contribution to the learning and development of our children." The teacher advisory council was opposed to recognizing one teacher a year. The decision, however, had already been put into movement.

At the next school board meeting, board members asked that the administration move forward in nominating a Teacher of the Year. A Teacher of the Year was nominated, recognized locally, and then recognized as a finalist at the state level—a wonderful recognition for the school district that was featured on the front page of the local newspaper and in major papers throughout the state.

The "rules of the game," however, had been violated, and this activity garnered increasing hostility among the teaching workforce over the next several years until the activity finally was dropped. Teachers began to complain about Dr. Judet's leadership, which they alleged "favored some" instead of "all." The image could not be overcome. It surfaced every time there was a problem and became the proverbial albatross around Dr. Judet's leadership, affecting to a certain extent each of the decisions regarding teachers in the future and certainly affecting her status with the teachers. This was the hard way to learn what the rules of the game were and the negative consequences for violating them.

Women are omitted from many of the rituals established between and among school administrators: Friday night poker games, Saturday afternoon golf games, traveling together to a ball game in another community, and so forth. Many "rituals" are developed through casual conversations at the poker tables and on the golf courses, which are the times when the "men" are together to maintain relationships and bonds. In fact, these are the kinds of activities that are routinely part of men's interaction with other men and that socialize novices for what they will need to think about and do as a school superintendent.

Climate

Climate is the feeling that is conveyed when you enter a business, school, office, or home. It is determined by the appearance and the way in which members interact with each other, with their clients, and even with outsiders (Schein, 1992). A middle school in Missouri has its large "Welcome All Learners" banner hanging from the entryway on the outside of the school. Entering into the school convinces students and others that they are welcome here, that their teachers look forward to being with them, that they are the "best and brightest," and that any needs that they have can be met at school. Positive thinking posters are everywhere. "You can do it!" slogans are also posted everywhere, along with signs that announce, "We believe in our students!" The entryway to the school, as well as other open areas, has comfortable chairs grouped throughout around tables with magazines, homework postings, and "activities of the day" postings. Teachers often are around the school entry at the beginning and ending of the school day to offer cheerful and encouraging words to students.

A neighboring school district has a middle school with signs posted on the entry doors announcing the hours the school is open on school days, where all visitors should report before going into the school's hallways and classrooms, that permission must be acquired prior to going beyond the entry hall, and, in bold letters, "No Weapons Are Allowed." Entering the school and walking briefly through part of the entry hall to the principal's office provides an overview of clean and shining hallways, no seating places for students or others, empty halls, no posters, the presence of a security officer, and a quiet and orderly school.

The culture's climate is easily recognized in each school. Principal and superintendent candidates always should request a tour of the schools, central office, and other school district facilities in order to pick up some of the details about the cultural climate present in the schools. Sociocultural values are visible on the walls, on the bulletin boards, and in the atmosphere established for children, teachers, and guests. However, a school's climate may not "tell all" that should be known about the community's cultural characteristics.

One of the women superintendents, who had been interviewed regarding the position from which she was dismissed (Dana, 2005), told about the newspaper editor who created continual difficulty for her in developing relationships in the new community. She was in her position for three years prior to being dismissed. When she arrived, the owner and editor of the local newspaper announced in headlines the "First Woman Superintendent" and printed an overview of the professional experience of "Mrs. Ehrman" (she had earned a Ph.D. a number of years previously). Within a week, two anonymous letters were published criticizing the school board for paying "the woman" a higher salary than the previous superintendent (a male). Dr. Erlene Ehrman immediately telephoned the editor and invited him to lunch, which she maneuvered into a monthly lunch. During the lunches, the newspaper editor called her "Doctor" to her face (never using her name) and he was pleasant enough. He had very little to say, however. Articles published in the newspaper referred to Erlene as either Ehrman or Mrs. Ehrman and letters to the editor regarding "Mrs." Ehrman continued to be published anonymously, finding one fault or another with the school leadership. The editor certainly established an unfriendly climate for Dr. Ehrman using the "voice" of the newspaper and fostered the same among members of the community. "The woman" simply was not the right gender.

Embedded Skills

Every community has residents whose skills are embedded in their existence and work, and regardless of their position, profession, or vocation, these skills are recognized and valued by other members of the community. The school board member who asked Dr. Helen Halloway in her interview if she would attend athletic events was always dressed in overalls and T-shirts. He did not appear to be the financial wizard he was, but the entire community knew that he owned thousands of acres of farmland and was worth several million. That was not easy for Dr. Halloway to discover. Only when this board member chaired a finance committee did she realize his insight and skill. It was fortunate that Dr. Halloway also was somewhat of a financial wizard, or she would not have lasted more than a couple of years in this superintendency.

Mental Models and Shared Meanings

When working with a school board to establish a foundation for the schools and serving the educational interests of the community, Superintendent Susan Radkin and school board members had identified families that had lived in the community for generations and some of the stronger leaders in those families whose leadership was rooted in the community. Dr. Radkin brought them together to help design, plan, and develop by-laws for the foundation. Using family legends and combining them in a way that created a foundation obviously supportive of community families and education provided evidence of the value of local longtime families in the community. Identifying the mental models of the community and operationalizing them in creating a leadership team to develop the foundation was a coup for Dr. Radkin.

There are shared ways of thinking—common mental models—that guide the perceptions and language used by group members. These ways are taught to children as they are reared within families and cultures. Because women are not usually observed in the more powerful leadership positions, cultures generally will not consider options of electing or appointing a woman to a position that has always been filled by men. When roles are clearly established and perceptions of family include dividing family responsibilities, change in that efficient and effective arrangement will be uncomfortable and likely objectionable for community members.

Even within cultural categories, there are shared ways of thinking about gender that reflect differences. Deborah Tannen (1990) presents considerable research of the difference in language use and meaning between men and women. One of the behavioral regularities within the American culture is women's "soft" language. This behavior becomes a stereotype for women and one of the main characteristics expected in the talk between men and women. Tannen says:

> Many frictions arise [between men and women] because boys and girls grow up in what is essentially different cultures, so talk between women and men is cross cultural. (18)
>
> If women speak and hear a language of connection and intimacy, while men speak and hear a language of status and independence, then communication between men and women can be like cross-cultural communication, prey to a clash of conversation styles. (42)

One of the many reasons why public and interpersonal relations are essential is that they allow for interactions to be acceptable and, often, supportive. The time together is what is needed for developing "shared meanings" and understandings. Of course, high-quality thinking involves always being ready to question one's own thinking and meaning regarding a statement, issue, or judgment. Nonetheless, shared meanings can become powerful, particularly in times of change when people do not want to lose any of what they have. Their interest is in greater personal gain, a typical and normal self-interest. The value for self-interest is shared among folks in a culture when someone with different cultural meanings suggests change. Women are more comfortable in their leadership if they share power "with" others rather than having power "over" something. However, if shared meanings of power are the latter, the culture will have difficulty perceiving the woman superintendent as having any power.

Root Metaphors

"Good Schools," "100% American," "Home grown; home owned" are slogans rich with meaning that have become "root metaphors" or symbols integrated within the culture. School athletic teams are known by their mascots. Plaques on school walls symbolize the value and support of community citizens and school personnel who have achieved.

Working within a culture without recognizing its traits and behaviors is akin to walking on land mines—particularly when some elements in the culture may be quite sensitive or "ready to explode." For example, if a woman superintendent has come from a family who believed in the American Dream and had always treated children equitably, regardless of gender, she may need to be careful about operating on an assumption that a community will value equity. People will verbalize their support of and commitment to equity, "talking the talk," but they often do not "walk the walk."

When women apply for a superintendent's position, they must be careful to do the homework about the school district and its community that will be helpful in determining their "fit" within the culture. To fail that task is to invite dismissal within a few years—or sooner.

Political Ideology

Recognizing the kind(s) of political culture in the school district community is essential to the success of any public school district superintendent. The American school superintendent was in a highly political position during the latter part of the twentieth century and continues to be there in the twenty-first century. One of the fastest ways to find yourself "at odds with" your community is to create a political faux pas. It's all too easy to do, which makes knowledge of the political culture you will be serving even more important. It's predictable that beginning issues for women superintendents will have to do with community politics, school board relations, ways of communicating, and learning to balance work and personal needs. Veteran women superintendents would agree that these characteristics actually continue to be important for women.

To initiate an understanding of political culture, it is helpful to know how experts have defined it. Fowler (2004) names and defines three dominant political cultures in the United States: traditionalistic, moralistic, and individualistic. The traditionalistic political culture is recognized by its "ambivalence toward the market and unrestrained commercial enterprise" (95, 97). The underlying belief system is political leadership should be provided by the elite and maintaining the established order must prevail. Although government is seen as a positive force, it must support the status quo. Political parties and political ideology are unimportant. Typically, traditionalist areas have a one-party system and major issues are decided within that party. Kinship, social connections, and personal relationships are very important. Politicians are expected to have and to maintain a broad and deep network of personal relationships.

A moralistic political culture believes that politics should be "a public activity centered on some notion of the public good" (Fowler, 2004, 97). People favor an activist government that initiates new programs when necessary and believe that participation in politics should be widespread. Fowler notes that the New England town meeting is typical of this kind of culture. Ideas and issues are very important and constituents debate them with great intensity: "Government and civil systems are viewed positively because both encourage the fair and impartial implementation of government policies" (97). Historically, the moralistic political culture has been the source of most of the "clean government reforms" in U.S. society. Fowler points out, "Sometimes, however, members of the moralistic political culture become overly rigid in their beliefs or veer toward fanaticism" (98).

An individualistic political culture (Fowler, 2004) understands politics as a type of operation in which utilitarian—primarily economic—purposes are served. The culture opposes intervention in private affairs such as business, family, and churches and believes any intervention should be kept to a minimum. The culture understands that individuals enter politics in order to advance—just like any other business. Consequently, politics is based on an exchange of favors and mutual obligations. Issues, ideas, and ideology are not as important as tradition. Loyalty and strict respect for the system of mutual obligation are primary values. At best, politics in this culture operates in a smooth, efficient, and businesslike manner; at its worst, it becomes corrupt.

Added to the above political analysis, leadership texts often identify four kinds of community power structures: dominated, factional, pluralistic, and inert. It behooves a school superintendent to be able to accurately identify the community structure within which she will be working. A dominated community power structure exists when decisions are made—either formally or informally and either overtly or covertly—by a few individuals who control or strongly influence policy decisions for the community, regardless of the nature of the decision to be made. A factional community power structure will have a number of groups, all of which have equal influence and which compete for control over policy decisions. Power is challenged at nearly every point by one interest group or another in a pluralistic community power structure, creating controversies within the external school community and often within the school district workforce. Inert power refers to community power structures that support the status quo and that may be latent, surfacing when something challenges the status quo.

Bjork, Bell, and Gurley (2002) point out that a superintendent's role differs depending on the nature of the community power structure. The schematic that they present states the superintendent's role as follows: In response to a dominated community power structure, the superintendent "identifies with and takes cues from dominant group; perceives her/his role as implementer rather than developer of board policies" (32). In response to a factional community power structure, the superintendent "works with [the] majority. When the majority changes, [the] superintendent must realign . . . assumes middle course on controversial issues, careful not to alienate minority factions, as majority may shift in the future" (32). In response to a pluralistic community power structure, the superintendent "acts as a statesperson giving professional advice based on research and experience . . . offers professional opinions, proposes alternatives in open, objective fashion" (32). Finally, in response to inert community power structures, the superintendent "initiates action, provides leadership for effectiveness . . . [and the] school board 'rubber stamps' proposals. Superintendent is constrained by the community values that emphasize status quo" (32). Failure to fully understand the nature of the community power structure and to behave in ways that allow leadership that will be acceptable is to risk disaster as a school superintendent.

Political ideologies raise their heads in a number of areas of decision making in public schools—often after the fact when decisions are announced or become evident and when controversy arises out of the differences in ideology. Curriculum decisions become controversial because of the differing beliefs about what should be taught to children. The debate around teaching evolution and/or creationism has become intense during this first part of the twenty-first century. Textbook selection often creates great challenge for educators because of the inclusion of or failure to include material related to varied ethnicities or cultures or genders. Innovative steps that have been identified for "reforming" schooling or for "improving" schooling frequently are controversial, based on a given political ideology.

In the past two decades, the innovation associated with outcome-based education (OBE) is one of the strongest examples of an educational movement that became surrounded with political controversy. The controversy undermined the efforts of superintendents who were focused on improving teaching for learning.

William Spady spent much of his professional lifetime in teaching and educational research, and he became a consultant-in-demand with public schools after he published a rational model for getting desired student performance results. The history of public education has always focused on educational outcomes (or results) for children and youth. Spady's outcome-based education model in the late 1980s incorporated new research on motivating children to learn, assessing performance, and achieving goals. Setting up specific outcomes to be achieved—or standards to be met, in other words—became understood by educators, and they grew enthusiastic about outcome-based education.

However, with fear of ideas not associated with Spady's outcome-based education model that were being labeled "new world order," "scientific exploration," "ungraded curriculum," "individualized education," and so forth, different religious sectors began to discuss outcome-based education in Sunday school and church fellowship meetings. Peg Luksic, often referred to as "Pennsylvania Peg," undertook the challenge of lobbying hard and long against the implementation of outcome-based education. The analogies she used were alien to Spady's model, but she claimed that the analogies illustrated what outcome-based education was. The philosophy, practices, budget support, and examples of implementation were alleged by Pennsylvania Peg to be beliefs and actions that would turn the children and schools over to federal government control. Peg Luksic's videotape about outcome-based education was distributed to churches throughout the United States. Those videotapes were widely distributed among church members in a congregation that found what she claimed to be believable. Gross exaggeration and open misrepresentation of the outcome-based education practices created fear and consternation among church families and others who heard about the video. Peg was articulate, persuasive, and effective in her efforts. The "anti-OBE" sentiments grew across the nation. Within a few years, superintendents in the country were very cautious about using the outcome-based education phrase.

Dr. Darlyn Balendin tells about a time very early in her first year in the superintendency when a secondary English teacher who had provided leadership to development of a K–12 outcome-based curriculum guide arrived in Dr. Balendin's office. The teacher reported efforts of faculty members in curriculum work and that there was some growing concern about outcome-based education. Darlyn probed for more information and then surmised that the problem was the community's lack of accurate information. She reassured the faculty member about continuing with the teachers' efforts to get this first curriculum guide functional—particularly in light of the forthcoming state review to determine accreditation based on new state standards. Dr. Balendin had been told that there were no other curriculum guides in the school district. After she had contacted each school board member and probed a bit about any awareness of problems with outcome-based education, she suggested to the school board that the first quarterly "hearing" that the board wanted her to hold be about outcome-based education.

On September 7, 1993, the first of four public hearings featuring their schools was held. Flyers had been copied and distributed throughout the community announcing "Outcome Based Education and the Marshfield Schools: Is There a Connection?" All necessary arrangements had been identified and delegated to the appropriate staff.

At 5:00 P.M., Dr. Balendin arrived at the high school, where the hearing was to be held, to check all the arrangements and equipment. She opened one of the double doors to the cafeteria, which seats 300, and in the front row were six women. Dr. Balendin quickly greeted them and apologized for interrupting. One of the women responded that there was no interruption—they were there early to be sure they had a seat. Flash! Dr. Balendin knew immediately that something was going on. She telephoned all seven school board members and every school administrator to be sure each would be in attendance.

The hearing was to be held from 7:00 P.M. to 8:00 P.M., as announced on the flyer. Beginning about 5:45 P.M., people began to arrive. By 6:15 P.M. the high school cafeteria was full. Dr. Balendin asked the custodians to hook up the "in-house" large television screen in the gymnasium and open those doors to the public. At 7:00 P.M., with approximately 500 school patrons present, Dr. Balendin welcomed everyone and began presenting the ten-minute "history" of outcome-based education that she had prepared, allowing forty-five minutes for guided interaction with participants. As she reports, "The only smart thing I did that evening was to ask everyone to sign in, providing names, addresses, and telephone numbers, so that they could receive a copy of the evening's notes and be invited to participate in future school events and on committees."

Before Dr. Balendin had spoken four to five sentences, someone in the audience raised his hand in a way that shouted, "I have a question!" Dr. Balendin continued with a brief comment that she would be taking questions in a few minutes. Two sentences later, another hand "shouted" into the air. At that point, Dr. Balendin said that she told the audience, "I can tell that you have something you would like for me to hear. Let me put my notes aside for now, and I will take your questions. Please speak out only when called upon and so that everyone can hear what you have to ask and say." She then spent the next three hours and seventeen minutes recording their questions, making sure that as she recorded them on a transparency, using the overhead projector, the person asking the question verified that it was written down as intended. At the end, she adjourned the meeting but only after saying that in the two and one-half months that she had served as superintendent of schools, she found that children were achieving, teachers were working very hard to do their jobs well, and citizens who had been in the schools were positive, complimentary, and interested in all of the students performing well. That was her initiation into the culture—and the community perceived for some time that she did not fit.

Another visible piece of evidence that political ideologies are powerful is seen in the gender makeup of our U.S. Congress. Both houses of Congress are composed almost entirely of men. The same is true for state congresses. Should political party association ever be set aside as the overriding influence on congressional members regarding how to vote, there still would not be enough women to garner a majority vote on tough women's issues.

Access to equity is one of the most visible examples of political ideologies at work. Susan Okin (1989) notes:

> We as a society pride ourselves on our democratic values. We don't believe people should be constrained by innate differences from being able to achieve desired positions of influence or to improve their well-being; equality of opportunity is our professed aim. The Preamble to our Constitution stresses the importance of justice, as well as the general welfare and the blessings of liberty. The Pledge of Allegiance asserts that our republic preserves "liberty and justice for all." Yet substantial inequalities between the sexes still exist in our society. (3)

Affirmative action legislation was passed with hopes of prescribing reasonable and bias-free actions for removing barriers to race, gender, and age in all organizations, agencies, companies, and communities. Yet, nearly three decades later, the evidence of the effects of affirmative action is very limited. Housing remains firmly segregated for the most part. Women continue to reach a "glass ceiling" in their efforts to rise to the top of organizational work, even though in 1991 the Glass Ceiling Act became national policy for purposes of furthering equity by increasing penalties for organizations preventing women and racial minorities from moving into top leadership positions.

Controversy has surfaced around quotas for race, gender, color, and ethnicity. The public has not supported striving for equity of results. Courts continue to make distinctions about what kinds of affirmative actions can be taken to reach racial equity. A compelling example is found in *Gratz v. Bollinger* (December 13, 2000), which addressed the University of Michigan's undergraduate affirmative action policy. The university's undergraduate admission policy regarding race used a point system rating all applicants on a number of criteria and providing additional points for minorities. A federal judge ruled that the use of race as a factor was constitutional. In regard to the University of Michigan's Law School's affirmative action policy in the case *Grutter v. Bollinger* (March 21, 2001), a different judge invalidated the law school's policy, ruling that "intellectual diversity bears no obvious or necessary relationship to racial diversity" (Brunner, 2004, 6). On May 14, 2002, the decision was reversed on appeal, ruling that the admissions policy was, in fact, constitutional. On appeal to the U.S. Supreme Court, on June 23, 2003, the Supreme Court upheld the law school's policy, ruling that race can be one of the many factors considered by colleges when selecting their students because it furthers "a compelling interest in obtaining the educational benefits that flow from a diverse student body." The Supreme Court additionally ruled that the point system was not acceptable and needed to be modified (Brunner, 2004, 6).

Other court actions that give notice to those who have worked diligently to assure that affirmative action regulations be met are the following. On November 3, 1997, Proposition 209 was enacted in California, placing a ban on all forms of affirmative action. On December 3, 1998, the state of Washington passed "I 200" and became the second state to abolish state affirmative action. On February 22, 2000, the legislature approved the "One Florida" initiative in which the "education component" was "aimed at ending affirmative action in the state" (Brunner, 2004, 5).

The lack of racial equity—and gender equity—in the United States is patently obvious. How many state senators are women? How many state representatives? How many U.S. senators are women? How many U.S. representatives? How many women serve on the Supreme Court? How many women are CEOs for the top 500 companies in the United States? How many women are public school superintendents?

Another point of interest is that the small number of women who reach high levels of leadership in politics, business, and the professions receive a vastly disproportionate amount of space in the media when compared with women who work at low-paying, dead-end jobs, including the millions who stay home working for no pay and who are not even acknowledged as working (Okin, 1989, 4). Gender-structured professions and gender-structured relations make women—and their children—vulnerable.

Over the past fifty years, the disparity between what men and women have been paid for the same jobs has been great. Although the disparity has been somewhat reduced, in 2003 women still earned twenty-one cents on the dollar less than men ("Women Deserve Equal Pay," 2004). Some of that disparity is influenced by the kinds of jobs women can attract and acquire. Much of the disparity is influenced by the very nature of our biological makeup. Most organizations in the United States do not provide paid pregnancy leave for women.

Most citizens support the notion of equal opportunity. However, there is hesitancy regarding equity. Affirmative action policies, established in the 1970s, are currently under attack by those with different ideologies and those who do not like some of the results of affirmative action efforts by companies and institutions. With each employment of a woman or racial minority in a coveted position, with each admission of a woman or racial minority to a select college, citizens with political ideologies focused on gaining and maintaining power and control begin to be reactive and activated. Efforts are mounted to challenge fine points requiring steps toward gender and racial equity. Interestingly, the ideologies expressed are often contrary or contradictory, making the ground for leaders and other decision makers swampy. If there is an interest beyond assuring that white men's opportunities are not limited in the workplace, it is unclear. Those who protest equity of outcomes do so from a definition derived out of white male culture and the ideology that supports it. Consequently, political ideologies become pitted against each other and efforts to expand equity to all without penalty to others becomes an improbability. This division is witnessed in the two political parties that worked to have members of their parties elected to national leadership in both the 2000 and 2004 elections for the legislative and the executive branch.

All of these practices on a national, state, and local level affect public schools and public school leadership. Because local leadership is perceived by community citizens as more easily influenced, women CEOs in public schools are readily available for community critique, direction, and even dismissal from their jobs if community citizens can make them big enough targets. Women are more politically vulnerable for two primary reasons: their gender and their failure to develop themselves politically.

Religious Ideology

Religious ideologies are quite varied and recognizable. Each religion has a doctrine that informs and conditions the perceptions, opinions, and practice of its constituency. Because in many countries, including the United States, religion, faith, and spirituality are embedded in the cultures of the countries and because the citizenry values religious commitment and experiences, doctrines become valued.

Religious doctrine is just as varied as doctrine related to socioculture and political ideologies. Generally speaking, the doctrines in each of the three ideological areas (sociocultural, political, religious) are ever present in one way or another when consensus on school issues needs to be gained. Further, ideological doctrine can lead to strong disagreements between and polarization of groups within a culture. When factions develop, power struggles begin. Positions are taken, and people "wage" both internal and external efforts to gain control of decision making. Of course, this can pose great challenges for school leaders, and when there are inherent biases that exist toward women leaders, the challenges are even greater.

Religions throughout the world largely deny women access to formal leadership positions within the accepted practices of the religion. For example, both Buddhist and Islamic religions allow only male leadership. Women are clearly subordinated. The Catholic religion prays to Mary, but women cannot be priests, bishops, or the pope. The formal leadership within the Catholic Church is entirely male. Many Protestant religions have a similar barrier. The Assemblies of God Church allows women to assume lower-level leadership positions; however, women have not served as deacons or the primary leaders of their churches. On June 14, 2000, at the Southern Baptist Convention, the Southern Baptist Church in the United States accepted and now uses the doctrine in a committee report titled "The Baptist Faith Message." In that report was the following language under "Section XVIII: The Family":

> A wife is to submit herself graciously to the servant leadership of her husband even as the church willingly submits to the headship of Christ. She, being in the image of God as is her husband and thus equal to him, has the God-given responsibility to respect her husband and to serve as his helper in managing the household and nurturing the next generation.

The wording makes an effort to imply equity. Unfortunately, the effort is not recognized because of the clear use of "submit" and the stereotypical placement of women in the "household and nurturing the next generation"—both contradictions in the doctrine.

Leadership within the church in a number of denominations is, indeed, limited to men, and nearly all churches are absent women CEOs—much like public schools. Church leadership responsibilities for women are associated primarily with teaching children or adults in Sunday school, serving as a music director, preparing communion, publishing the weekly bulletin, and other stereotypically "women's" roles. Not only will women superintendents be seen as unique, maybe even unusual, as CEOs, but also consciously or unconsciously those people for whom religion is a very high priority will expect a woman CEO to respond to and/or follow the lead provided by men.

A woman superintendent, Dr. Beth Perkins, recalled when one of her school board members called her and told her to communicate to the teaching staff that they were to begin logging their arrival and departure time because "folks in the community are observing that several of them cut their workdays short." Beth listened and responded that she would need more specific information and that it would be appropriate for the school board to place a request for the information at their next meeting or study session. During Beth's dismissal from her position, the school board member reminded her that one of the reasons she was being dismissed was that she did not "submit to his instructions about notifying teachers to keep a time log, which was insubordination!"

Religion works to influence public schools in many ways. For years, the Gideon Society distributed Gideon Bibles to children at schools. Then in December of 1989, the courts ruled against the distribution of the Gideon Bible at school in response to action initiated by the *Freedom Writer* (Gideon

Bibles in the Schools, 2001). It was a surprise to Superintendent Sarah Medley when an elementary principal asked her if she would like to come join the Gideons in the morning for coffee before they distributed their Bibles. Sarah asked the principal to tell her more specifically about the presence of Gideons at school and what they planned to do. She learned that nine local members of the Gideon Society would join the principal for coffee before school and then distribute Gideon Bibles to every fifth grader who was in class. The Society members would explain what the Gideon Bible was and why they were there to provide copies for students who would like to have one. Dr. Medley agreed to be present in the morning.

Immediately, she returned to her office, telephoned the school district attorney, reported to him what the principal had reported to her, and asked his assistance in working with the school board. The school district attorney took the lead. At the next school board meeting, he met with board members during executive session. The school board president and vice president were Gideons and had routinely helped in the distribution of Gideon Bibles. The discussion was long and anguished. The school district culture was such that to end nearly a century of distribution was going to be difficult. In particular, with two Gideons on the school board, the issue assuredly was going to be quite difficult for them.

Dr. Medley reported that she had intentionally removed herself from this issue and discussion, thereby allowing the school board attorney and school board to make the decision. To the credit of the school board president and vice president and following much discussion among themselves and with the school district attorney, the school board placed the item on the open agenda for the following school board meeting. At this meeting the issue was discussed and then placed on the agenda for action at the next school board meeting. The action was to discontinue distribution of Gideon Bibles on school campuses. The item included a board president recommendation that the school district discontinue distributing the Gideon Bibles on school district grounds. However, the school board did encourage the Gideons to distribute their Bibles from the sidewalks in front of the school to children arriving on buses.

The church community was angered, even those who were not Gideons. Dr. Medley became the target because she failed to maintain the custom and was viewed as responsible for creating the issue and giving religion yet "another blow."

Since the mid-1980s, churches have become political in their public education interests. Triggered by a report, "A Nation at Risk" (National Commission on Excellence in Education, 1983), commissioned by then President Reagan, the public began to accept the language used by Terrence Bell, Secretary of Education, in describing the achievement of students in the public schools as "mediocre." The report identified problems in student achievement, school leadership, and teaching. The public began to voice interest in having schools become significantly more accountable than they were. As Dr. Kim Janie recalls, about five years later the Christian Coalition published a reactionary and strongly political guidebook for Christians for "Taking Back Your Schools." One of the first tenets advised not to speak to the school superintendent or any other administrator under any circumstances. Dr. Janie recalls a year when only two citizens declared their candidacy for the open positions on the school board. Her usual practice as superintendent was to deliver a copy of the previous three school board meeting agendas, attachments, and minutes; a copy of the forthcoming school board meeting agenda and attachments; a copy of the school district budget; and a full copy of all school board policies to each candidate.

When delivering materials to a school board candidate, usually during lunch, Dr. Janie would explain to the candidate what the school board identified as her leadership goals for the current school year. She intended to perform her usual practice. However, one of the two candidates, whether influenced by the guidebook or not, would not return telephone calls. The candidate would not agree to have lunch with Dr. Janie and returned materials that she or her secretary had sent or delivered to him.

Another incident illustrates the disruptive effect that the Christian Coalition's guide to "Taking Back Your Schools" had on another woman superintendent. Following election and after the victors were sworn in as members of the school board, the school board president, Mr. Keckman, called the meeting to order and asked Dr. Arlene Franklin to address the first discussion item. The public agenda identified what would be discussed but did not include attachments explaining the information the school board had read and studied. Dr. Franklin began to provide the background to the item, per previously agreed-upon procedure and so that others in attendance would know some of the background for school board discussion and action. With only a few sentences spoken by Dr. Franklin, one of the new board members interrupted her and demanded,

"Why is *she* talking?" Dr. Franklin turned to the board president and quietly said, "I think this is your question." Mr. Keckman explained that every summer the school board held a two-day retreat and made a number of decisions about the protocol they wanted followed at their meeting: "One of those decisions was to have the superintendent introduce the item and explain the background, and then school board members would begin to discuss the item. This coming summer we will once again address the protocol and you will have a voice in how the school board decides to discuss the item. Are there any other questions?" The new school board member replied, "This is a school board meeting not the superintendent's meeting!" Mr. Keckman turned back to Dr. Franklin and asked her to continue.

In the general culture of the United States, masculine culture prevails not only in most organizations but also in most public schools and their school communities (Schmuck, Hollingsworth, & Lock, 2002, 98). The challenges for women who wish to ascend to the superintendency are, indeed, major in terms of the sociocultural, political, and religious ideologies that exist and that have conditioned others in their attitudes, opinions, prejudices, and discriminations.

Case Study: Religion and the Superintendent

Dr. Meg Smith had been on the job just thirty days and counting. This was her first superintendency. She was prepared, she thought, for the challenges of the school district. They were the same challenges as superintendents faced in most school districts—finances and student performance. Meg had spent several months gathering information about the school district, and she had arrived before her contract began to be in the school community, visit with citizens, visit with employees, and develop a personal assessment of the school facilities and employee operations. All the challenges were clear and manageable, she thought.

Mr. O'Connor was a school district veteran teacher. Like so many, he had graduated from the school district, earned his teaching and coaching credentials, and returned to progress through the ranks. Because he had been successful in developing and coaching state championship football teams, he was viewed as a successful educator and received a series of promotions. Meg recognized in him the characteristics of a "good ole boy." She had worked with many good ole boys. What did surprise her were his comments when she was visiting with him before school started in the fall: "Dr. Smith, we weren't surprised the board hired a woman. We *were* surprised the board hired a Catholic."

No graduate class had prepared Meg to look at the issue of religion in the school community. She was familiar with separation of church and state and curriculum conflicts that may arise as results of personal beliefs and values. But she did not realize her personal religious practices could be in question. She thought that that issue had long since been settled by the courts.

Meg soon learned there was a large and powerful local church in her school community. The school district employed many members from their congregation. Two members of her seven-member board were also highly involved leaders in this church. The church pastor was known to vocally support political candidates and encouraged certain members of his congregation to run for local offices. Meg also learned that the past two superintendents had been men from this church. The pastor preached and the church membership believed and practiced that women should remain at home, rearing the children.

Church members served on curriculum committees and parent organizations and had challenged certain instructional materials. These vocal members were becoming increasingly visible at meetings and events. The school board election was in several months, and three candidates from the church had filed candidacy papers. It was clear to Meg that she needed to begin identifying how she was going to work with this school board and other constituents of the same church who probably had strong beliefs about schools, leadership, and religious faith.

Chapter Questions

1. What are the potential issues? What information suggests what the issues are?

2. Who will these issues affect? How might they be affected?

3. What ideologies are represented in this chapter and what helped you recognize them?

4. How will these issues affect the superintendent?

5. What plan of action, if any, would you recommend for Dr. Meg Smith to take?

POWER AND CONTROL

"The position belongs to me!" he said. "Maybe," she said.

G ender structuring over the ages has conditioning effects on women's access to powerful positions. Consequently, all too frequently, women leaders are viewed through the lens of male leadership and face confounding biases toward them when they use the entitled power of a position, of their expertise, or of their legitimate authority. Tannen (1990) noted:

> There are many kinds of evidence that women and men are judged differently even if they talk the same way. This tendency makes mischief in discussions of women, men, and power. If a linguistic strategy is used by a woman, it is seen as powerless; if it is done by a man, it is seen as powerful. Often the labeling of "women's language" as "powerless language" reflects the view of women's behavior through the lens of men's. (224–225)

C. S. Bell (1988) explored how contextual features shape the negotiation of authority between women superintendents and school board members. Her findings were that sex ratios, gender-related expectations, and male dominance of power structures further created challenges of authority in this governance relationship. Bell points out, "The woman superintendent's gender is interpreted as a symbol of overriding difference and risk" (55).

As Charol Shakeshaft (1989) said, "Power means different things to men and women" (206). A number of studies of women superintendents' work have found that when women are uncomfortable in using directive, authoritarian behaviors to assume the power of their positions as school superintendents, it's mostly because of the consequences, that is, others see them as behaving inappropriately (Lips, 2003). Because of the cultural conditioning of gender roles for men and women, women who can be authoritarian and directive choose to have "power with" their superiors, peers, and subordinates rather than "power over" them.

Brunner, Grogan, and Prince (2003a) note, "This 'power with others' model of leadership is authentic" (30). That is, "power with" emanates from the tendencies of women—conditioned or not—to nurture, to work together, to collaborate and make sure others have a voice in the collaboration, and to support others in working toward a goal for the common good.

> Thus, the collaborative model of power is not only a feminist idea that represents the experiences of women; it may also be an increasingly emergent paradigm of power. In other words, feminists view orthodox conceptions of power as incorporating masculine preoccupations with how people control one another to secure their personal wants, and they suggest that such conceptions must be complemented with more feminine concerns about how people can effectively organize themselves to solve social problems and transform their environments. (Brunner, 1999b, 72–73)

Psychological Needs and Power

For many years, we have known that people have a primary survival need. They also have four basic psychological needs. All people have a psychological need for power to some degree. As Lips (2003) notes, "Women are just as likely as men are to be motivated by a need for power" (466). Belonging, fun, and freedom are the other three psychological needs that all people experience, and all needs vary in the degree of their intensity (Glasser, 1998). The power need for men and women is the need to have some control regarding their own destinies. As superintendents of schools, men and women also need to develop some degree of power in effectively leading the organization, or the consequences may be dismissal from the position. Women often face difficult struggles if they aspire to positions where leaders are expected to have power "over" others rather than empowering others. One of the reasons is that women who work to establish power "over" are not well received in a culture where sexism or sex-role stereotypes are inherent. Such behavior contradicts well-established norms.

Because of women's socialization as nurturers, the primary modus operandi for them is to develop and use power "with" others in fulfilling their leadership responsibilities. They achieve power "with" others through the meaningful engagement of others in the decision-making processes of the school district. Women pass through decades of socialization, using a communication style that Lips (2003) describes as "sharing ideas, turn-taking in speech, and listening," and men are socialized to develop a communication style described as "asserting ideas, interrupting, and holding the floor" (467).

Brunner's study (2000b) of "unsettled discourse" of twelve successful women superintendents describes women's "experiences of inequality." Brunner states, "In no small measure, although they occupied the most powerful position in public education, the women experienced gender bias" (106). When they talked about power, the "unsettled" talk was of power as dominance and control. Gendered talk that was described by Brunner as "settled" was of power as shared.

Power is an interesting phenomenon. We all need it to some degree. The extent of the need seems to be more pronounced in the leadership of superintendents who are directive and authoritarian. A large number of leadership studies have identified the kinds of power that leaders have available to them and use in their work. Bolman and Deal (2003) point out, "Social control is essential to those in formal positions because their authority depends on it. Officeholders retain authority only if the system remains viable. If partisan conflict becomes too powerful for the authorities to control, their positions are undermined" (168). In addition to position power, other kinds of power exist. Expert power is associated with those who have developed a strong knowledge base and competencies in management operations required for school district leadership and "know-how" to solve problems and make decisions. Being able to control awards and recognition provides another kind of power to school leaders. Establishing relationships, alliances, and networks provides essential support for a leader to gain and maintain power. Developing this kind of power is where women can be successful—if the men in the organization or in governance support it. Control of agendas establishes an important level of power, as well. Skill in framing the meaning and use of symbols important to the culture will increase the power a school leader has, and persons with charisma, strong communication skills, and political acumen can build essential power to acquire and maintain CEO leadership positions (Bolman and Deal, 2003, 169–170).

Trying to establish and use the kind of power that is most appropriate to the occasion or situation poses more challenge to women than it does to men. Women have greater and more subtle restrictions placed on them by the socialized culture of the organization.

Conflict around issues and decisions can surface very quickly, thereby influencing power struggles. Like leadership in general, men and women tend to handle conflict resolution differently. As nurturers, women tend to shy away from conflict unless they become angry, while men find conflict to be healthy at times. Essentially, women report that the reason they hope to resolve issues quickly is that—even when they understand and welcome some degree of conflict—during a conflict, their voices are often not heard or heeded. One woman explains it this way: "My size and somewhat smaller voice seem to invite interruptions when I'm using conflict resolution inquiry methods. Also, men more frequently than women tell me that I don't understand the issue, when I do understand."

In a single-case ethnographic study, C. Cryss Brunner (1999b) presented the following inference:

> Since the male power wielders in a given community are a dominant force, and the position of superintendent is viewed as a powerful and masculine person, then a woman wishing to be a superintendent must define and use power in the same ways as the community's male power wielders. She must define and use power in the same way that male superintendents before her have. (63)

What she actually discovered in her study, however, was that the "male power network had different definitions and uses of power than . . . [the] female power network" (71). Specifically, "others have shown that contemporary political scientists and sociologists have largely conceived and analyzed power as command, control, and domination" (71).

The twenty-first-century experience for schools and school districts to date is clearly connecting (a) the development of collaborative efforts to improve teaching for learning and (b) shared decision making about school improvement with improved student performance. Leaders who build their power "with" others through collaborative and shared decision-making processes are experiencing greater performance gains for their teachers and their students. It would seem that when collaboration is such a value-added practice and women qualified for the superintendency are strong collaborators, steps to achieving equity in service as the school district superintendent are closing the gender gap. The data, however, do not reflect a significant closing of the gender gap.

Personal Challenges Undermine Access to Power

For any superintendent, the tenuousness of the job is worrisome. The job is very public. In order to be successful, superintendents are expected to be visible, attending a large number of meetings, events, and activities. Metaphorically, superintendents live in "glass" houses. The superintendent's family is directly affected by support or nonsupport of the superintendent by the community, school board, and employee workforce.

For a number of years, the average tenure of a public school superintendent was approximately 2.5 years. Although tenure has increased over the past ten years, there continue to be personal challenges. Carter and Cunningham (1997) point out the tenuousness of such a public position where educating the community's most valuable assets, children, is the purpose for the work of educators in public schools. Not only do superintendents have a most precious resource for whom they are responsible, but they are also expected to be the educational leaders of the communities. They are expected to make decisions that contribute to the welfare and successes of the communities, to influence others on behalf of the public schools and their communities, to generate resources above and beyond those provided by the communities, to participate in partnerships that will benefit all parts of the communities—and to be likable.

When a school board grows crosswise among themselves or with the superintendent of schools, the dissolution of relationships often means the ultimate dismissal of the superintendent. The personal challenge and effects of being dismissed are great. Holding such a public and visible position and then, in public, facing failure in maintaining the position brings anger, humiliation, blaming, and other relationally destructive behaviors. A woman superintendent explained, "I feel completely discarded—of no value anymore." It takes strong self-confidence and belief in oneself to seek another such position following dismissal. Those who do continue to seek out superintendent positions maintain their own confidence level by believing that they were doing the right things and were earnestly serving the needs of the children and both the internal and external communities. The inference persistently is repeated that, following dismissal, men more often than women continue to seek out and work in another superintendent of schools position. Early research findings of Dana (2006) suggest that men do keep working as superintendents of schools—even when dismissed from one or more school districts—while women move to a lesser position in school district work or accept a position outside of education.

Barbara Pavan (1999) interviewed and observed four women superintendents. In the discussion of her findings, Pavan stated, "Working with the board and individual members required enormous amounts of time, which continued to be necessary; however, there was some evidence that the emphasis on data, children's needs and open communication was influencing some board members in this study" (116–117).

As indicated earlier in this volume, women enter the superintendency approximately eight to fifteen years later than men do. Consequently, their age is a personal factor that has some effect on their ascending to the CEO position in public schools.

Women are sometimes place-bound and unable to make a move without separating from the family, a step that has been judged in the sex-role stereotype for women as unwise, particularly if there are children at home. Fortunately, commuter marriages are becoming more common, particularly after the children have left home to pursue their own education and life experiences.

There are stereotypes that reinforce perceptions of women as more emotional than men. Women are acculturated to be nurturing and more emotional, and although many are developing the skill and behaviors that indicate more strength in facing potentially emotional situations, the sex-role stereotype persists. Kamler and Shakeshaft (1999) recorded a consultant's summary about board members' and other school community members' view of women candidates for the superintendent of schools:

> My sense is that there are myths about women . . . women are too emotional and can't see things rationally and so that affects their decision making. The other thing is that women are nurturers to a greater extent than men are. That doesn't sit well in the superintendency; we [superintendents] have to make these tough decisions . . . women are not as strong in dealing with the major issues as men would be. (56)

In *Sacred Dreams* Pavan (1999) cites Lindle's (1990) findings that board relations provided the largest source of conflict for both male and female superintendents in her Pennsylvania study, yet Glass (1992) found that "only 16.7 percent of superintendents reported this reason for leaving their last superintendency" (117). It would be interesting to disaggregate that percent by gender.

Participation in women's networks where contextual insights can be introduced, illustrated, and strategically discussed can be quite beneficial for women who aspire to the superintendency or who already have a position as a school superintendent and hope to maintain it. Support groups and mentors, in particular, are helpful in building the confidence and competency of women in the school superintendency. Established networks are few and far between, and developing a relationship with a mentor can be daunting. The best mentor for women aspiring to the superintendency or in their first superintendency is a successful woman superintendent. A number of women have reported informally at conferences about the difficulty of finding a mentor— one who is a successful superintendent and has the power and skill to be an advocate and interest in guiding the development of the beginning superintendent. Not many women superintendents step forward or are available to mentor other women seeking a superintendency or simply trying to succeed in the superintendency they have. All of these potential constraints are mentioned because of the extreme importance for women in building political coalitions and support and in fully understanding how they can gain and keep power while serving as school superintendents.

Women superintendents experience higher productivity, work longer hours, and have higher entry scores to preparatory programs than do men. They would have good substantive experiences to use in coaching other women who aspire to or are beginners in the job of superintendent of schools.

On all fronts, including with their own gender, women who hope to be successful school superintendents often are thwarted. The findings from a few research studies suggest that not only do current women superintendents fail to step forward to coach members of their gender, but also other women do not generally support their women superintendents (Funk, 2004b).

It is certainly a personal challenge for women to control the intellectual and emotional swelling of a defeatist attitude. Maintaining determination, energy, and enthusiasm for "going after" CEO leadership opportunities is overwhelmingly challenging when gender—something that cannot be readily changed—is the major constraint. Women simply do not have access to the socialization that must occur in order to be consistently competitive in the CEO market. Their socialization does not prepare them in the way it prepares men for firming up their own leadership power, identifying and avoiding political land mines, and developing relationships with powerful people who will provide very strong sponsorship. Women know through firsthand experience about the advantages men have as a result of structurally prejudiced leadership selection and the disadvantages women have in culturally conditioned and prejudicial arenas, such as the school district superintendency, where they long to provide service.

Dr. JoLyn Gaines described the difficulties she had in acquiring a position as a school superintendent. She had taught high school mathematics for twelve years and served as an assistant principal for eight years and a principal for four years when she first began to apply for central office positions as assistant superintendent for business operations, assistant superintendent for community relations, assistant superintendent for buildings, grounds, and transportation, and so forth. She said, "I have had sixteen interviews in the past three months and even moved to one of the 'final three' on two occasions. Every time a man was selected before I was. Once a man with only two years of classroom teaching experience and five years in school leadership was selected!"

Discarded Leadership

Even more challenging is acquiring a position as a school superintendent and then being dismissed from that position within the first few years of service. A superintendent dismissed from her first job is confused and saddened, and although the problems that led to her dismissal are probably clear, she wonders why what she was taught in her superintendent preparatory program did not work in this school district.

The title and theme for this book, discarded leadership, comes from a common practice of the American public to "discard" that which they do not want or no longer want, regardless of its quality, capacity, competency, life, and vigor. Webster's (1996) defines discarding as "to cast aside or dispose of; get rid of: *to discard an old hat*." Many "old hats" have not become

HAVE I GOT A SCOOP!

nonfunctional or overly worn. Like discarding that old hat—which has served multiple purposes over several years, yet still has quality, capacity, and appropriate function—discarding the knowledge, capacity, understanding of a school district's operations, commitment, results gained, and talent of school leaders is wasteful. Often a "discarding effect" occurs because of some influential person's dissatisfaction with a superintendent's decision, anger at the leader's choosing a different approach to a problem, or not liking her/his personality.

Like unnecessary divorces, discarding school leaders creates at least a temporary instability within the school district workforce. Where school district superintendents have been discarded every two or three years, a culture of instability develops within the employee workforce, which ultimately creates morale problems and provides disservice to the children who are being educated in that climate. Discarding can also refer to failure to employ the leadership and skill that is available from women. That leadership does not achieve full actualization, benefiting many, when the knowledge and skill are limited to classroom work instead of schoolwide or school districtwide work.

Teaching for learning is complex and difficult. The standards for student performance are high, as are the standards for licensing and performance of school leaders. It is most difficult to meet those challenges, even to make incremental improvement, when a school district team is working together over several years on the same objectives. Changing school or school district leadership every few years provides a rotating door to changing the school district/school objectives. After a period of time, the faculty workroom walls will hear veteran teachers telling novice teachers, "Don't worry about learning all of this. There will be another superintendent (or principal) in a year or two, and she or he will want us to use another approach—whatever 'fad' she or he fancies."

Although substantive research on the dismissal of women and men superintendents has not been broadly pursued, women superintendents tend to be more vulnerable to dismissal than men because of the barriers posed by their gender. Not only in school leadership is discarding visible; in other areas there are clearly visible examples of discarding of leadership. Such certainly is the case in politics, where a small number of women have worked successfully.

Geraldine Ferraro was the first woman to be selected as a vice presidential candidate. She completed the Democratic ticket of Walter Mondale-Geraldine Ferraro in 1984. Teacher, attorney, and congresswoman, Ferraro was committed to the elderly, persuading her colleagues to preserve access of the elderly to Social Security and Medicare. She advocated for women's rights, spearheading efforts to pass the Equal Rights Amendment and Women's Economic Equity Act and taking many other steps to assist women and homemakers. Her leadership work has continued in service to the International Institute for Women's Political Leadership and the United Nation's Commission on Human Rights. Ferraro faced a strong challenge to her place on the Democratic ticket. Allegations developed regarding her husband's financial practices, implying that there was guilt and associating that guilt with Ferraro. Tannen (1990) noted,

> An article in *Newsweek* during the 1984 presidential campaign quoted a Reagan aide who called Ferraro "a nasty woman" who would "claw Ronald Reagan's eyes out." Applied to a man, *nasty* would be so tame as to seem harmless. Furthermore, men don't claw; they punch and sock, with correspondingly more forceful results. The verb *claw* both reflects and reinforces the stereotypical metaphor of women as cats. Each time someone uses an expression associated with this metaphor, it reinforces it, suggesting a general "cattiness" in women's character. Even when seeming to praise Ferraro, the article used terms drenched in gender. She was credited with "a striking gift for tart political rhetoric, needling Ronald Reagan on the fairness issue and twitting the Reagan-Bush campaign for its reluctance to let Bush debate her." (242)

Tannen also captured the influence that words have in contributing to Ferraro's public image:

> In his book, *The Language of Politics*, Michael Geis gives several examples of words used to describe Ferraro that undercut her. One headline called her "spunky," another "feisty." As Geis observes, *spunky* and *feisty* are used only for creatures that are small and lacking in real power; they could be said of a Pekingese but not a Great Dane, perhaps of Mickey Rooney but not of John Wayne—in other words, of any average-size woman, but not of an average-size man. (242)

The attacks were undermining Geraldine Ferraro's gender, not her experience, qualifications, leadership capacities, or the issues she represented and around which she was campaigning.

When Bill Clinton won the U.S. presidency in 1994, he appointed his wife, Hillary, to chair a commission to develop a health care program to propose to Congress. Hillary Clinton was highly educated and had been active on a national level since high school in civil rights and child advocacy work and in supporting health care for children, senior citizens, and the middle class. She has never lost her strong interest in a comprehensive health care plan for all U.S. citizens. Hillary Clinton has been sharply criticized, even by women, for being too ambitious. This criticism would not have been used to describe a male politician. The public was uncomfortable with Hillary Clinton's role as a leader for a national decision-making group. Apparently there was difficulty in comprehending that a First Lady would have policy interests and that her intelligence and talent were important contributions to policy design and decision making.

A major objection arose when, to avoid potential public distortion of the committee's efforts prior to the completed work of the committee, she and other leaders decided to keep the sessions closed while committee members worked to develop a comprehensive health care plan that would serve all citizens. That Hillary Rodham Clinton as First Lady was invited to and accepted leadership of a national committee to study, discuss, and develop recommendations for health care of the nation's citizens was negatively and judgmentally played out in the media. The media and political opponents to President Clinton questioned Hillary Clinton's role and assignment, unlike they had ever questioned that kind of leadership from men. The committee's task was to produce policy recommendations for the executive and legislative branches of government to meet one of the nation's greatest needs.

Interestingly, just eight years later, when Vice President Dick Cheney pulled together a task force to develop recommendations related to the U.S. energy policies, the meetings were closed and the press and public did not know the membership of the task force or have access to the minutes, decisions, or recommendations: a similar situation—a man instead of a woman. Vice President Cheney never had to make his meeting public. Public protestations were loud, but the media treated the situation in a mediocre fashion. To this day, the public does not know the membership of that task force and has no way to determine whether or not the major oil entrepreneurs, of which Dick Cheney was one prior to his election to the vice presidency, were present and influenced the stance the task force took in formulating policy recommendations. Oil entrepreneurs would gain or lose from whatever the recommendations were; they would have a conflict of interest in serving on this national committee. Also, it is unknown whether the members had a conflict of interest in participating in recommendations to not sign the Kyoto Treaty, to propose drilling for oil in Alaska significantly changing the Artic wilderness, to deny that there is global warming and other antienvironmental protection positions that came from the recommendations of that closed meeting task force.

Elizabeth Dole has dedicated her life to public service and public safety, including serving as President Reagan's secretary of transportation, serving as President George Bush's secretary of labor, working for eight years as president of the American Red Cross, and serving as the national director of Education and Information for Hospice. During her appointment as secretary of transportation, Elizabeth Dole "earned the derisive nickname 'Sugar Lips' because she achieved some political victories by charming congressmen with what some people thought of as fake sweetness" (Lips, 2003, 462). When Elizabeth Dole developed an interest in running for the U.S. president in January 1999 and declared her candidacy, she was characterized as being "too robot-like, even too 'ladylike'" (Reed, 1999, 178). Elizabeth Dole decided to enter the campaign for a U.S. Senate seat in South Carolina, won her campaign, and is now serving as a U.S. senator— but not the U.S. president.

Former Attorney General Janet Reno, one of the most powerful women in the country during the Clinton administration, was also treated derisively by the media who used descriptive language to sharply criticize and satirize her in ways not experienced by men in the president's cabinet or by congressmen and congresswomen. Attorney General Reno came to the cabinet with a strong record of breadth of service and consistent application of the law. Yet, while tackling challenging legal issues, "people focused on her appearance and commented on her hair, her glasses, and her dresses in a way that simply does not occur with male political figures" (Lips, 2003, 462).

These women political figures simply tell the tale of how challenging and difficult it is for women in pursuit of any top-level job. Discarding their leadership at top levels is prefaced and accompanied by criticism of their femaleness and using language that reinforces gender structuring and prejudices that are deep-seated.

Case Study: Winning Is Everything

Her presence took over the room. All eyes focused on her as she entered the annual superintendents' conference. While she was deemed attractive by most standards, the attention had very little to do with her physical characteristics. Her presence could only be described as commanding. Her colleagues described her as charismatic, a word usually reserved for men.

Dr. Anna Steinberg had taken her profession by storm. She was a strong and successful teacher for a number of years, coaching students in debate so successfully that other coaches and schools dreaded being paired to meet in a contest with her students. Being one who continually sought out challenges and opportunities to move into leadership opportunities of increasingly higher status, it was not long before she set her goal to serve as a superintendent of schools. She entered the superintendency in her late thirties and moved to increasingly larger school districts to provide leadership. She was recruited by search firms to interview for prime superintendent positions and became the leading candidate in many large school districts.

Anna wanted even more influence. She positioned herself to lead one of the nation's largest administrative organizations. She obviously had the skills, ability, and talent to serve in this capacity. The question was, Did she have the support to secure the nomination, election, and position?

Dr. Steinberg and her male colleagues were known for their competitive nature, wanting to improve test scores, secure the largest grants, attract the best leadership to the school district, reform, reorganize, rebuild. While some did this with finesse, others appeared ruthless. Dr. Steinberg's finesse bordered on ruthlessness, and she quickly developed a reputation as a "bitch." She knew about this descriptive—and ignored the source. After all, many of her male colleagues had similar behaviors and were given support for their leadership. Why shouldn't she?

Anna was running for this leadership position against two male colleagues. The three were alike in many ways, she thought, and dismissed any other comparisons. She felt that it was more important to talk with her colleagues about her interests, how she could represent the state on a national level, and how she could hold her own with the "bigwigs." She sent out flyers to her colleagues, announcing her interests and soliciting their support.

During the annual conference, where the vote was to be held, a session was scheduled for each candidate for this national office to present her/his vision for the organization and how they planned to implement that vision. Each candidate spoke briefly about their ideas and then distributed the key components of their plans. Dr. Steinberg spoke last. She had delivered speeches hundreds of times, and this was not any different.

Voting occurred throughout the conference allowing attendees to share with their colleagues their opinions and views on the candidates for leadership. Conversation appeared to favor either of the men who were candidates. Comments regarding Dr. Steinberg's candidacy ranged from "Her plan is too ambitious" to "She is just not the right fit."

Dr. Anna Steinberg was stunned when the results were announced. She did not like to lose and could not remember the last time she had been unsuccessful. She was always successful—or so she thought.

Chapter Questions

1. What points in chapter 4 help discuss this case? How do they apply?

2. If you had been Dr. Anna Steinberg, would you have done anything differently? Why or why not?

3. Would you have been able to predict the results of the vote? If so, what specifics from the case study would you have used to predict the results?

4. If the superintendent had been Dr. Allan Steinberg (rather than Dr. Anna Steinberg), would he have behaved differently?

5. What can Dr. Steinberg do differently in the future to improve her opportunity to be elected to a state or national position, for example, the presidency of a state or national organization?

TEACHING AND LEADERSHIP

The pool of female leaders may be deep and wide, but few are able to make the tough trip upstream.

Gender, color, religion, ethnicity, and age. What do any of these factors have to do with leadership? Why are America's classrooms filled with women teachers and America's central offices filled with white men? Why does the predominantly female leadership talent pool who work in our classrooms trickle to a puddle at the leadership level? Why has there been little change in a system that has been in place since the beginning of the common school experience? What reduces the number of women candidates who aspire to the principalship and superintendency? What creates and inspires classroom leadership? What defines it? Why doesn't it translate into the school, the central office, and the boardroom? Why are we suffering a crisis in educational leadership when the talent pool appears to be broad and deep—and found in the classroom? These questions and more will be addressed in this chapter.

Who Teaches and Why

From the inception of public education in America, timeless issues have plagued our system. While student discipline concerns have become more pronounced, the system itself has always relied on a body of qualified teachers as the backbone of our common schools. In 1830, Congressional Minister of Education Samuel Hall noted the need to improve teacher preparation (Gutek, 1991). Hall was head of teaching at Philips Andover Academy and authored a text, *Lectures to School-Masters on Teaching* (1833; as quoted in Gutek, 1991). In his text, Hall cited the following weaknesses in our system:

1. Political and religious divisions within school districts that weaken community support.

2. Community unwillingness to finance schools adequately and supply them with needed equipment.

3. Upper class enrolling their children in private schools.

4. Deficiencies in the qualifications of teachers. (p. 190)

These four issues have not disappeared and continue to plague the quantity and quality of teacher candidates. Most would agree that the first three are significant contributors to number four. If we were to view public education as a business, why would men and women want to work for a company that has a divided base, inadequate revenue, and little to no appeal to the upper class? Why would women or men want to work in a system that is experiencing increasing competition?

Teaching has typically not been a time-honored profession. Teachers of the common school were not well prepared and often held no formal schooling beyond their common school education. The majority of teachers were individuals earning money to support themselves on their way to a *real* profession—law or medicine.

During the colonial period teaching was largely male dominated and teacher certification was based on the candidate's religion, political views, and practices. A teacher's mastery of the content was secondary. Today these priorities have changed. Women have been allowed into the workforce and dominate the teaching profession. Competence has been the standard for public school teacher certification, not political and religious preferences. While the standards for teachers have increased, the compensation has remained below other professions with similar entrance requirements.

With all these barriers, why do young people and those changing careers enter the teaching profession? Many come out of commitment, a desire to help others, a belief that they can make a difference in the lives of those they teach. Others enter the profession as a second career after spending time in careers that were more financially fulfilling but may have been personally unsatisfying. Teacher candidates come because they want to; they come because they could not gain admittance to the career path of their choice. Still "most college graduates under the age of 30 hold teaching in high esteem and can see a variety of benefits to a teaching career" (Farkas et al., 2000). The majority of new teachers have what it takes to get the job done—passion to teach. Most agree that they are underpaid but would gladly trade higher pay for improved working conditions such as better student behavior and parental support.

While those in the teaching profession still view their jobs as ones to be held in high esteem, much of the general population has a different view. Teachers are often mischaracterized as "incompetent know-nothings" (Usdan, 2001, 1). They are underpaid and dignity-challenged, suffering the wrath of irate parents and the demands for public accountability in federal, state, and local communities. They have little input into how their jobs are to be done. While they hold the future of our children in their hands, they are often without the standard equipment of most businessmen and women: phones, computers, offices, or work space. They are 2.8 million in number, notably women, and frequently the sole support of their families. Teachers are expected continually to take classes to improve or retain their credentials and are given little time or compensation to do so (Usdan, 2001).

With attention to the need for improved teacher quality, the rigor and consistency of teacher preparation programs have improved over the years. A parallel process has also occurred, that of alternative teacher certification. This certification method is intended to increase the pool of candidates and appeal to those already possessing a degree. Most practicing educators do not believe this alternative entrance to the profession is as rigorous as standard certification. The majority of new teachers report that their training program did a good or excellent job preparing them for the classroom but these programs have placed too much emphasis on theory, thereby reducing opportunity for application of learning to practice. (Farkas et al., 2000). Most teachers feel they are poorly prepared to teach low-achieving students effectively and are frustrated by this lack of preparation. This day-to-day frustration takes a toll on new educators, often leading quickly to educator burnout.

These factors and more have contributed to a teacher shortage. And urban educators are feeling the applicant crunch more than suburban educators with 26 percent of urban administrators reporting a teacher shortage compared to 11 percent of suburban and 83 percent of urban administrators reporting a shortage of minority educators (Farkas et al., 2000). Is it any wonder why many young people choose another profession and veterans are exiting at alarming rates?

Teacher Leadership Defined

School and school district leadership itself is essential to the retention of new teachers. Teachers will accept a teaching position in a school district or school with lower wages in exchange for strong leadership. Teachers cite the need for administrative support for everything from student discipline to parent complaints about grading. Administrative support is a key component to teacher efficacy and effectiveness (Farkas et al., 2000).

Teachers desire and need strong leadership at the school and school district level. They also believe they, too, should be part of the decision-making team. Teachers want to be involved in the decision-making process and desire a choice in addressing the very reasons they chose to enter and leave the profession. Much has been said about the need for teacher involvement in school and school district decisions, but little has been done to make it happen. Seventy percent of teachers feel left out of the decision-making loop, and little attempt is made to include them in the process (Farkas et al., 2000). Teachers are left to implement decisions that they have no involvement in making.

Teacher leadership is not about power or control or about position. Teacher leadership has evolved based on need, the need for schools to get better, to serve students in a better way, to improve test scores, and to use all the brain power available in the school. While the words "teacher leader" have become an educational term de jour, they are often only that—just words. Teachers attend professional development activities to learn about empowerment only to return to a school that is stifled under existing leadership with old paradigms. And we wonder why things don't improve.

Unfortunately, we develop principal leaders for schools they are not in. We allow them to be stifled in schools where leadership is underdeveloped and there is little guidance or support for collaboration. Most of these teacher leaders are female, with female aspirations and leadership traits that frequently are out of sync with the male-dominated leadership. These teacher leaders are fighting an uphill battle, attempting to change a system that was created centuries ago and has withstood the test of time. This educational system is still male dominated with male characteristics and a male culture. The system remains patriarchal and is not willing to compromise. The new female leadership that is trying to emerge remains thwarted and oppressed. Any attempts to revolutionize the system are met with opposition, leaving the new leadership trying to chisel away at the status quo. These new leaders must analyze their style of leadership and review how they tackle the system.

What is leadership? How do we define it? "Leadership is the process of persuasion or example by which an individual (or leadership team) induces a group to pursue objectives held by the leaders or shared by the leader and his or her followers" (Gardner, 2000, 3). Given this definition, the master leader is indeed the obvious—*the classroom teacher.*

Teacher Leadership Roles

Teacher leadership roles have expanded beyond the traditional department chair to other formal and informal roles. These leadership roles include involvement in everything from curriculum development and materials selection to defining professional development activities and formulating school budgets. Barth, writing in the *Phi Delta Kappan* (2001), cites at least ten areas of teacher involvement, involvement that is essential to the "health" of a school:

- choosing textbooks and instructional materials,
- shaping the curriculum,
- setting standards for student behavior,
- deciding whether students are tracked into special classes,
- designing staff development and in-service programs,
- setting promotion and retention policies,
- deciding school budgets,

- evaluating teacher performance,

- selecting new teachers, and

- selecting new administrators.

While the literature about teacher leadership is sparse, Miller (2002) does report:

> Teachers with leadership qualities often find their leadership options limited to administration, activities-type teacher movements, or becoming involved in union affairs. Teachers who become leaders experience increased personal and professional satisfaction and a reduction in isolation; effective teacher leaders are risk-oriented, collaborative, role models for students, and effective mentors; and teacher leaders need administrative support and tangible resources such as time, money, and professional development opportunities. (6)

Teachers who are truly involved in leadership roles in their schools have increased job satisfaction and are candidates for leadership succession in their school or school district. Meaningful teacher involvement in leadership roles can lead to meaningful change. The leadership decision makers continue to place more men than women in leadership roles.

Additionally, teacher leaders demonstrate the following behaviors (Wynne, 2001):

- exhibit expertise in their instruction and share that knowledge with other professionals;

- are consistently on a professional learning curve;

- frequently reflect on their work to stay on the cutting edge of what's best for children;

- engage in continuous action research projects that examine their effectiveness;

- collaborate with their peers, parents, and communities, engaging them in dialogues of open inquiry/action/assessment models of change;

- become socially conscious and politically involved;

- mentor new teachers;

- become more involved at universities in the preparation of pre-service teachers; and

- are risk takers who participate in school decisions.

What the studies seem to agree on is the need for a change in governance in order to sustain this model. Leadership is not a position; it is a process, a state of being. Educational leadership is a set of behaviors and actions. These behaviors include:

> a bedrock belief in what [leaders] were doing; they had the courage to swim upstream in behalf of their beliefs; they possessed a social conscience, particularly on issues of racism and poverty; they maintained a seriousness of purpose, holding high standards and devoting years of service to their causes; and they exemplified situational mastery, the happy marriage of skills and accomplishment. (Goldberg, 2001, 757)

Our antiquated system is filled with roadblocks and barriers for those who possess these commonalities. The system pushes back those that push ahead, and it eventually wins the prize—maintenance of the status quo.

Women Teacher Leaders and Equity

It is an old phrase—the glass ceiling. We have heard it and used it, and some have been its victims. It has been applied to the business world for decades while women have inched their way into male-dominated fields. The glass ceiling has yet to be shattered by a significant number of women. In 2003, women constituted 46.6 percent of the U.S. workforce and 50.5 percent of managerial, professional, and related positions (Catalyst, 2004a), while accounting for only 10 percent of senior managers in Fortune 500 companies and less than 4 percent of topmost executive ranks (Meyerson and Fletcher, 2000).

As published in the *Harvard Business Review*, Meyerson reveals that gender discrimination in the workplace impacts everyone's productivity. Gender discrimination is not as obvious as it has been in the past. It is embedded in the culture of how we do business. While women have tried to address this issue, changes in the culture of the workplace have seen limited progress. Women remain largely relegated to lesser roles than their male counterparts even though they share the same aspirations (Catalyst, 2004b). And since teaching is a predominately female profession, this presents an even larger problem.

A recent Catalyst study of female executives indicates that women face barriers to advancement related to gender-based stereotyping (Short, 2004). These stereotypes have persisted through decades and continue to impede advancement efforts by women, resulting in exclusions from informal networks such as golfing groups, poker clubs, and other male-dominated social groups. These social outings are often the place where promotions begin. And sometimes membership in these groups equals survival, as the following story will illustrate.

Concerned with her job longevity, an urban female principal, Eunice Robinson, began socializing with the superintendent, his male deputy superintendent, and two other male principals. The five went on golf outings and other social activities. Eunice Robinson had been hired from outside the organization by the superintendent and was placed in a hostile school where union leadership supported the incompetent staff she was trying to improve or remove. While the superintendent remained in his role, she was able to improve things in her school, transferring some staff and improving instruction in some classrooms. However, soon the superintendent was on the receiving end of a hostile board of education. He began packing his bags and was headed out of town. Rumors began about Ms. Robinson's longevity in the school district. She soon experienced a visit to her school by several school board members. The principal saw the writing on the wall, updated her resume, and left the state while the male principals remained unscathed.

Was this situation gender biased? The male principals with similar circumstances did not experience these concerns. They did not feel the need for ongoing protection from the male hierarchy. The organizational culture was not hostile to them.

Old habits and time-honored gender roles are resistant to change. Gender-biased, time-honored behaviors, such as paying women less for the same job, impede progress and productivity in our country. Corporate America exemplifies this behavior. Female wages remain far behind their male counterparts, and, given our current rate of progress, women will not achieve wage parity with men for fifty years (Catalyst, 2004b)!

Nowhere is the lack of parity more evident than in the top leadership positions of corporate America. The proportion of women in executive suites in their field remains nearly unchanged after three decades, despite females composing the largest group in the applicant pool (Woody and Weiss, 1994). While women, particularly white women, were one of the major beneficiaries of the 1964 Civil Rights Act, they remain disproportionately behind in percentage of senior-level job market share and compensation. The educational hierarchy parallels corporate America.

There is an increasing need in education for the leadership skills women possess. These skills include collaboration, consensus building, and empowerment of others (Jacobs, 2002). Yet the support of these skills remains elusive and informal at best. Education is no different than business and has many of the same issues, concerns, and barriers. One of these issues is the lack of a family-friendly environment for the working parent, specifically the working mom. While many women choose to enter the field of education because of a family-friendly calendar, this calendar becomes less family-friendly as individuals are given more responsibility and are promoted. The decision makers view the policy of providing family-friendly environments as requiring expensive practices such as providing child care. They also view women educators as providing a secondary, rather than primary, income for their families, so the motivation for providing family-friendly policies is lessened.

Take the case of Linda Mora, a middle school principal with young children. Teachers in her school reported to work at 7:30 A.M. It was an expectation that school district administrators were to be at their jobs earlier—much earlier. Dr. Mora knew this but spent many evenings at school, supervising games, attending parent meetings, and providing support for after-school programs. She rarely saw her young children since they were in bed prior to her arrival home. So she chose to spend a few additional minutes in the morning with them, arriving when the teachers did.

Early one morning, Dr. Mora overheard a comment from one veteran teacher to another: "What is she getting paid the big bucks for anyway? She can't even get to school on time. Roger, her assistant, beats her to the door every morning. He should have gotten the job, not her." Both teachers snickered, and Dr. Mora knew what those comments meant. They

were an attack on her credibility. Her experience as a successful administrator did not matter.

Despite 51 percent of women and 43 percent of men reporting difficulty balancing work and personal lives (Short, 2004), reconciling home
and work responsibilities seems to be largely a woman's role. This barrier is
a primary concern with advancing women in educational leadership. The
demands of the current administrative workplace leave little flexibility for
family needs and concerns and little room for family matriarchs, women.

Schooling and its structures have changed very little, resulting in
many teachers believing the best place for women is in the classroom
where gender bias is less, the network for advancement is unnecessary, and
a family-friendly structure still exists. The exponential growth of women
in the teaching profession emanates, in part, from its family-friendly
schedule. Teachers with school-age children generally follow the same
work calendar that children follow as days of nonattendance required at
school, therefore requiring little need to place their children in everyday
child care. Other professions do not accommodate a parents' child-care
schedule and can be inflexible toward a parent's desire for time to attend
school functions and events.

Prepared for Success

The new school family-friendly culture of collaboration and team building
is the kind of environment that "fits" and supports girls' and women's performance. Our culture still encourages blue and pink thinking, behavior,
and marketing. Barbie dolls remain a favorite toy for girls, while toy guns
and other violence-related toys for boys fill prime-time advertising in the
media. Boys are encouraged to participate in boy games such as football
and war. These games teach winning above teamwork and drive home the
importance of a competitive environment (Helegson, 1990). Girls, on the
other hand, are encouraged to play cooperative games such as house,
school, and jump rope. These activities have fluid rules that encourage collaboration and building relationships. In essence, the upbringing of young
girls contributes to their preparation and success as classroom teachers but
prepares them little for leadership roles outside the classroom walls.

The moral development of women is different from that of men as
well. Women are reared to be caring individuals who value relationships

over power making. Men believe individuals have certain basic rights and morality imposes restrictions on what individuals can do. Women, on the other hand, feel responsible for others, so their moral imperative is to care for others (Gilligan, 1982). While the female code of caring for others is perfect for the classroom, this mind-set creates conflict in the boardroom where decisions are made based on who plays golf with whom instead of who cares about whom.

Experienced in Failure

Gender-distinct morality is one reason that job segregation is evident in many occupations. The medical profession mirrors education with its ratios of female nurses to female doctors. The legal field parallels education as well with women constituting 49 percent of all law students yet making up 29.1 percent of all lawyers (Catalyst, 2004a). In 2002, women constituted 46.6 percent of the labor force and only 15.7 percent of corporate office positions. While this number has increased, it has done so at a turtle's pace.

Why are women who enter their chosen fields failing to progress up the leadership ladder at the same rate as men? Do they choose to opt out or take a break in their career paths to get married and raise a family? The difference in career paths accounts for some decline, however, it has limited impact on these statistics. It is not about the occasional teacher who takes a leave to rear small children or care for an ailing parent. The number one barrier to workplace advancement is gender prejudice, pure prejudice. This factor has remained steady for decades (Morrison, 1992). Prejudice keeps women in job-specific roles that continue to limit them today.

A secondary key barrier "keeping women in their place" is lack of attention and guidance in their early careers. This contributes to missed opportunities and an isolated work environment. Without guidance, mentoring, and social contacts to promote them, women are left to their existing networks that lack the business savvy and organizational knowledge (Morrison, 1992). This lack of knowledge excludes them from the promotion track. And any attention to needs of the family further isolates women. Time spent caring for the needs of the family is viewed as lack of commitment to the job. The pool of female leaders may be deep and wide, but few are able to make the tough trip upstream.

Pink Versus Blue

Corporate America and education alike speak and think in gender-biased languages. Women use words that elicit feelings and emotions while men's vocabulary is packed with action words. Soft versus hard language has been the subject of research and books (Lichtenberg, 2004). This language difference has been referred to as pink versus blue. In fact, pink is often viewed as PSL, Pink as a Second Language. While male conversation is laced with figures and facts, women discuss relationships, removing themselves from conversations about conflict. The language men and women speak is distinct—pink and blue.

Women are conditioned to emphasize relationships through both language and behavior. Women want to know about the person(s) they are working or doing business with; they discuss feelings and personal information and allow time to process decisions. In contrast, the male gender does not encourage or allow the discussion of feelings. With men, roles tend to be respected more than the individual. Satisfaction comes from discussing how to tackle a task, not whether or not it is to be tackled at all. Communication among management personnel is tainted blue, not pink, and women are poorly prepared for immersion in this second language.

Let's listen in on a pink and blue conversation between Director of Elementary Education Dr. Barb Soloman and her male boss, Dr. Shipley.

> "Dr. Shipley, I have prepared the agenda for the principal's meeting next week. It is our first meeting since June, so I thought everyone could share vacation photos. Alice took her kids to the beach, and Arturo vacationed with his mom in Hawaii. This is all Alice and Arturo can talk about."

> "We have a lot to do, Barb. I don't think that would be a good use of our time. Those two frequently complain about the amount of time we spend in meetings, and you know how I hate complainers! Barb, I think the board is interested in your interviewing for my job when I retire, but we have to spend time on school business, not family business."

Barb believes relationships are important and wants to help build a positive culture for change, a needed change in her district. But Barb clearly is going to need to change her language to blue if she wants to fit into the male-dominated world of educational administration, making her emotional words neutral and reducing personal conversation. If Barb wants to blend into her school district culture, she needs to reduce the relationship building in her role and become more businesslike. But does education need more of the same?

Today's women are prepared to be successful in an environment that is not ready for their leadership style. The business and education world talk about the "new leadership," one that is collaborative and process oriented and emphasizes "we" instead of "me." But those who select the next leaders are the me's, not the we's. White males dominate executive offices and boardrooms. Add skin color to the pink style of communication and the barriers to advancement become higher and broader.

A woman's voice is quieted, becoming pale pink, before she becomes a woman. She has less encouragement and less opportunity to lead prior to entering college. The fate of collecting a number of "less" descriptors begins early during a girl's upbringing and contributes to future limitations. For example, during 2004, for every eighty-five boys taking the Advanced Placement test in computer science, there were only fifteen girls (College Board, 2005). Advanced Placement classes are only the tip of the iceberg. More boys than girls continue to take high-level math and science classes, courses that open doors into a male-dominated world.

Conversely, boys are less well prepared than girls in many areas but are more frequently encouraged and accepted into leadership positions. Reading and writing skills of high school boys are consistently below that of high school girls (College Board, 2005). Is this a matter of male ability, planned pedagogy, or an accident of the culture into which boys and girls are born? Most agree it is how our schools and society work—but little has been done to address these inequities in educational preparation of girls and boys. Sexism may be evident in both pink and blue during our school years, but it becomes increasingly pink as we grow into adulthood.

A Woman's Place

The question is how much influence do women have in shaping this gender-prejudiced world in which we live? Are women a part of the problem? Do women perpetuate the gender-based roles in children, only shouting "unfair" as an adult? Do teachers play a significant role in gender typing boys and girls? If you were to look at the data, the answer is a resounding yes (Sanders, 2002).

Teachers do not join the teaching profession to purposefully harm children. Teachers want to help children. They do not look at each boy and girl thinking, "Ramón is going to be an engineer, and Cecilia should be a teacher." Teachers do not intentionally believe that boys should make more money than girls and girls should never have equal opportunity for a management or leadership position. But it happens. Gender prejudice is not unique to the upper levels of educational management and leadership, either. Unfortunately, it begins in preschool. Most educators do not realize the potency of the roles they play.

Teacher preparation programs do little if anything to instruct candidates on these issues. These institutions may provide discussions on equity awareness issues, but gender equity instruction is usually optional and appears only as an elective course. In these unique courses, preservice teachers become better prepared to close the academic gaps between boys and girls. But rarely is the school or district supportive of such efforts. Individual teachers cannot do it alone.

Classroom Confines

While classroom textbooks have become increasingly friendly toward multicultural and gender equity issues, the nation's marketplace remains driven by sexual images and violence to women. Advertisers clearly know that "sex sells," using images of scantily clad young women to market everything from fast food to cell phones. High-selling video games with women being verbally and physically abused and woman treated as the "property" of men are marketed to today's teens and young adults, which strongly promotes women as sex objects. It is no wonder young boys struggle with appropriate interactions with girls and young girls are so obsessed with body image.

While some improvements have been made in the classroom to address gender inequity, society as a whole has made limited progress. When children enter kindergarten, there is much work to be done by teachers who have little preparation. To illustrate, a kindergarten teacher was orienting her young students on the first day of school when a bright-eyed, vocal young boy was heard saying, "Our teacher is SEXY!" Educators hope that children will come to school with a strong vocabulary but would prefer the vocabulary be acceptable and matching a commonly and developmentally appropriate list of words.

Gender differences do not stop with language and marketing. Males and females seek value and self-worth from different sources. Generally girls look to others for their self-esteem and boys search within themselves. In terms of developing self-esteem, the ways girls and boys seek affirmation is extremely critical to what occurs in schools. Girls are validated by what is done and said to them. They have a greater fear of looking foolish in front of others, more concern about being perfect. So the impact of a teacher in the lives of young girls is more powerful than for boys (Orenstein, 1994).

Girls are more concerned about appearance than boys, and appearance becomes even more critical to their self-esteem as they get older. Thinness equals beauty and quiet equals acceptance. Acting too smart and too unfeminine can contribute to social distancing in school. Girls still are supposed to be the homecoming queen, and the queen is expected to be beautiful but not necessarily intelligent. Take the example of Emma, a blonde, blue-eyed sixteen-year-old whose goal is to be homecoming queen. Emma's mother was homecoming queen at the high school Emma now attends, and she views Emma as her successor. Emma was elected to numerous school leadership positions through popular vote and clearly desires to maintain her popularity. Emma's mother tries to help her by hosting high school parties and providing transportation and a meeting place for Emma's friends.

Emma does work hard to maintain her grades, seeking the help of a gifted girl in her class, but chooses not to socialize with this same girl outside of her private tutoring sessions. Emma is willing to do anything to remain popular, dating older boys, hosting parties at her house, and so forth. She laughs at boys' inappropriate jokes, perpetuating the "dumb blonde" stereotype. But Emma is far from dumb. She knows how to use this stereotypical technique to achieve her high school dream— homecoming queen.

Girls themselves can break this cycle of need for outward recognition and validation of appearance. They can learn to value their own efforts and realize their own self-worth. Some factors affecting the upbringing of young girls can be influenced and others can even be controlled. However, after decades of awareness of the issue we have done little to change the outcome for girls. It is past time to tackle the classroom through teacher preparation programs.

We know that girls and boys work and play differently. Each gender responds uniquely to rewards and recognitions and communicates at different levels, reacting differently in the classroom. Girls thrive on cooperation, and boys excel at competition. In schools, our practices remain the same. Changes in society occur at a rapid pace, yet schools are slower to change. We have yet to apply changes to our pedagogical practices about the way we deal with gender differences.

Patriarchy

Much has been said about the significance of a positive male role model for the lives of children. The importance of fathers in the lives of girls is evident when studying children from single-parent homes. Girls have less information than boys about how to maneuver in a male-dominated world and tend to have fewer interactions with adult males. With less male attention during these developmental years, girls lag behind boys in their exposure to the inner workings of the male world that dominates our educational culture.

Male teachers also are cautioned about classroom relationships with female students. They are fearful that their actions can be misconstrued as anything other than professional so they, too, separate themselves from girls, being cautious not to spend time alone with them. In a previous era this time between a teacher and student served as a positive experience for teachers in mentoring students, working with them both on an academic and personal level, and for students, who received appropriate attention and interacted with a potential role model. Teachers served in lieu of an absent parent, providing that natural bonding a classroom can offer. With the advent of lawsuits and the threat of careers on the line, student and teacher interactions have changed. Girls and boys no longer receive the maximum benefit of a strong, positive student and teacher relationship that reflects the healthy role of mentor/protégé. Instead the roles are formal and less intimate.

This lack of closeness also is exemplified in the relationship between teachers and principals. Teachers try to maintain with their students the kind of professional closeness that attracted many of them to the profession. However, the closeness ends at the classroom door. Principals try to maintain professional closeness with teachers; that effort ends with the potential for misperceptions about the professional relationship. The concern about behaviors that could be misconstrued has contributed to this distancing.

Relationships between principals and teachers can be strained based on the demand for accountability, union contracts, and increasing responsibilities for both roles in meeting the ever-present threat of low test scores and their resulting consequences. This relationship can be even more strained if the principal is male and the majority of teachers are female. Female teachers who aspire to leadership roles are left out of the inner network where promotions are discussed. They feel forced to demonstrate their leadership skills through long hours, often working in excess of the very supervisors whom they hope to impress.

Perceptions, not reality, contribute to the need for women to exert additional effort to attain the role of school principal. Management attributes that are favorable for men are viewed as unfavorable for women administrators (Hudson and Rea, 1998). Once appointed to a leadership role, women are not viewed as having legitimate authority, thus decreasing their real or perceived power and the ability of women to progress up the educational hierarchy.

Teachers' View of Principals

The teaching field possesses a pool of predominantly female candidates who have the necessary characteristics required for today's schools. Yet those in charge of selection are mostly men who view female attributes as less favorable than male attributes. These decision makers base selection on the role of the traditional principal, not that of the leader for today's schools. If the decision makers assessed the perceptions of the teachers whom principals serve, they would clearly understand that there is little difference between the needs and desires of male and female teachers (Hudson and Rea, 1998).

Creating Our Own Crisis

We have heard the cries of a leadership crisis in education today. School administrators are retiring by the thousands each year, and school districts are concerned about the reduced quantity and quality of applicants.

Applicant pools seeking leadership positions are smaller and more variant today. In some areas there is a great need for qualified applicants—such as in rural areas. It is difficult to attract qualified leaders to rural areas. While the country cries for compassionate educational leaders who demonstrate commitment and quality, the system bars many from entering.

Recent reports show there is no shortage of qualified administrators to take the helm of our schools as administrators retire or transition to other districts or roles (Ringel et al., 2004). Indeed, the problem does not lie in the quantity or even quality of applicants.

Several recent Rand studies reviewed the career paths of school administrators. Included in the studies were the issues of gender, race, and ethnicity of administrative applicants. While there was an adequate amount of qualified applications for each position, practices in human resources offices prevented many applicants from entering administrative ranks (Ringel et al., 2004).

One of these studies reviewed the career paths of Illinois administrators. The study noted a 24 percent increase in demand for school administrators from 1987 to 2001. This increased demand did not result in a reduced candidate pool (Ringel et al., 2004). While 70 percent of qualified applicants applied for positions, only 40 percent were employed as school administrators.

The number of female administrators in Illinois did increase. Illinois data would also indicate that efforts to remove the barriers for women in attaining an administrative career were far greater than typically experienced. Men are still three times more likely than women to become principals and 2.5 times more likely to become assistant principals. Additionally, men are 2.5 times more likely than women to go directly to the principalship without ever becoming an assistant principal (Ringel et al., 2004)!

These data suggest that the barrier lies somewhere at the point of entry, when a candidate decides to enter the administrative field. Some candidates have strategically placed themselves in positions where promotion is imminent. These candidates have typically moved themselves into the social circles of the decision makers, developing a network with key influencers. The candidates have easily attained a mentor/protégé relationship with someone in the community or district. The relationships have developed naturally on the golf course or at the poker table. Other candidates have not had or created the opportunity to develop a similar relationship. Their interests and schedules do not fit those of the decision makers. Candidates for promotion are typically the primary caretakers for their families and often have conflicts with social functions. And yes, those within the circle of decision makers are mostly men while those on the outside are predominantly women.

The perceived administrator shortage has led to other methods of developing additional opportunities for men while limiting those for women. Politicians and state boards have repeatedly heard about an educational leadership crisis and have reacted by creating alternative certification paths that open doors for more men than women (Tallerico and Tingley, 2001). Many states have increased access for those with a business or military background, male-dominated careers, to enter the public school administrative ranks. At the same time, states are increasing standards for those in traditional preservice preparatory programs. More white men are eligible for the alternative certification route than women or minorities, while those in traditional certification programs are predominantly women. Could these new policies be considered discriminatory? Some would answer a resounding "yes."

Who are the policy makers who make the decisions about the need for alternative certification and who should be eligible? Our state and federal government offices are filled with white men who create policy resulting in continuing discriminatory practices. Policies, such as approval of alternative certification to license or certificate school administrators, limit even further access to quality women candidates.

Succession Planning and the Absence of Women

How can inherently prejudiced ideas of men about the need for leaders who are "more like me" be changed? How does the system learn to accept and support the leaders in our midst and not continually search for more of the same? What can be done to change policies and practices that result in hiring the best candidate for the job, not just the best man? All three questions can be answered simply: men and women in the field need to set aside their own prejudices and condition themselves to a gender-neutral approach to recruitment, screening, and selection. We have all contributed to a culture where gender prejudice is tolerated and gender structuring is the norm. Cultural change means changing behaviors, attitudes, and practices. This is not an easy task.

Case Study: A Moral Imperative

All she wanted to do was help children, she thought. That passion is what drew her to teaching. She knew she could help children, having taught Sunday school, worked in the community, and worked at a local day care center. Deloris Raymond was skilled at developing positive relationships and always seemed to brighten the faces of those she touched.

Teaching was a natural for Deloris. Her mother and father were both professional educators. She grew up around the teaching profession and was well aware of the time and talent it took to do the job well. Deloris's father was a school principal. He took the position initially to increase the family income, but he grew to love the job.

Deloris saw her father's passion and hoped to follow in his footsteps. She also had natural leadership inclinations and felt she could positively impact more children as a school administrator. Her idealism and passion for children was evident.

Deloris believed education for all was our "moral imperative." She was a compelling teacher and believed that every child deserved a quality teacher and a quality environment. That commitment and the time she spent in her instructional role influenced the growth of perceptions that she was a strong instructional leader. She completed a doctorate in educational leadership and even there was described as a leader who had her priorities straight regarding the purpose of education. Within just a few years, Dr. Deloris Raymond applied for and was promoted to a central office position as the chief instructional officer. She was delighted because she believed she could make a bigger and broader difference for children. Her belief in the need to serve all children with the best of teaching and with consistent learning opportunities had not changed; in fact, it had strengthened.

Eventually as chief instructional officer, Dr. Raymond was offered the position as superintendent. Her first year was tumultuous. While she was a master of instructional leadership, she failed miserably as a politician, a key skill she lacked. It did not take her long to provide effective leadership for aligning curriculum, raising test scores, and excelling in other areas, but she demonstrated less than adequate political skill. Deloris did not have a mentor as a superintendent, she did not experience socialization to the position, she had strong teacher leadership skills, she was missing some key essentials in leading as a school district superintendent.

School board members and community residents came at Deloris Raymond from all sides with special requests. First, she was approached by the city to seek support for offering tax incentive credits (TIFS) to three new companies considering purchasing property and establishing their headquarters in the community. All Dr. Raymond thought of was the loss of potential revenue for serving the educational needs of students. She was resistant and decided not to join the coalition courting the companies. Two school board members advised her that her decision was unwise. Then the girls basketball team members and their parents requested a private meeting with Dr. Raymond for the following Saturday morning. At that meeting, team members and parents lodged a number of complaints against the coach. He was too much of a driver. All girls on the team did not get to play in many of the games. They thought that this woman superintendent would be empathetic and would support their position. Dr. Raymond explained that they needed to visit with the coach first, then with the athletic director, and if their needs were not resolved, they could meet with her again. The group quietly left the meeting. Deloris was so focused on the needs of the students, her moral imperative, that she brushed aside most of these inquiries or demands. Soon complaints began to arise about Deloris Raymond's treatment of community members and her lack of acceptable interpersonal skills. The school board's mid-year evaluation of her performance during her first year was less than glowing.

The next school board elections changed the composition of the membership, replacing two veteran school board members with candidates who ran on a platform of change, which meant dismissing the superintendent of schools. The first action the new school board took was to dismiss Dr. Deloris Raymond from the position as superintendent, leaving behind the instructional focus of the superintendent and gaining some political acumen by employing a different superintendent. Deloris's reason for aspiring to the superintendency became the reason the school board wanted a change.

Chapter Questions

1. In what ways was Deloris prepared for the superintendency? In what ways was she not prepared for the superintendency?

2. What points in chapter 5 are illustrated in "A Moral Imperative"?

3. What could Deloris have done from the start of her superintendency to define her work with the school board and community? Provide a rationale for your answers.

4. What would you have done differently in response to patrons requesting that their needs be met?

CHAPTER 6
EMERGING LEADERSHIP CHALLENGES

There was a student on the interview team. He was an attractive boy, a sophomore. He seemed genuinely interested—sincere in his task of giving input as to who should be the next superintendent. His question was simple enough—but I had not rehearsed my answer. "Dr. Brown, why should you be our next superintendent?" Maybe it was his innocence, lack of pretense that created my response; maybe I was tired of the political formalities—so I answered, "Brandon, most superintendents are white, male, and in their fifties. And in case you hadn't noticed, I'm white, too."

—Diedre, superintendent, 2003

And so it goes. There continues to be a traditional profile of the American School Superintendent and American leaders in general. They are white males in their fifties. They always have been. Most of them are successful in their roles, and as Americans, we like to replicate success. So we hire more of the same—much more of the same. If the system isn't broken, why fix it? The utilitarian answer is, it is an issue of supply. The altruistic response is our schools need to move toward more caring and innovative organizations using practices that are prevalent with women leaders.

Dr. Mary Marian sat in the offices of a superintendent search firm, one of national prominence. She was in the market for her first superintendency, eager and waiting for the opportunity. Mary had not really thought through all the issues surrounding job placement; she had not done her homework. No one had told her what to look for or what to do when determining if the job is the right fit. To her this issue was secondary. After all, she was competent and highly educated and she had a successful track record. Mary prided herself on her competence and commitment.

Prior to interviewing, Mary decided to meet with several successful veteran superintendents. So she asked her superintendent, Jim, for recommendations. Jim recommended several white males, and Mary proceeded to set up dinner meetings with each and every one. They all had longevity in various school districts and were well regarded by their colleagues—other white males.

Each superintendent gave Mary great advice, she thought. One told her to make the school board her priority, take the members out for drinks, call them regularly, and take them to state and national conferences. Another advised her to have strong relationships with the unions, keep them "on your side." And the third had excellent suggestions as well. When asked by Mary what words of advice or encouragement he had for her as she proceeded on this career path, Dr. Tanton stated the following: "Mary, there are three things to remember, and each one is equally important. You always need to have your resume ready, money in the bank, and an unconditional friend to tell your troubles to. The superintendency can be lonely, and you may not last long, so be ready."

Mary did not stop to think why a woman wasn't among the mix of successful superintendents she met with. These superintendent role models were all white men in their mid-fifties. Mary did not have a mentor in her own school district, at least not anyone she would consider for that role. She was the most senior-level woman in her school district. No one had offered to help her on her way to where she was. Mary had worked hard to get to this position, putting in many long hours exceeding that of her male colleagues and having to leave her two children frequently so she could complete the next project or return that last phone call.

Now she pondered the thoughts of these three superintendents as she sat in the search consultant's office. Mary had a successful career history, and she believed this next challenge to be no different than the last. Mary was sure she was ready for this new role. But was she really?

Mary was offered and accepted a position in a medium-sized school district. She was the first female superintendent with a school board that had progressed very little in the past fifty years. They had told her how impressed they were with her credentials. Within the first month on the job, a veteran assistant superintendent said to her, "We all were surprised they hired you, I mean a woman."

Mary was determined to be successful in her first superintendency. She put down roots, buying a home in the community and placing her children in the same school system she led. Her task was to improve student achievement, accommodate growing district enrollment, and lower the tax levy. During the next several years Mary did all that and more—and then she was fired.

Public outcry over Mary's dismissal was loud and long. Even though the school board took a verbal thrashing, their decision remained unchanged. The school board had been "talked into" hiring a woman and no longer wanted to continue the relationship. They wanted someone different—a man to do the job. And that they got. Mary hired an attorney and negotiated a contract buyout.

Now, after a contract buyout, Mary was sitting in another search consultant's office, this time one of lesser prominence, waiting for an opportunity to discuss her next job prospect. She was not so eager this time. Mary was cautious and uncertain about her desire for another superintendency. Mary believed that everything she knew, everything she stood for when the school board chose to dismiss her, was shattered.

The search consultant walked in the room. He was a veteran educator, African American, and a former superintendent. Charles had reviewed Mary's resume and her situation and talked with her about possibilities. "Are you willing to move?" he asked. "Are you willing to go to a smaller school district, take a cut in salary, take an assistant superintendency?" And so on. Why was he asking her these questions? Mary's performance in the previous school district was nothing less than outstanding, she thought. So what if the school board decided to fire her? She knew they fired her because she was a woman and they did not like her style. It wasn't because of job performance because she had met every goal the school board had established. Mary had watched white male superintendents with a history of dismissals get job after job. She asked Charles what her chances were in securing another superintendency. He hesitated, then explained, "After being fired, it is much harder for women and minorities to get a second chance. Much harder."

Mary went through months of interviews for the superintendency. She was a finalist for several positions, but each required uprooting her family and moving out of state. During some interviews she was aware that she was the token female in the interview pool. Her name was on the short list just so the school board could say, "Yes, we interviewed one of them." Mary thought long and hard about her options, now realizing the superintendency could be migrant work, packing up every few years to move to a distant community and going through the resettlement process all over again.

While she knew a superintendency position would eventually be offered, Mary withdrew her name from the candidate pool. She changed her children's schools and her career path. The passion for the role she once held so dear has not returned—and neither has Mary returned to the superintendency.

Superintendent candidates like Mary choose to leave the field due to frustration, not desire. They are capable, experienced applicants who have been scarred through the dismissal process and find the additional barriers in the selection process difficult if not impossible to maneuver.

Aspiration Is Not the Issue; Opportunity Is

The data report that there is no supply chain crisis in school administration. The literature supports this. Policy groups have stated this. So why does the general public not believe it? Could it be the headlines? Is the media marketing a false crisis? Are we actually in a manufactured leadership crisis? How many strong performers like Mary do school boards and school districts not give a second chance, let alone a first one?

According to the U.S. Census Bureau, the superintendency is the most male-dominated executive position of any profession in the United States (Glass, 2000). School administration programs now enroll more women than men, but there remains a comparatively low number of women employed as school leaders. These enrollment figures indicate that for women *aspiration is not the issue; opportunity is*. Barriers to women's advancement, not competence, are of primary concern when it comes to increasing the numbers of women in school administration preparatory programs. Clearly gender prejudice is number one on the list of barriers.

But first, how does a woman acquire her first superintendency? The entry to the superintendency begins with the assistant principalship where women, regardless of their qualifications, are hired far less often than men. The assistant principalship is the primary entry point into administration for women. A suburban high school recently advertised for an assistant principal, with applications received from eighty qualified applicants. All were screened by the assistant superintendent for human resources, then forwarded to the high school principal.

The principal spent several hours reviewing the applicant pool to determine who would be interviewed. He selected four men and two women to move to the interview level. The interview team was composed of several faculty members, both women and men. The team spent hours meeting with candidates and reviewing their credentials. They narrowed their choices to a young man who was an administrator with five years in the classroom and two years experience as assistant principal in a small district. The other candidate was a veteran woman educator who had strong, supportive references for her work and fifteen years teaching experience, two years as assistant principal, and one year as principal at a small high school.

After the interviews, the team discussed these finalists. They thought highly of the woman, but she was in the later half of her career compared to the young man. He "had a lot of energy," they said—code words supporting his youth in comparison to her maturity. He seems to be able to handle the discipline, a teacher said, although there was no evidence to indicate that the female candidate could not. The committee discussed at length the experience and credentials of each candidate and agreed that discipline was a priority.

The position was offered to the young man with limited experience. The woman applicant had a proven track record of success as a classroom teacher and administrator, but the committee focused on the perceived "energy" of the young man. "Won't he make a great principal one day?" they said. What they did not speak about was that the woman candidate already had been a great principal.

Women applicants tend to be older than males when applying for administrative positions. They also have more years of service in education than their male counterparts. Women have a track record in education that provides a history of their skills, leadership style, and competence. Male applicants are in the early stages of their educational career and have limited experience, less time to learn, and less time to demonstrate leadership skills (Tallerico and Tingley, 2001). Search committees at all levels often base their selection on the history of leadership in their organization, an organization composed of white men in senior leadership positions.

Our culture perpetuates this selection process, hiring men over women at an astounding rate. As educators climb the educational ladder, the rate of selection of men over women becomes increasingly disproportionate. Why is this? Individuals and search committees making the selections base those choices on their interactions and experiences with leadership, which is white and male. These decision makers have had limited exposure to alternative types of leadership such as those provided by women and minorities. While the criteria for selection may be identified in the job description or profile, the selection process itself is based on experiences and biases of the committee members. Evans (2003a) notes: "My research shows that women get promoted based on their performance, while men might get promoted on their potential. Women are doing a job for 10 years before they get promoted because they must prove they know how to do it" (36).

Aspiration Is Challenged by Lack of Opportunity

To address the belief of the public that candidates for the superintendency are few and far between, alternatives could include seeking a broader pool of administrative applicants and accepting candidates with alternative certification. However, the reality is that both of those alternatives still would provide a predominantly male pool of applicants when a qualified pool is already in existence. Those candidates can be found in state department of education's certification files, in our schools, and in leadership preparatory programs. Preparatory program students provide an applicant pool that is self-selected beginning with a primary interest in leadership. Unfortunately, there still is one potential shortcoming with that applicant bank— an admissions process could easily set up selection of those who look and sound like what is commonly considered "superintendent material," using descriptors that describe white men superintendents.

The typical superintendent candidate proceeds through the ranks, first as teacher, then principal. He usually looks like the traditional school administrator, a white male. He attains his doctorate somewhere throughout this time and then applies for his first superintendency, initially in a small school district and progressing over time to a larger one. He has gone through the educational chairs but did not sit long in any one of them.

School boards value a candidate having gone through the chairs, but apparently they do not want them to spend too much time in any one position. Female candidates spend half or more of their professional career in the classroom, usually ten to fifteen years. Consequently, school boards may view women as having a teacher mentality, which may pose considerable challenge in transitioning to the role of school administrator. They may view women as too child centered, without experience in important areas such as finance and student discipline. School boards look at the fifty-something female candidates as nearing retirement and past the age for entering this challenging position as an administrator. In general, school boards believe most women applicants who have followed this career path—a large number of years of teaching before becoming qualified as an administrator—are too old!

Length of time spent in each administrative position (assistant principal, principal, central office position) is equally as important as a candidate's level of administrative experience. School boards value candidates with secondary administrative experience over those with elementary administrative experience because they believe the secondary administrative experience is more rigorous than elementary administrative experience (Tallerico, 2000). Elementary principals are afforded greater anonymity than secondary principals because there are fewer demands for public appearances. High school principals have a high level of visibility, often even greater than that of superintendent. They are well known and are seen at events with high community participation such as athletics, music concerts, and graduation ceremonies.

Successful high school principals are viewed as having strong management and leadership skills. They are celebrated as heroes if one of their sports teams wins a state title, or warriors if they survive difficult matters like school violence. Although there has been an increase in the number of women serving as high school principals over the past two decades, the strong majority of high school principals are men.

Women predominantly serve as elementary principals, curriculum co-ordinators, or staff development coordinators (Hodgkinson and Montenegro, 1999). Unlike the male-dominated positions as high school principals and assistant principals, elementary principals operate below the radar screen in most school districts. The children in their schools love them and, consequently, so do the children's parents. Persons in these jobs generally receive limited attention from the school board or community because they work with an "easier" population to lead. The primary exception to their community visibility beyond their schools will be when students at an elementary school have not performed acceptably according to annual student achievement scores on state standardized tests. Then the principal of that school feels public pressure from everyone to provide the kind of leadership that will result in improved student achievement scores. While the roles traditionally occupied by women provide a valuable service to the school district, search committees and school boards view them as less significant and less challenging than the role of high school principal.

Experience at the superintendent level is also considered positive when applying for the position. Women are less likely to have had any experience as a superintendent at the age when men are applying for their second or third role at the helm of a school district. While men begin their administrative careers in their mid to late twenties, women begin their administrative careers during their thirties (Shakeshaft, 1989).

Search firms who commonly assist school boards in recruiting and employing superintendent candidates, also commonly referred to as "headhunters," frequently screen out female applicants for superintendent positions: "It's the headhunter who makes the first cut of superintendent candidates, eliminating anywhere between 5 and 100 applications before forwarding (typically) 10–12 on which the school board can focus" (Tallerico, 2000, 76). Of even greater concern is that women applicants are at a distinct disadvantage before they even apply.

The Road Most Traveled

Hodgkinson and Montenegro (1999) report: "Two primary traditional paths have been reported in the literature: teacher to principal to superintendent, and teacher to principal to central office administrator to superintendent" (12). The unwritten list of qualifications that screens a candidate in or out includes experience in many male-dominated positions. While more women fill middle management staff positions, men enter line responsibilities at the school principal or assistant principal position at a rate of 2.5 to 1 (Ringel et al., 2004). This promotion rate ensures that women will have great difficulty closing the gender gap between male and female superintendents.

In addition to these career paths, search firms and school boards prefer superintendent candidates who have spent limited time in the classroom, have been high school principals, have some experience at the superintendency or central office level, and are in their early forties. While these criteria do not include the word "men," it does imply: "Most women need not apply." The professional characteristics for the typical female applicant for a first superintendency include: ten to fifteen years' teaching experience, age in the late forties or early fifties, and a limited time in administration (Tallerico, 2000).

Most search consultants do not just wait for applicants to apply. They actively recruit candidates for the role using historical predispositions about "best qualified" (Tallerico, 2000). School boards receive information from search firms about the "top" candidates, the ones the search firms have determined best meet the desired superintendent characteristics that the school boards they serve have supplied. School boards rarely receive the applications of all candidates. The top candidate pool is based on the applicant's experience and credentials, not necessarily competence required for the school district's specific needs, and commitment, and the candidates in that pool are those selected by the search firm. Affirmative action is out of favor in contemporary society, leaving the less experienced, minority candidate at the bottom of the stack of applicants and therefore not passed on to the school board in the form of a recommended candidate. "People on search committees need to be exposed to alternative models" (31) for identifying, recruiting, and selecting superintendent candidates, says Dr. C. Cryss Brunner (Brunner et al., 2003a):

> I would rather just say that the variety of models (of leadership) need to
> be visible. Women need to know that the way they practice is acceptable,
> especially when they find themselves practicing in ways not mentioned

in books on the superintendency. Otherwise, they will feel alone and experience limited support because board and search criteria are based on
white male norms. (Brunner et al., 2003a, 31)

Recently a superintendent vacancy came about in a local school district. The well-respected school district superintendent was retiring after
many successful years in his position. The school district was doing well
financially and making strong academic progress. The retiring superintendent was well known for his expertise in facilities and finance and had
done an exemplary job at both. He had left the key responsibility of instructional improvement to his capable assistant superintendent, a
woman, who had come through the ranks as teacher, then middle school
principal. Dr. Karen Campbell was well respected by the school board and
staff and had demonstrated both competence and leadership in her role.
She had just turned fifty, and her only child was out of the nest. Karen was
ready for this next challenge.

The school board hired a well-known, local search consultant to conduct a search, focusing on in-state candidates. The consultant was typical:
white, male, in his early sixties, and a former school superintendent. After
meeting with the school board regarding what the preferred characteristics
for their next superintendent were, he met with staff to let them know the
school board was looking for someone with experience as a superintendent.
During his remarks, he made eye contact with Karen, the assistant superintendent. Karen clearly received the impression that she was not welcome
to apply.

Karen, who had contemplated applying, quickly backed down from
the application process. The board's profile for the next school district superintendent stated "experience as superintendent required." Karen expressed disappointment regarding this "disqualifier" and made her
decision to not apply. A female colleague encouraged Karen to change
her mind and focus on attaining the position. After rethinking her original decision, Karen decided to apply for the vacancy and let several key
school board members know her intentions. Karen also met with her retiring boss to seek his support. While he was not sure Karen was capable
of handling his role, he did believe she deserved an interview so he made
sure she was in the interview pool. She was successful in the interview and
was hired by the seven-member board.

"It was a 50/50 chance going into the interview," she said. Karen knew that particular school district inside and out and had been the driving force behind the school district's academic success. The school board knew that as well and realized without her their district could falter. "The search consultant, Dr. Wilson, tried to push a couple of men," she said. "These are the same men he has pushed for several other superintendent searches he has led. However, the school board finally realized I was the right fit for the job, even though I was a woman."

Karen easily transitioned from assistant superintendent to superintendent. She required no time to acclimate herself to school district norms since she helped establish them and easily continued district progress. Karen hired a quality replacement for herself, a woman, whom she is mentoring for a superintendency—perhaps replacing her when she retires.

Search firms and school boards are the gatekeepers to superintendencies. Their lack of exposure to alternative leadership styles and beliefs about whom and what creates a good superintendent contribute to eliminating women applicants from the pool.

Men School Board Members and Superintendent Selection

School board member demographics can have a negative impact on women and minorities in superintendent selection. Karen's board was 100 percent Caucasian, 71 percent male, and 29 percent female. The white male-dominated board was searching for a "like me" leader: white and male. Nationally, school board member demographics are 85.5 percent white, 7.8 percent African American, and 3.8 percent Hispanic, and 61.1 percent are male (Hess, 2002). School board membership reflects, to a degree, two gatekeeper variables in superintendent selection, white and men.

Between the white men school board members and the white men search firm recruiters, their prejudice more strongly affects women and minorities. Approximately 14 percent of all superintendents are women or minorities. According to a 2000 study of American superintendents, over half of the superintendents surveyed reported that the "good ole boy" approach to hiring still exists and it dominates the superintendent search process. Many practicing search consultants are members of this "good ole boy" network, creating additional barriers for women applicants (Glass et al., 2000).

Let's face it; women do have a more difficult time being hired for the role of school superintendent, whether it is their first, second, or third superintendency. Like Karen, they may not make it through the application process because they lack "experience." They also suffer from lack of informal networks, do not have mentors, and are often older than their male counterparts. For those who do make it through this obstacle course and into the superintendent ranks, preconceived ideas about leadership and gender often add roadblocks to an already rocky path.

Conflict on the Job

So what about the women who do end up being hired for the position? Are they successful? What additional barriers, if any, do they face? What conflict might they face as they move into their new role?

Men, Women, and Power

The responsibilities of the superintendent of schools makes the position potentially an extremely powerful one. In many communities the school district is the largest employer; thus the superintendent is the CEO of the biggest business in town. The school superintendent is seen as having majority control over the quality of the school system, impacting housing values and real estate costs. The school superintendent has the ability to seek tax rate hikes or reduce them. The superintendent controls staff hiring, vendor contracts, and coaching selections that can make or break a small community's identity. The quality of a school system can also impact economic development, serving as an attractive place for businesses to locate or creating a declining environment where businesses fail. The roles and responsibilities can make a superintendent highly influential, if not controlling.

The roles for a woman superintendent may be very different from that of her man counterpart. Most women and men have differing leadership styles in the way they define and use power. Men superintendents tend to define power as control or authority using a top-down approach to leadership. Women utilize a more collaborative approach, building on relationships and involving others in decision making (Mountford, 2004). In the woman-led environment, the goal is to collaborate—for everyone to win. This contradicts historical norms for the superintendency where men lead through control or, if there is any collaboration, it will be limited and a man will continue to control the results. A woman's style of collaborative leadership challenges the status quo, often creating discomfort for school boards and those she supervises because "control" is spread throughout the organization.

Place yourself in the situation of Superintendent Marlena Fitzwater—fifties, new job, and new community. In addition to her new role as superintendent, Dr. Fitzwater has just become a grandmother, a natural role for her after successfully rearing three children. Marlena has successfully been through school district positions as teacher, assistant principal, and principal. She has now accepted her first superintendency in a small district, a three-hour drive from her current home. She remained in state so she could easily commute back to her hometown where her husband, Steve, resides. Marlena's spouse is the longtime owner of an insurance agency with a strong client base. If he were to relocate with her, Steve would have to rebuild his client base. So Marlena and Steve decided to maintain two households for the time being and create a "commuter marriage."

Marlena had searched for a superintendency closer to home but was always edged out of the final selection. She had made it to the final interviews for two superintendent positions, but the positions were offered to men who were well known in the "good ole boys" network. Marlena never focused on membership in the "good ole boys" group. Instead she had spent the past twenty years balancing the rearing of her children, her career, and helping Steve with his business. She had little time to network with her male colleagues. Opportunities to attend lunches and golf outings were turned down to spend time at her children's soccer games and music programs. Other "free" time was spent on job-related tasks, often spending time at the office on the weekends to catch up with the unlimited supply of paperwork. Not until Marlena decided to apply for a superintendency outside of a daily "commute" area did she get the nod.

Because she lacked a mentor, Dr. Fitzwater walked into the superintendency wearing rose-colored glasses. She was thrilled with her first superintendent offer and accepted the position immediately. Marlena failed to assess the school district and community to determine if it was the right fit for her. She was eager to tackle the challenges of this small but growing community and was delighted with the opportunity.

The applicant pool had been small. While the school district had typical struggles, that is, finances and student achievement, the school board thought Dr. Fitzwater could handle the position. After all, she had been a high school principal and had managed interscholastic sports and a complex school budget. The board, six men and one woman, voted unanimously to hire Marlena. And then the trouble began.

The president of the school board had held his president position for three terms and had run the school board uneventfully for the past several years. Mr. Kramer believed in top-down leadership. He ran a successful auto body shop and was well known in the community. Mr. Kramer and the previous superintendent determined what the school board agenda would be while they were at the local coffee shop having coffee and a donut and conversation with the local constituency. Anything Mr. Kramer did not support was removed from the agenda before it was finalized, making school board meetings extremely short. In fact, if the state did not require a regular meeting of the board of education for the purpose of conducting business, there would be no need for a meeting in this school district. As with any business, according to Mr. Kramer, school business should be handled quickly and quietly.

This was not Marlena's style of leadership, and it was clear in her mind that things needed to change. Marlena believed that all school board members, not just the president, should be involved in decision making regarding policy and practices. According to Marlena's quick assessment, major issues were pending in the school district and Marlena needed to alert the school board immediately. Marlena had analyzed the budget and concluded that the district was not being fiscally prudent, and fund balances were declining at an alarming rate. Additionally, student performance was below state standards, and the school district was scheduled for a state accreditation review in a short eighteen months. Things were not as rosy as they appeared to be according to board meeting actions and reports.

Dr. Fitzwater spoke with Mr. Kramer, and he reluctantly agreed that things needed to change quickly. He expressed his concern over these changes. "Were they necessary?" he asked. "Couldn't we resolve this budget crisis another way?" But Marlena conveyed increasing concern over these impending problems and wanted to have everyone's input. With Mr. Kramer's reticent approval, Marlena began to schedule meetings and organize several school district task forces to study these issues and make recommendations to the school board. School district staff had never been required to attend so many meetings, and rumblings were heard throughout the community and school district. Additionally, Marlena wanted to have study sessions with the board to review the committee findings.

The superintendent communicated task force and committee information in weekly board notes, another new school district activity. The school board president, an original supporter of Marlena's, began to receive complaints from other school board members. In turn, school board members were receiving complaints from school district staff. The positive, collaborative culture Marlena had hoped to establish became one of staff compliance and school board complaint. The school district stakeholders just were not interested in participating in the decision making outside of the "way it had always been done."

A contract extension for the superintendent was on the agenda of the upcoming January school board meeting. In the past, the contract extension normally had been a "slam dunk" for the superintendent. The public part of the January school board meeting was uneventful, as usual. Closed session came, and Marlena was asked to step outside the room. She had been included in these sessions before, although closed sessions in her school district were few and far between. Time ticked by slowly as she sat outside the meeting room door, alone. The door slowly opened, and the school board president asked Marlena to step into the room. The school board had decided, he said, not to extend her contract. The school board had made an error when Marlena was hired, and she was not the "right person" to lead their school district. She could stay and look for other employment or leave now and Gary, the high school principal, would serve as interim superintendent until the board could select her replacement.

Marlena was stunned, as she sat in silence and listened to the pronouncement of her fate. She was absolutely speechless. What happened? she asked herself. She had done everything right, she thought, meeting routinely with the school board president, working with the school district staff, determining together the changes the school district needed to make, moving the school district toward a solid financial future and improved student performance. What had gone wrong?

It was clear that Dr. Marlena Fitzpatrick's collaborative leadership style was not a match with the school board and school district culture. Historically, decisions had been made using a top-down approach in this school district. Marlena wanted to involve those affected by the decisions in the decision-making process, believing that they should be involved. The male-dominated senior leadership team, consisting of the school board and superintendent, had established norms for decision making, and Marlena violated those norms, creating dissonance at the school board, faculty, and staff levels. The school board members viewed themselves as being successful in the past. There had not been conflict until Marlena arrived. Prior to then the stakeholders—teachers, employees, and students—seemed content. They had not been involved with a leader like Marlena before, a woman with a collaborative leadership style. It disrupted their routine. Originally a supporter of Marlena's, Mr. Kramer weighed the complaints against her and decided she was the one who needed to leave.

Collaboration Meets Conflict

Dr. Marlena Fitzwater clearly had a conflicting leadership style with the school district employees and school board. Prior to Dr. Fitzwater's employment as superintendent, the school district had been conditioned by top-down, authoritarian superintendents. Although the previous superintendent, who was a man, may have appeared to minimally collaborate with the school board president, he clearly knew his place in the male-dominated hierarchy. Involvement of the school board was limited to board meetings, and the staff remained essentially uninvolved in district decision making.

Marlena Fitzwater wanted to change the entire male-oriented culture of the school district by developing collaborative leadership both at the employee and school board level. She believed those affected by the outcome of school district policy and other decisions should have input into the decision-making process. Marlena knew, as superintendent, the buck stopped with her, but she believed that participatory decision making is a highly effective leadership tool that can greatly improve organizations. In Marlena's case, it may have enhanced the organization, but it significantly reduced her tenure as school superintendent.

This woman superintendent was caught in a conflict of power and style. As chapter 4 pointed out, men define power by authority and control and women believe power should be shared (Brunner, 1999c) This male-dominated board, previously led by a male superintendent, hired Marlena based on their perceptions about what a high school principal should be able to do, serve as school district superintendent. This school district was not ready for this woman superintendent, nor was Marlena ready for the school district.

Hopefully Marlena will pursue another superintendency. There are other women who aspire to fill this role and are looking for opportunity. Writing to this opportunity, Houston (2001) states:

> Nearly two-thirds of the current staff members in district offices are women, and many of them have mastered the skills of affiliation and collaborating through the process of acculturation that we seem to reserve for little girls. We must find ways of shattering the remnants of the glass ceiling and making the role attractive to this new kind of leader. (431)

The key is not only to find the right fit but also to create the opportunity.

Might things have been different had there been mostly women on the school board? A recent study on motives and power of school board members found that women school board candidates tend to campaign for a school board position for altruistic reasons, providing service to the community. These women conceive of power as collaborative, rather than top down (Mountford, 2004). Their perception of power is similar to that of female superintendents, thus leading to the inference that if school boards were composed of a majority of women, more women superintendents would be hired, leading to collaborative practices in schools. This trickle-down effect could significantly change the culture and climate of public education.

Unfortunately for aspiring women leaders, women who have already arrived in a position of leadership often forget how they got there. They tend to forget the struggles that occurred prior to securing their first leadership opportunity. Men support and reward those who helped them achieve promotion. Men superintendents will reciprocate through networking: providing job leads and finding positions for those who helped them achieve theirs. This is a practice women leaders should replicate if there is desire to increase both the quantity and quality of women leaders.

Who Goes There?

Who are these brave souls who choose a career path leading to a position as superintendent of schools? "I once had a school board president who told me that my job as a superintendent was to be a quick-healing dartboard. And he was a supporter of mine!" (Houston, 2001, 428). Therein lies the sentiments of many school board members. The reality of the modern-day superintendent is different from the first-generation school superintendent who made sure there was enough coal in the boiler room to heat the school. Yet many still find it their calling, and some return for a second, third, or fourth superintendency, even after devastating personal or professional experiences.

Working as a school superintendent today places women and men in a position where they are targets for criticism both from the school district workforce and from the external community. It is not uncommon that student performance on state assessments will disappoint teachers and parents and the person in the position "where the buck stops" will be held responsible for failure to lead effectively. Likewise, as budgets need to be developed and tough decisions need to be made for reductions, a circumstance created by nationally waning revenue so far in the twenty-first century, school superintendents once again are targets for those who have complaints about what is selected for reduction. The experience of having one's tenure interrupted by conflict and controversy is familiar for superintendents. Yet many still have the passion that brought them to the profession to begin with, the desire to make a difference in the lives of children. Many find the challenge of leading a school district a thrill of a lifetime, and they return to educational service year after year.

Regardless of the passion, dedication, and commitment, too much conflict and controversy can mean the end of service as superintendent to a school district. This experience is most familiar when a woman is the superintendent.

A Matter of Style

Smart women use their natural, nurturing side to build relationships with others and, consequently, develop collaborative power. They do not believe they need to act like a man to be accepted in their leadership role. Women who are successful in their professional lives act like themselves, remaining positive, using their natural traits to build relationships, increasing productivity, and producing positive results (Evans, 2000).

However, strong women can make both men and women feel uncomfortable. Their style challenges feminine norms, in particular, women's leadership. This strength, if not exercised properly, can create discomfort and distance with school board members, school district staff, and the community. The words "aggressive" and "bitchy" have been used to describe "strong" women.

The dominance of men on school boards and in school administration establishes a context within which conflict between women superintendents and the school boards they work for might readily occur—particularly if there are some underlying cultural prejudices that exist for both genders. Sometimes this difference makes women feel a need to act like men or display behaviors typical of men. Some women feel they need to create an "alter ego" because their natural self could not possibly be successful in a male world (Evans, 2000). These women display their alter ego during their professional life while leaving their natural, feminine side at home. These women hide their natural traits, their nurturing side, their intuition, and their femaleness—characteristics that definitely are needed in school district leaders.

Dr. Judy Parvil, a veteran superintendent, used locker-room language and cigar smoke to gain entry into the male administrators' networks. Judy would not sit with women colleagues at monthly superintendent meetings or attend the state women administrators' network group. Her alter ego was most evident at out-of-town conferences, where she would lead the male superintendents to the next drinking establishment while being the only female in the group. There she would dance into the night, drinking and using profanity throughout the conversation.

Dr. Parvil's behavior carried over to her interactions with school board members. She would interact socially with the male school board members who occupied the majority of her board member positions, emulating their behaviors. Meeting her school board president for drinks after work was commonplace. Judy socialized with school board members at out-of-town conferences, skipping conference sessions in order to play golf and drink at the clubhouse. She was rarely seen with her two women school board members.

During a conference dinner where women superintendents were "accidentally" seated at the same table, a women superintendent questioned Judy as to why she did not attend the state women administrators' group meetings. After all, the colleague said, we are all working on the same goals, increasing the number of women in school administration. Judy replied, "Those organizations are a waste of time. The meetings are just bitch sessions where women whine about the lack of opportunities and why they haven't gotten this job or that one. If you want to make it up the ladder, you have to run with the big dogs. I don't believe in encouraging fluff groups. That is not how you get ahead." In her mind she was absolutely correct. Networking with her male colleagues had helped her secure her first superintendency. A male golf buddy retired, and Judy had sought his support to be his replacement. Her strategy was successful.

One of Judy Parvil's professional goals was to win election to a post in a well-known school administrators' organization. Realizing that 50 percent of the organization's membership was women, Judy knew she could not win election without the women's vote. Judy spoke at the executive board meeting of the women's group and asked if the group could send correspondence to their membership encouraging the support of their members and providing endorsement for Dr. Judy Parvil as a candidate. Some members of the women's group were concerned about taking this step; they perceived that Dr. Parvil had not provided much support for them or for the association they had on behalf of women. However, it was decided to support this woman's candidacy and move forward with the communications. Judy Parvil's belief about "running with the big dogs" seemed to help her be elected, although by a very slim margin. The support of the state women administrators' organization may have been what helped Dr. Parvil move from a close majority vote to the majority vote, becoming the deciding factor in the election. Interestingly, Judy Parvil was so busy and occupied that she did not return to another meeting nor ask for ways the organization thought she might be able to use her success to support other women.

Altruism and the Female Superintendent

Perhaps it is because most female superintendents are mothers (Brunner et al., 2003b). A strong majority (77.2 percent) of female superintendents have reared or are rearing children. Perhaps it is because women have volunteered their time in the schoolhouse before being paid for it. Perhaps it is because girls are reared to care for others and build relationships. Or perhaps it is the fact that women administrators have spent more time in the classroom than their male counterparts. It appears that much like their female school board counterparts, women choose the superintendency for altruist reasons. They have a desire to make a difference in the lives of children, to positively impact schools and communities, to build stronger families. Women view school improvement as a moral imperative—the need for all kids to be successful. But altruism can inhibit one's ability to see the speed bumps, detours, and land mines that may lie ahead.

When Dr. Riboniat attained her position as superintendent of schools, the male administrators in the district could not understand how she got there. Who did she know, they asked? What connections did she have to community leaders and school board members? They clearly could not understand her success. She was the first female superintendent in the school district as well as in the county. They had never had a woman leader, they said, and this change of gender seemed to frustrate and puzzle them.

The school district was of significant size for the state, and this was Dr. Riboniat's first superintendency. She had many challenging positions on her way to the superintendency and was still young for a woman superintendent, a mere thirty-nine. She must be out for herself, or worse, they murmured. She is using the school district and the school board as a strategic career move to her next position. Dr. Riboniat must have some unspoken spell on the school board. The board, they knew, would have never hired a woman; they were sure of that. They just knew she was a witch, so the veteran male assistant superintendents proceeded to slowly light the fire that would burn her career at the stake.

Dr. Riboniat had walked into a hornet's nest of trouble. The current school district's assistant superintendent for business was among the applicants who had applied for this superintendency. Dr. Bob Branson had many colleagues who supported him for the position, his own good ole boy network within the school district. He deserved the job, he thought. He was next in line, had been loyal, and had been through the school district's administrative chairs.

Dr. Riboniat was the antithesis of Dr. Branson, a collaborator, scheduling meetings, moving things along quickly. She pushed hard, eliminating afternoon golf outings and extended employee lunches. Dr. Riboniat expected all assistant superintendents to spend their lunch times eating at the school cafeterias and working late into the evening until their tasks were complete. The group hated her for that. They hated that a woman was disrupting their routine, the status quo. This small group of veteran assistant superintendents banded together over their dislike of Dr. Riboniat. They soon decided she had to go.

Their action was plotted for three years, talking with school board members and creating conflict. Some of the assistant superintendents had gone to school with school board members so it was natural to drop by their houses or meet them for coffee at Bill's Café. They made comments about Dr. Riboniat, implying that she was keeping the school board in the dark about school district issues and that employees did not trust her. These comments from trusted, veteran employees were enough to send the school board on a witch-hunt.

Dr. Riboniat should have seen it coming. There were signs—several, many. But she was there for the children, she thought, and things were going very well for them. Class sizes were reduced, technology was in place, new schools were being built, and achievement was on a steady rise. All performance indicators were up. The school district was having its best year ever, or so she thought.

Then it came—the closed session, the dismissal, Bob Branson sitting with the other assistant superintendents, huddled in a corner. Judy Riboniat was gone. She was leaving, one way or another. Her tenure as superintendent in the school district was over.

Bob Branson sat there and grinned. His issue was not her leadership style, although he abhorred it. It was not her professional performance because he knew the school district needed to improve. It was the fact that a woman was in the ultimate position of power in the school district, and he wasn't. Dr. Branson wanted to ensure her failure as a leader, but he couldn't. Dr. Riboniat was persistent and worked too hard at being successful. So instead, he created distrust of her among the administration and school board. After all, he had known them the longest, and whom would they believe about what was truly happening in the school district?

The editorial in the paper the next day read that if Dr. Riboniat were CEO of a large corporation, she would have received a raise, not a pink slip. But she wasn't. Dr. Branson had spent three years successfully orchestrating a coup. To Bob, it wasn't about her; it was about him. He deserved that position; it was his turn. He deserved the power, respect, and compensation that went with the position.

Dr. Riboniat had aspired to the superintendency because she loved children, and she knew she could make a difference; it was her moral imperative to help all children learn, preparing them to succeed in life. She had known this was her calling since she was a little girl and played school with the neighborhood children. She had accomplished much of what she had planned to accomplish as school superintendent. Based on what she believed about the superintendency, she should have been recognized, not dismissed, for her collaborative leadership.

However, her belief system was now shattered, and so were her spirits.

Case Study: The Superintendent and the Search Consultant

The phone call seemed to come out of the blue. A superintendent search consultant representing a national firm telephoned to see if Dr. Natalie George was interested in applying for a superintendency in a prominent school district. Natalie had been in her current position for less than two years and was enjoying the challenges this small school district presented. She had such a good relationship with her school board members, teachers, support staff, and community. It was satisfying to provide leadership as a superintendent of schools for this school district. However, the invitation delivered by the consultant was both appealing and flattering. She would think about it, she said.

Dr. George began acquiring information from the Internet about the school district the consultant wanted her to consider for application. She did some essential research and made telephone calls. The more she heard, the more she favored submitting an application, even though it meant uprooting her daughter again. Family had become extremely important to her since she had been a single parent for three years.

Natalie updated her resume, spoke with her school board president, and submitted her application for the "new" superintendent opportunity. Surely, the telephone call from the search consultant meant that she was a top contender. She waited for the next call.

The search consultant called again and asked her to fly to Chicago for a screening. Natalie made her flight reservations. By now her administrative team was aware of the possibility of her departure and several senior members began posturing for this vacancy. Natalie did not like what she noticed in the behavioral change of her administrative team.

The screening with the search firm seemed to go very well. The search firm's interview team reported that they would be bringing her name forward to the school board. The school board wanted a female candidate on the slate, and Natalie would be "the one," they said. "The one," Natalie reflected. What did that mean? Natalie was somewhat dumbfounded by the comment. She thought she knew what these comments were intended to mean, but she was not sure.

On the return flight home, Natalie focused more and more on these last comments. The school board wanted a female candidate on the slate. She "was the one," they said. Natalie knew "the one" meant the only woman on the list. The more she thought about it, the angrier she became. She had been recruited for appearances only to be the only female candidate. The search firm and the school board knew full well that they were going to hire a man superintendent, not a woman. She was the token woman; she had allowed herself to be used.

Chapter Questions

1. What, if anything, did Natalie George risk when she applied for the superintendent position?

2. How might her application to another school district impact her effectiveness in her current role? Can she control that? Explain your response/position.

3. What steps should Natalie take now with her current school board and administrative team members, all of whom know that she has interviewed for a different job? Explain your answers.

4. What is the responsibility of the search firm to recruits as it works to recruit applicants?

5. What did you learn in chapter 6 that can be applied to this case? Explain the application.

CHAPTER 7
THE POWER OF NEGOTIATION

While friends remain relatively constant, the opposition multiplies like rabbits.

This was Dr. Maria Carpenter's first superintendency. The position served an average-size district but larger than the one she was leaving. In her previous assignment she had served as high school principal the past six years. Maria was leaving her high school position for the "plum" superintendency in the county and she was the school board's top choice. The new location would make it a long commute from home, but Maria did not need to relocate immediately. Maria's husband was already retired and had numerous hobbies that occupied his time. He was willing to relocate with Maria. "It was her turn," he said. He meant it was her turn to fulfill her career aspirations. He had already fulfilled his, a successful small business owner.

The couple decided to put their house on the market. This new school board did expect their superintendents to reside in their community within a short period of time from the beginning of their service, and Dr. Carpenter was no exception. Maria's house sold quickly, and she and her husband moved before the school year began.

Once employed, Maria began the task of assessing the school and community to determine its strengths, weaknesses, opportunities, and threats. Maria was extremely outgoing and enjoyed meeting and talking with people so the task of talking with school district stakeholders came easily to her.

She was out of her office and in the schools and community every day, listening and learning.

It did not take long before Maria ascertained that there was a tremendous need to improve the school district's aging facilities for both safety and cosmetic reasons. Additionally, state funds were being cut and the school district needed to seek a tax hike to support current staffing levels and programs. Maria organized a school district finance committee to analyze and discuss these issues and make recommendations.

Within a short time the group was recommending that the school district seek a tax increase. The increase had to be approved by the school board and placed before the voters for approval. With most school boards, determining whether or not to seek a tax increase is a politically challenging task. The local community was known for its frugality and already questioned many school district expenditures. Only after several work sessions and the committee's recommendation did the school board approve placing the issue on the ballot.

A community campaign committee worked diligently to seek support for the issue. Phone lists, surveys, flyers, and ads were developed and distributed. Voter registration was carried out in all the schools, and school employees contacted school district patrons reminding them to register and answering questions about the ballot issue. As the election neared, teachers called parents and reminded them to go to the polls. Teachers were aware that school district employee layoffs could occur should the issue not pass.

To Maria's and the school board's surprise, the ballot issue failed miserably. Community feedback indicated several reasons. First, there was a belief that the school district had as much money as it needed and facilities were adequate. Most voters had attended these same schools and remembered them as they were, not as they should be today. Secondly, the patrons believed the school district superintendent was promoting her own agenda, not the community's.

Convinced that a second time before the voters would make the difference, Maria asked the school board to place the issue back on the ballot during the next election. With state revenue declining, she said, the school board would need to make significant cuts to remain financially solvent. The board reluctantly agreed. Employees were disheartened with the results of the last issue and gave minimal effort to this initiative. With little fanfare, the issue went before the voters again, only to go down to defeat, this time by a larger margin.

When impending cuts were announced, community members became enraged. Patrons called school board members nonstop and appeared en masse at the next school board meeting. The school board began to look to Maria as the source of this failure. She alone had pushed this tax issue, they said. It was her agenda. The school board was not about to cut any programs or staff. The school district was the major source of employment in the community, and cutting programs meant cutting paychecks from neighbors and friends.

At the next school board meeting, Maria was the topic of executive session. The school board was terminating her employment and appointing the assistant superintendent as interim superintendent, effective immediately. The school district security officer, whom Maria had hired, was to escort her to her office. She was to pack up her office that night. Her compensation was also terminated, effective immediately. The attorney for the school board handed Maria a letter explaining that she was working without a binding contract and thus her dismissal was immediate.

Maria was devastated. She knew the school board was blaming her for the failure of the tax issues but was shocked with this turn of events. She thought she had a valid contract. Like most women, when she was hired, she did not negotiate her salary. She accepted what was offered and the terms of the contract—a one-year renewal, or so she thought. The contract had not been signed by both parties and was not binding, wrote the attorney. Not only was she without a job, she was without severance pay.

Distraught, Maria contacted a colleague to seek advice. What could she do, she asked? Should she hire an attorney? Should she file a lawsuit? What recourse did she have? After listening to her story and asking questions, the colleague advised her to negotiate a letter of reference and leave. Maria had no recourse; she had not taken care of herself or her family by securing an acceptable contract. Maria left herself vulnerable to immediate dismissal. With an unsigned contract, the school board would receive no criticism by the taxpayers for a contract buyout. While the school board was in the clear, Maria clearly was without a job, a paycheck, and, at the moment, a future.

Doing What Doesn't Come Naturally

Negotiating does not come naturally to women, especially when it involves salary. Women are often underpaid and undervalued and leave their decision regarding their monetary worth to their employer, not themselves. It is not that they do not value their own work; it is because they do not want to create potential conflict with those who employ them.

Women are focused on relationships and prefer that people remain friends or colleagues, not adversaries. Tasks such as negotiating and debating do not come naturally to their collaborative nature. Women give away their talents such as time, advice, consultation, and mentoring when men charge for similar expertise. Women are service oriented and naturally want to help others. When it comes to helping themselves, women can be doormats, allowing colleagues, bosses, family members, and friends to usurp energy, skills, and resources with little or no return.

Maria was no different. When it came time to negotiate a contract, she did not negotiate at all. She wanted this first superintendency and took it without question. She assumed that compensation was not an issue and what she was being offered was what the job was worth. She did not question what was offered, signed or unsigned. Clearly, she undervalued herself. Maria failed to create any safety net for herself should the school board make the decision to dismiss her. She devalued herself by letting others control her professional future. She failed to establish the worth of her work and ensure that she would be compensated adequately, no matter who decided to terminate the relationship.

If stereotyping holds true, the only thing women ask for that men don't is directions. Of course, stereotyping does not define the actual person. A woman's conditioned failure to negotiate and check all of the details connected with negotiations can affect them profoundly over a lifetime. Women have been reared to collaborate, not negotiate. Negotiation clearly has the potential for conflict and discomfort. Women do not want to offend others, and frequently they feel that they have little control over their future.

Second-Class Citizens

In fact, men have controlled much of women's lives until recent years (Babcock and Laschever, 2003). The worldwide political arena is a key example of our male-dominated culture. Male politicians provide the leadership for most governments, and the United States is not an exception. No woman has ever been elected president or vice president of the United States and less than 16 percent of state senators and congressmen are women. Not until the 1920s did American women even have the right to vote!

Historically women have been treated as second-class citizens. Women have been denied the right to a formal education and to property ownership. Education has been the right or privilege of men and still is in many countries throughout the world. In countries where these gender restrictions exist, women are accustomed to seeking approval of men for everything. In the United States, women still wait on men to ask them out on a date or seek their hand in marriage. It is customary. It is no wonder that women are reluctant to seek adequate and comparable compensation for work they have performed!

Salary and contract negotiations are a critical juncture for women in terms of gender equity. Starting salaries can impact lifetime earnings of everyone. Women will seek no more salary than they believe others will pay. They do not seek what they believe they are worth. This behavior has added to the disparity between compensation for men and compensation for women with women demanding less for themselves than their male counterparts. Males allow and often are directly responsible for approving payment to women for comparable work performed to be of less monetary worth than that performed by a man.

For Dr. Lorraine Andrews, the role of superintendent was what she had aspired to since she began teaching. She was deemed a "go-getter" by her principal and later named Teacher of the Year. Leadership came naturally to her, and career advancement seemed obvious. However, her role of school superintendent in her school district sent two different messages to her. First, she knew she was a leader, in charge and in control, at least of most things. She had the ability, authority, and power to make things happen, to call a meeting, to organize a task force, to create the necessary structure to improve test scores.

The second message was distinctly different. Lorraine's school board was composed of members who were mostly men. They referred to her as "ma'am" and pulled her chair out to help seat her while at the school board table, a behavior to which she was not accustomed. They frequently complimented her on her appearance and opened doors for her when she walked into a room. The school board clearly recognized Lorraine as a woman first and superintendent second.

Although unaccustomed to the chivalrous behavior, Lorraine decided that was a behavior she could grow to accept, or at least tolerate. She occasionally appreciated a door being held for her. Lorraine was just a bit concerned that this behavior was an example of the traditions and practices the school board held dear and to correct them might be counterproductive. Any counterproductive actions might create some tension, influencing board members to resist Lorraine's more important recommended changes, such as increasing the number of women's sports teams to comply with Title IX.

Soon Lorraine experienced gender bias from school board members at school board meetings. When discussing the budget for the upcoming school year, several school board members referred all finance questions to the veteran school business manager, a man. When Lorraine attempted to share her expertise in this area, school board members asked the business manager to validate her answer.

Lorraine definitely needed to determine who was in charge of what decision. She was accustomed to having authority and responsibility for everything under her supervision. She believed her authority was being compromised and her responsibilities as superintendent diluted.

Lorraine needed to have a discussion with the school board about roles—hers and theirs. This discussion was going to require give and take. She spoke with the school board president about these concerns and requested a meeting. The school board seemed unaware of their actions and were surprised about Lorraine's concerns, but they soon agreed to clarify each other's roles in the school district's decision-making process. With these written guidelines in place, Lorraine's relationship with the school board improved.

Negotiation is not just about money; it is about ideas, values. Contract negotiations can include working conditions and superintendent and school board roles and responsibilities. These discussions should be held prior to assuming the new position. Lorraine should have included this discussion when negotiating her employment contract. She will know to do so the next time.

Men negotiate with more frequency than women, four times more often (Babcock and Laschever, 2003). Negotiating an initial salary can generate hundreds of thousands of dollars in additional compensation over time. Women are decades away from closing the compensation gap. In spite of what is in the media, in some fields women are losing financial footing compared to men. The Breaking the Glass Ceiling Foundation reports between 1995 and 2000 the gap between male and female earnings widened for full-time managers in seven fields. These fields include entertainment and recreation services, communication, finances, insurance and real estate, business and repair services, retail trade, and professional medical services, indicating a negative trend in the economic power of women (Break the Glass Ceiling Foundation, 2005).

The Art of Negotiation

The art of negotiation can also be used in contract discussions with current and potential vendors, unions, and other entities that work with the school district, decreasing the school district's operational expenditures significantly and providing cost savings. Superintendent Williams's school district had just passed a sizable bond issue to build a new elementary school and renovate existing schools. Dr. Williams was in the process of finalizing the new school facility contract and working with her chief financial officer to address the issue of cost overruns. This had been a problem with the last new facility constructed by the school district and several school board members were waiting to discuss cost overruns at the next school board meeting.

Superintendent Williams decided to propose an agreement that would prohibit the contractor from exceeding the stated amount, no matter what the circumstances. This construction company had provided quality service to the school district in the past but was known for its costly overages. The school district's veteran chief financial officer expressed concern that the general contractor would not agree to such an arrangement. Dr. Williams choose to lead the discussions with the contractor, and much to the business manager's surprise, the contractor agreed to these new terms. The school board was pleased with this new arrangement.

Although Dr. Williams did well with this contractual arrangement, women who choose to negotiate often do not have the results that men in similar situations have (Babcock and Laschever, 2003). Women will often ask for and accept less. Whether they are negotiating a contract or dealing with professional responsibilities, women do not believe they are valuable to the extent that men believe in their own value. Women have experiences outside of negotiations in using assertiveness in discussing their expectations. Often that behavior in women is described as aggressive behavior, and others may perceive them as "difficult" or "bitchy." So, in negotiations, they make an effort to avoid potential controversy and confrontation.

Assertiveness is a trait that is gender specific. Assertiveness may be a positive descriptor for men, but it often is viewed as negative when applied to women. Men use their assertiveness to initiate discussions involving negotiations while most women wait silently for an offer to appear. Women have been reared to be polite and to wait to be asked instead of asking. In other words, women sit patiently waiting for an opportunity to appear while men create that opportunity.

Men, Women, and Negotiating

Why do men seek more opportunity than women? Why do men seem to recognize and act on opportunity and women wait for opportunity to present itself? Women are not sure they deserve the opportunity, whether it is in the area of compensation or recognition. Therefore, they tend to be content with what they have instead of allowing themselves to be to discontent and wanting more. While women remain content in their leadership, men receive the advantages of opportunity after opportunity and climb up the corporate, institutional, or academic ladder four rungs at a time while women sit back, watching. Additionally, women may feel insecure with their own abilities to negotiate effectively and, therefore, may be hesitant to initiate the negotiations process—or to set the expected results of negotiations at a high level of accomplishment.

When you look at a wine list, what do you believe is the better wine, the more expensive wine or the least expensive? You may choose to purchase a moderate or inexpensive wine, but you have been conditioned to believe the higher-priced wine has the better flavor. A similar value is perceived with salaries. A school superintendent making $300,000 per year is viewed as more talented, capable, and valuable than one making $125,000, thus having more appeal as a candidate for other school district superintendencies.

In addition to monetary recognition, women fail to seek other honors such as awards and praise. Men and women alike work harder when recognized for efforts and accomplishments. Men ask others to submit their name for recognition while women wait to be recognized. The lack of female mentors and sponsors for women adds to this conundrum. Mentors can play a key role in providing opportunities for recognition. In general, men spend more time and effort looking out for themselves than do women.

Culturally, women are reared to focus on the care of others, another reason self-recognition is so difficult. Women are nurturers. They are the primary caregivers in the home. Laura Banks, a forty-year-old administrator, worked sixty-plus hours per week as an elementary principal. She and her husband had a small child, and both were exhausted by the time they arrived home each evening. They spent little time with their daughter and less time with each other. Laura had the majority of the responsibility for child care, picking up Alecia from day care and bathing and feeding her. Her husband worked the same amount of hours but came home and sat while she completed task after task before collapsing in bed exhausted. Laura felt like a hamster on a treadmill with no union break.

A woman's focus on others carries into the workplace as well. Women will seek and ask for things on behalf of others instead of themselves. They will spend time helping others with their work, then stay late to complete their own tasks. They will nominate colleagues for achievement awards and feel very uncomfortable nominating themselves.

Beulah Abrams had been an educator for thirty-two years, fifteen years as principal of Rosemont Elementary School. She was a pillar of the community, beloved by Rosemont alumni and endeared to many. Beulah had not only raised test scores in this poor rural community, but also she had rid the school of vandalism, started a thrift store for families, and was often seen taking bags of groceries to local families.

Rosemont teachers and students had received many awards, thanks to Beulah. Beulah took every opportunity to complete nomination forms, call the local newspaper, or develop awards of her own. However, rarely was she the subject of the award. Beulah seemed to shy away from recognition.

Upon retirement, the faculty wanted to plant a garden at the school in her honor. She said "as long as the children benefit." When the staff wanted to give her and her husband a weekend getaway, Beulah told them to give the money to the thrift store. With each gift, recognition, or honor, Beulah declined again and again. Beulah had earned these rewards and more. But in her eyes she did not deserve them.

Just Ask!

Let's face it: women don't ask. Girls were reared not to ask, to wait to be asked, and to politely decline when appropriate. Women give away their power, their recognition, and their salary to others. Our male-dominated culture expects women to behave in this manner.

Our culture expects women to take a lesser role in society, to seek less of the credit, to remove themselves from the limelight. "Behind every great man stands a good woman" is a saying that both genders are familiar with today. Significant change does not appear to be near. Can one imagine a time when the White House would introduce the President and First Gentleman? This drastic, symbolic change will not occur for decades, if ever.

Why don't women change? While girls grow up playing school and boys play competitive games, each gender develops its current and future behavior around these ingrained, culturally reinforced experiences. Perception becomes reality. Perhaps the only way to begin the process of changing is to assure that a positive, equitable, self-fulfilling prophecy is established for girls to grow up and behave in ways that will promote equity. As an example of a self-fulfilling prophecy, when a respected science teacher tells his students over and over that they are going to be excellent scientists, his students begin to believe what they hear. Even those who disliked science become more interested in the subject. The teacher encourages them at every opportunity. Students begin to succeed at the task of learning science and are reinforced with each success.

Like the students in the science class, boys and girls are conditioned by expectations. Girls learn to be quiet, not seeking what they deserve, being happy with what they are given. Boys learn to win and want more. Boys are encouraged as a gender to strive for the top. Men's successes are measured by the rise on the corporate ladder and the number of zeros at the end of their salary.

Their friends, their maternal instincts, the decor and condition of their home, not the money in their bank account or the title on their business card, are women's measure of accomplishment. Others view women this way and women view themselves this way, making it less comfortable to demonstrate their talent and expertise through climbing the corporate ladder or educational hierarchy. As a child, sharing accomplishments and seeking promotion was viewed as bragging and frowned upon. These memories and cultural patterning are embedded in the minds of women, and they resurface in response to multiple stimuli.

To a major extent, it is this cultural patterning, this kind of conditioning that influences women to fail to seek honors and public recognition for their accomplishments. Ellen Marshfield, a high school principal of five years, offered to host the Regional Athletic Directors Conference. Ellen is the only female principal in the conference, and she has done an outstanding job of increasing both the quality and quantity of high school sports at her own school. Additionally, she has hired an excellent coaching staff, thus increasing the overall school win-loss record and student participation rates.

Each year the Regional Athletic Directors Association seeks nominations for association president. Association members can volunteer to have their names placed on the ballot or be nominated by others. Ellen has been a senior member of this group. She thought someone would nominate her, but she did not seek a sponsor. Ellen learned early in life that nominating oneself for such positions was boastful, so when time came for nominations, Ellen sat quietly while others were nominated. Ellen had demonstrated school leadership on her own school campus, but the male-dominated athletic directors' group was not willing to recognize her as their leader, and neither was she.

Ellen was being nice, too nice. She had spent years fitting into the good ole boys' network and had finally arrived. They accepted her as one of them, except in instances such as these. As actress Sally Fields exclaimed at the 1984 Academy Awards, "I can't deny the fact that you like me. Right now, you really like me!" Like Ellen, Sally had worked so hard, not for her own recognition but for acceptance from her colleagues. This is the unspoken sentiment of many women who have made it into the male-dominated world of educational administration. Women acquiesce to the male perception of female leaders and carry out the role of leader with little fanfare. Recognition, honors, and strong compensation are left to the male gender. Even when women work harder, produce more, and expect less, their work is viewed as inferior to their male counterparts.

After her two male colleagues had gone home for the evening, Dr. Irma Wrisinger was often seen in her office working into the night, returning phone calls and completing paperwork. This left little time to spend with her two teenage boys. She was vying for a promotion to assistant superintendent.

It did not surprise her when her male colleagues were home and she was burning the midnight oil. She had worked many extra hours to attain her current position. While she thrived on the challenge of each new role, she also needed the additional salary to pay for upcoming college tuition for her sons. Irma did not think to ask for a raise in her current position. She assumed she was earning the same as her colleagues at this level. What Irma did not know was that she was at the lowest level of this salary grade and her male counterparts had asked for and received placement on the high end. After five years, each of these colleagues had earned in excess of $15,000 more than she had, an amount that was enough to make a dent in her children's college fund.

Destinies of Men and Women Following Dismissal

The doorbell rang at 7:00 A.M. as she was heading out the door. It was a courier with a letter addressed to her. The return address was the school board's attorney's law firm. The school board had held an executive session last evening, without her. She was awake most of the night thinking about the school board meeting, knowing that her exclusion from executive session was not a good sign.

The rest of her family was readying for work and school. She sat in the dining room, alone, reading the contents of the letter, the allegations against her, charges she knew were not true. The letter banned her from school property, her office, school grounds, and from her children's school functions.

It was June, not the best time to seek employment. The school board was attempting to fire her and avoid buying out the remainder of her three-year contract. "There are only two kinds of superintendents: those who are in trouble and those who don't yet know they're in trouble," reports Jim Murphy, executive director of the New Jersey Association of School Administrators (Pardini, 1999). Transience in the superintendency has increased in recent years. Change in the school board, state, and federal pressure to improve student performance and uncertain finances have all contributed to this change. While most superintendents leave their jobs voluntarily to move to larger school districts or seek employment in the private sector, others leave due to conflict with the school board.

School Boards and Politics

Politics can play a key role in the decision for the school board and superintendent to separate. Religious right, charter schools, back to basics,
or a disagreement over federal funding can impact this decision. School
board members can be as passionate about their politics as superintendents are about student achievement. "He lobbied against accepting money
for a preschool grant," said Rosalyn about one of her school board members. "Can you believe that? His rationale was that it was government in-
terference and the government should not be telling us how to raise our
children. Doesn't he realize where the rest of the school district funds
come from?" The school board membership had changed, and the school
board grew to support this lone board member's thinking, signaling the
beginning of the end for Rosa.

Politics alone should not be confused with performance. An aspiring
superintendent was discussing her professional goals with her superintendent. She was applying for her first superintendency and was as eager
as they come. Jim walked over to his desk and gave her a copy of a school
district strategic plan he had been reviewing. After glancing through the
document she said, "Quite impressive." Jim replied, "The superintendent
accomplished almost everything listed, and was fired anyway." While performance may help with contract renewal, it is not at the top of the school
board's list.

School Boards and Religion

Religious beliefs and practices by school board members can impact
both day-to-day and long-term school district decisions. Many religious
doctrines are gender structured and create gender-based organizational
hierarchies dominated by men. Male and female board members alike can
carry these practices over into their role as school board members. "He ac-
cused me of not being submissive," reported Dr. Christy Heyer. "He said
women should submit to men. He didn't want a woman as superintendent anyway, but since I was already in the position, he would make sure I
did my job—his way." The conversation left no doubt regarding this
school board member's beliefs and intentions. It was clear there was no
place for a woman in the role of superintendent, and certainly not for
Christy Heyer.

Most superintendents are optimists and find it difficult to pay attention to these warning signs. Their beliefs that all children can learn and succeed, and that they can turn around a failing system, often spill over to the belief that they can turn around a difficult school board. School boards with beliefs about a "woman's role" or the acceptance of federal funds leave very little room for discussion. These beliefs are usually unwavering and based on doctrine, not on analysis and discussion. When school board members display this type of behavior, the superintendent is already on her way to being out.

School board–superintendent conflicts are the reasons that approximately 16.7 percent of all superintendents leave their jobs and approximately another 10 to 12 percent are forced out involuntarily (Pardini, 1999). Most of these dismissals are the result of school board–superintendent conflicts over values or philosophies, including gender-based leadership. School board members who do not believe a woman should be in a leadership position often have values that correspond with other conservative ideologies. These values include what the content of curricula should be and how to teach the content, how facilities should be used and the extent of public access to school facilities, and which clubs and activities should be approved for student participation. Conflict between the district superintendent and school board can first display itself in the presence of issues about providing school building access for churches, scheduling public prayer at graduation, or the teaching of creation verses evolution in the science curriculum. All it takes is one passionate issue to bring a superintendent's tenure to a close.

Dismissal based on gender is usually not as blatant as Christy Heyer experienced. The seeds to dismissal are planted—and need to be recognized by women superintendents—in comments about a conflict of style or comments of lack of support from the school board on any issue. In hearing or sensing comments of discussions about either of these characteristics, a woman superintendent's internal antennae should go on alert. An indicator of the potential for such experiences occurs when women administrative candidates are presented as employment recommendations for any of the administrative positions open and are discussed by school board members as "women." Another indicator of potential future problems with school board–superintendent relations that should alert women superintendents is commentary that is in any way negative regarding sexual harassment. Understanding the school community culture will help a superintendent know

145

how to approach and deliver decisions related to sexual harassment issues. Anything related to the topic of sexual harassment or harassment of women can be one of the land mines that women superintendents do not recognize as anything except something that must not exist in the school district. That may not be part of the inherent belief system that male school board members have. These issues alone may not be cause for alarm. A pattern of behavior is.

"I was shocked," exclaimed Dr. Doris Moreau. "The school board had just renewed my contract, now this!" Doris had walked in unwelcomed to an executive session of the school board. She did not realize they were meeting behind closed doors. Her secretary, who also served as the school board's secretary, had typed and posted the meeting notice without Doris's knowledge. Now Doris understood the conversations that ended when she walked into the room; the subject of conversation had been the document her secretary typed that she never saw: "The board was in there with the school district lawyer discussing the quickest way to get rid of me. You would have thought it was the Board Mafia the way they were hiding. Why didn't they just talk with me about their concerns?"

The school board's concern about Doris could not be openly addressed. She was a female leader whom they did not want. The board did not have a legitimate reason to fire her. School district test scores were up, finances were strong, and the community was content, except for the school board majority. School board membership had changed since Doris was hired and so had their values. Doris was on the losing end of the vote.

A superintendent has no ability to change this type of board. She does have limited ability to control some of the resulting fallout. Negotiating does not end with the initial contract. It is a skill that can be strongly used during dismissal. From negotiating a positive reference to obtaining a buyout package, the art and skill of negotiating is never as important as when facing dismissal.

Negotiating during Dismissal

The school principals had received a call the night before. A school board meeting was scheduled for 4:00 P.M. the next day. The purpose of the meeting was to dismiss the superintendent. Most of them thought positively about Dr. Terri Riley. She had been at the helm of this large urban district for less than two years. How could the school board fire her so quickly? Veteran principals knew this school board had made demands to violate their own nepotism policy and hire friends and relatives. Dr. Riley refused to recommend candidates unless they were the best of the candidates for a position. She was adamant about following policy and procedure.

The school board meeting room was packed. The school board meeting went on for hours with community members and staff testifying on Terri Riley's behalf. A tall, older man sat close to the board proceedings. Administrators knew he was Terri's longtime friend and mentor, a former superintendent. He was present to negotiate Terri's buyout.

Whether it is an experienced colleague, an attorney, or the superintendent herself, it is critical for someone to negotiate a settlement. A new job search can take months, even a year. "I just wanted what they owed me," she said. "They approved a three-year contract, and they should pay me for the remaining year. The school board, not I, violated the terms of our agreement."

Job Security No More

Job security in the superintendency has gone the way of typewriters and coal stoves. In our highly mobile, fast-paced society, the tenure of a superintendent has changed accordingly. Starting over in this role is not new to many. Dr. William Jackson was on his fifth superintendency when the most recent buyout occurred. He would continue his career path in other school districts before retiring. Jackson had negotiated buyouts from three previous school districts, only to move on to another superintendency after each buyout. His short tenure in communities was well known and was not viewed negatively. He was willing to move to another state to secure continuing employment, if necessary.

Many of Dr. Terri Riley's male colleagues had similar job experiences with at least one dismissal in their career history. Others had less than glowing separations from superintendencies in their past, but they continued on to superintendency after superintendency. Some do not fare as well, becoming depressed and even suicidal. After one fired New Jersey superintendent took his own life, a superintendent's Wellness Committee was organized to support superintendents dealing with health, addiction, or forced unemployment (Pardini, 1999).

Job Stressors

Chapman (1997) reports a number of job-related stressors for first-time superintendents. These include high visibility, diverse constituencies, employees who are incompetent or charged with sexual assault, pressure from right-wing political groups, decisions regarding whom to trust, and lack of people in whom to confide (12).

Working through and with these stressors contributes to both building your enemy base and building a coalition for dismissal. Where do superintendents go to discuss their problems? Educators who have climbed the mountain to the superintendency find the view very lonely, and the loneliness associated with the superintendency has a powerful impact on people serving as superintendents.

Whether woman or man, superintendents amass adversaries and enemies over time. As adversaries join forces, friendships are tested. "I thought I knew who my friends were," said Mary Jane. "But once the news of my firing spread, I quickly learned who I could count on."

No matter how hard a superintendent works to build strong public relations, engage stakeholders, and work with associations and unions, the list of those wanting a change in the CEO generally increases. While friends remain relatively constant, the opposition multiplies like rabbits. It is not a matter of whether a superintendent is going to be fired or not; it is a matter of when.

Legal expenses can mount, even when superintendents do not oppose their dismissal. Negotiating a contract settlement or asking an attorney to review an existing contract and serve as an intermediary between the superintendent and the board can be expensive tasks. To help offset pending legal expenses, some state associations supply their membership with financial assistance to apply toward legal bills. Having a local attorney in place to support the superintendent through difficult transitions is a wise decision.

Separation from the school superintendency does not spell the end of one's professional career, but it can mean a delay. After dismissal, it may take a year to secure employment. Dr. Dena Lake was sitting in the hotel room after an excellent interview with the school board. She was a finalist for a high-profile superintendency after being dismissed from her previous position. Dena had accepted an interim position with the state after her dismissal, and she had debated her future. Her dismissal had been public, political, and painful.

Dr. Dena Lake was a candidate listed with several search firms, but she questioned the sincerity of her candidacy with two of these firms. One firm used her as a "token" woman candidate in the interview pool. Another told her it would be too difficult to attain a new superintendency, and she should look elsewhere. She finally found a search consultant who knew her value as a superintendent and promoted her candidacy. She soon had what she thought was a legitimate interview.

This particular interview had gone extremely well, she thought. The school board was responsive, and they seemed to have a natural connection. But after the interview, there was a knot in the pit of Dena's stomach. The phone rang. It was her husband. "How did the interview go?" he asked. "What's the matter? You don't sound well. Are you afraid you aren't going to get the job?" "No," she replied slowly. "I'm afraid I *am* going to get it." Just as she hung up the phone, it rang again. The school board wanted Dena to stay over and meet with them the following day.

It was at that point that Dena realized she no longer had the passion for the superintendency, the commitment she once shared with her colleagues. Her public dismissal and its fallout had scarred her both professionally and personally. Dena had given her heart and soul to her previous school district, and the dismissal tore right through her. Several colleagues throughout the country had committed suicide over their terminations (Westerhaus, 2004). Dena did not want to be a casualty of the profession. By all accounts, Dena bounced back rather well from this dismissal. But she was not sure she could handle dismissal a second time.

Several of her male colleagues had been through buyouts and less than glowing transitions without a hiccup in their resume. Dena took it personally. The relationship with the school board turned sour, and relationships were important to her. A man would have reacted differently, she thought. Like rambunctious boys on the playground, a fight ensues; there is a winner and a loser. Girls toss words around, verbally sparring, hurting each other's feelings. Dr. Dena Lake's feelings were wounded and so was her pride.

Why do men seem to rebound from dismissal and women take longer to get back on track? While men move on after a conflict, women analyze issues, feel guilt, and are concerned about disrupted relationships. Women want to be liked, to enjoy positive relationships with colleagues, staff, and the school board. They work hard at this aspect of their professional life. The fired female now has a perception that since she was no longer wanted in her last school district, she may not be wanted in the next.

Your Job Is Your New Best Friend

Women often view their jobs like a relationship. If the jobs are not going well, neither are their relationships. A positive or negative relationship with the job can impact all aspects of their lives. Men often see jobs as possessions, something to be gained and lost and gained and lost again. When women lose a job, they feel as if they have lost a relationship. It is as if they have had a falling-out with a good friend and they try to find ways to salvage the relationship.

Women go through stages of grief over loss of employment. The stages mirror loss of a loved one; they include: denial, anger, depression, and acceptance. As with the loss of a loved one, women take the loss of employment personally, asking themselves, "What did I do to deserve this?" and "How could this happen to me?" Women may believe they could have prevented the dismissal, blaming themselves for this severed relationship.

Anger follows as others are blamed for the loss. Emotional outbursts may occur, lashing out at family and friends. Anger is often followed by depression, not being able to visualize a professional future. And the last stage is acceptance, being able to accept the loss of employment and move ahead with future plans. The length of these stages of grief varies, but each takes time. Moving through each phase impacts one's ability to be a viable candidate for other positions.

A woman's perception of herself is much like a mirror, based largely on how others see her. Women measure their own competence through others' comments and recognition. However, when dismissal comes, many women have developed personal coping mechanisms, including close friendships that can provide an emotional outlet during the grieving process.

Superintendent Longevity

While there may be debate about the average stay in the superintendency, one thing is in agreement—the tenure has not significantly increased. Increased accountability and political demands have placed additional expectations on this already isolated position. Searching for a superintendent can be time consuming. The average superintendent can be hired and fired within a three-year span. This leaves little time for her to work on the business of school improvement.

A study of Texas superintendents who left their position identified significant turnover due to being "pushed out" (Czaja and Harman, 1997). During a one-year period, 183 Texas superintendents left their positions. Eighty-five of those remained in public education. Out of twenty-three random interviews, fifteen changes in employment involved poor working relations with the school board. Five of the fifteen were terminated or resigned under pressure, and four of these received a buyout. The superintendent initiated three of the four buyouts after intolerable events.

Concern for the superintendent's own mental health was an issue. Participants in the study reported major health problems prior to resigning, including weight gain and cancer. Yet just one sought professional counseling.

School districts, like government and corporations, seek heroes, knights in shining armor to charge ahead. Once recruited and in place, the heroes' actions can often produce unintended consequences, resulting in a once-supportive school board changing its direction to support the superintendent's dismissal.

Public Cost of Discarded Leadership

There are many variables involved in the process of dismissing a superintendent, none of which have received adequate study and research. Dismissal often creates community turmoil, school board dysfunction, administrative uncertainty, and a loss of leadership momentum. Sometimes this leadership change is necessary and good, but more often than not, the last ones considered in the decision making are the children. During most superintendents' tenure, they have put in place policies, programs, and practices that, if given adequate time and support, will result in positive change for the children. Instead the superintendent's tenure is shorter than the time it takes to create lasting change in a school district, and a "new" school district leader generally turns the ship in another direction.

After a leadership loss, school districts need time to grieve. Some stakeholders may experience loss as the superintendent departs, and others may find it a welcome change. As with any change, there is a cost, the cost of change, discarding old programs for new, new supervisors to report to, and reorganization. There is a clear disruption of school district communications and operations. The bottom line: abrupt changes in leadership do affect the most important stakeholders in the school community—the children. They are affected by a change in philosophy, different expectations for their school leaders and teachers, changes in curriculum that disrupt the alignment of their total learning process, and changes in pedagogy that leave behind one methodology for a new one for which professional development, risk taking, and practicing strategies in the classroom occur. All of these might be positive, but the general effect is "on hold" behaviors of the employee workforce and some withdrawal of commitment to what they were being held accountable for by the previous superintendent. These effects are what move passionate educators to ask, "Shouldn't the children matter?" There has to be an improved way for a school board to provide direction, support, and stability to a school district. Of course, that is asking quite a bit when every year one or more school board members pass through the election process to join the school board and one or more leave the school board. The systemic overlay on public school operations is, indeed, a challenge for whomever is a superintendent of schools. And she had better be quite skilled in negotiations.

Case Study: They Gotcha!

It was the day after the school board meeting. The school board had informed Dr. Monique Ellerby that they were not renewing her contract and this current and third year as superintendent would be the last of her service to the school district. Monique was visibly shaken by this turn of events. She had been the superintendent of schools in the school district for nearly three years and things were headed in the right direction—at least that's what she thought.

Monique decided to seek alternatives to this turn of events and to see if there were options for her. Her first call was to a retired superintendent who was now a search consultant. Her call to him resulted in a breakfast meeting the next day.

Monique appeared distraught as she sipped her coffee:

Gary, I don't want to leave my job. I like the school district, the people in it, the community, and my home. My family is settled and happy here. Can the school board just do this? They told me three years ago that this first three-year contract could be renewed for another three years during the last year of this first contract. Aren't I entitled to due process? I've done the job they have asked me to do and have done it well! I've met every school board goal that was set for me and I have evidence to approve it. I even have my performance evaluations that the school board completed all three years and they rated me "very good" or "excellent" on every item! You helped me acquire this position, Gary. Do you have any advice for me?

Gary was seated directly across the table from Monique. While she was talking, he was reviewing her contract to see if there were any loop holes. He sat quietly after her last question and finished his drink. After a few more minutes, he looked up from the pieces of paper and softly said, "They gotcha, Monique. I think they gotcha."

Chapter Questions

1. What lessons have you learned in chapter 7 that can be applied to Dr. Monique Ellerby's situation?

2. What do you think Gary meant by his comment "They gotcha"?

3. How should the contract have been set up in the beginning to avoid this situation?

4. What is the best action Dr. Ellerby can take at this point?

5. What would you plan throughout each year to try to avoid the occurrence of Dr. Ellerby's experience in your own superintendency?

6. Acquire copies of several different superintendents' contracts; discuss how the contracts are similar and how they are different; then create a contract that reflects the lessons you've learned throughout all of the chapters in this book so far.

CHAPTER 8
DILEMMAS AND DISCARDED LEADERSHIP

"The superintendent is often the lightning rod for everything related to youth within a community."

—Carter and Cunningham (1997)

A lovely day begins, but by noon the clouds have moved overhead and the rumblings of thunder can be heard. Within a short hour, rain begins to fall and lightning juts out of the clouds "looking" here and there for something to strike. Thunder grows louder, clouds begin to roll, and lightning cracks loudly. All of this occurs within a very short time—much like serving as a school superintendent must seem for the many who experience dismissal or who begin to bring closure to their leadership work because dismissal is imminent.

Women, in particular, have experienced lovely days that turned rather quickly into thunder and lightning extravaganzas, rain, hail, and tornado- or hurricane-type winds—the kind that put them in the eye of the storm. They have experienced the frustration and lack of ability in controlling or dissipating the storm's fury, which is overwhelmingly bigger than they. In fact, when the storm has wreaked its fury and begins to clear, women superintendents often find themselves alone, without a job. That's how it seems—the results of a major storm.

Dilemmas faced by women who want to be school superintendents lay the groundwork for experiencing ultimately some of those storms—either personally or professionally. At either the personal or the professional level, some dilemmas are resolvable; others are not.

155

Place Bound

"You can be anything that you want to be" is the familiar refrain. However, it is not the complete story. There is always context—and sometimes cultural values and beliefs—that determines somewhat "being anything that you want to be." To accurately represent the choices available to women seeking a school superintendent position, the saying should be amended to add: ". . . but you cannot be everything that you want to be." The addition helps women be realistic about what they want to be. Being place bound is a context that illustrates this point. Being place bound proves to be a very frustrating dilemma for married women with children or unmarried women with family or other commitments that cannot be met from a distance.

Betty Olivette and Jody Simpson were teachers in their community's schools—high school and elementary school, respectively. They learned about a new graduate studies program at the state university that provided opportunity to acquire certification at the school principal and school district superintendent levels. The state university, about sixty miles away, offered a new, easy-access program of graduate studies in educational leadership. The classes were offered from 5:00 to 9:00 in the evenings and on weekends. Both sought and were provided admission to the program of graduate studies. For four years, every fall, spring, and summer semester, Betty and Jody traveled 120 miles two times a week to complete their studies, research, and degrees. It was an enlightening and growth-producing experience. Leadership was fascinating, and effective leadership, particularly servant and instructional leadership, made so much sense.

Even before graduating, both women were thinking about and discussing the administrative positions that they would begin to seek. Given that both had families and both had husbands whose work was tied to the community in which they lived, their options for opportunity to acquire an administrative position were limited. They were place bound. Also, they both would be novices as administrators. Of course, both recognized that they could drive to another school district that was within a reasonable distance and provide service there—if that other school district did not require their administrators to reside in the school district. They even considered the potential of taking their children with them and schooling them in the school district that would employ them as administrators.

As assistant principal positions within a forty-five-mile radius opened, each woman would submit an application for the position, if it was one at the level for which she was licensed. Jody even submitted one application for a coordinator of curriculum position because she felt quite competent in providing curriculum leadership and oversight. Neither had an interview—not even one. So, thousands of dollars later, there was not hope of an increased salary to help make payment on student loans.

Even though married women now routinely work and progress from entry-level jobs to jobs of greater responsibility and leadership opportunity, a sizable number remain bound by cultural expectations—filling the expected roles of wives, meeting the responsibilities of domestic labor, caretaking of children—and, consequently, they are place bound as well. Certainly in small school district communities, a woman who enters her profession as a classroom teacher has limited opportunity to seek promotion in status. Assuming that a college or university is within reasonable driving distance, women can acquire the necessary course work and meet the necessary requirements for certification as a school or school district principal, like Betty and Jody did. However, the acquisition of the certificate does not automatically open doors for becoming a candidate for leadership positions.

Small school districts frequently have a school principal, a special services coordinator, and a school superintendent. That's it! More often than not, persons filling those positions have many years ahead of them before they retire. Unless those hired leave their positions for one reason or another, several years can pass before a vacancy occurs. If the school district "raises them up from the inside," the person(s) "raised up" are more likely to be men than women.

Mid-sized school districts experience this competition for leadership to an even greater extent because there are more applicants for a vacant position, and more than one current school district teacher or principal usually will apply for the assistant principal, principal, or superintendent position. Often suburban school districts, and even metropolitan or urban school districts, not only develop their own internal candidates but they increase the competitive edge for candidates by also looking at candidates from outside their own workforces to fill administrative positions. Because of the competition for administrative vacancies, it is quite challenging for women who are place bound to be able to acquire opportunities to enter an educational leadership position.

Known as an excellent teacher and encouraged to "move up the ladder," Louise Franks applied to graduate school, was admitted, and for three years drove fifty miles round-trip every week to complete the required coursework. She had some hesitancy about the decision at first—a creative tension between a personal desire to move into increasing responsibility and some "guilt" connected to taking even more time away from home, husband, and three school-aged children. Louise admitted that she had frequent thoughts about becoming a school superintendent, but she had chosen family as her first priority and career as her second priority. Her story involves three years of solidifying her knowledge about learning theory and best practices for school leadership. She came home from class energized and upbeat, and her husband even commented frequently that he thought she seemed happier, although busier.

Louise began to explore available positions after earning certification for a school principalship at the kindergarten through eighth-grade level. Within a year, the superintendent and the middle school principal in her school district retired. The high school principal was hired to serve as the school superintendent. The middle school principal was moved to the high school; the elementary principal was moved to the middle school.

Louise had taught in the one elementary school in the school district for eleven years, providing leadership for curriculum development and innovative practices and setting up programs to serve children in academic need before and after school on a regular basis. She applied and was interviewed for the elementary principal vacancy.

The school board employed Paul Jarvis to serve as the elementary principal. Paul had middle school experience but no experience at the elementary level! When describing her reaction to the board's decision, Louis stated, "I was stunned! I was humiliated! I was a pretty darn good teacher and had a wonderful reputation as an excellent educator in this school district! Not only was I not hired, but a stranger from another community who was a man without elementary school experience was hired!"

That experience motivated Louise to look for an administrative position in neighboring communities—including those seventy-five miles away. Without contracted administrative experience and unwilling to live in a different community from her family, Louise viewed her studies and efforts as being "in vain" and "unwise"—at least in terms of local opportunities.

Louise's place-bound circumstances are not unusual. In a 1992 study by Grady regarding whether women who complete preparatory program course work for school administrator certification acquire administrative positions, of the 129 respondents who had not applied for an administrative position during the past five years, 29 percent reported that the reason was "no vacancies in the area" (84).

Being without local opportunities for school leadership and being place bound, surely a wife and her husband would want to explore opportunities to move where both would have better jobs and conditions. However, there is one hitch that could create some family stress—clearly identifying for whose benefit the move will be made. Watkins, Herrin, and McDonald (1993) note:

> Few women have the luxury of relocating in order to attain job advancement. Ninety percent of women reported they would relocate only if their husbands secured employment. Seventy-five percent of men would relocate for a better job with or without the spouse's employment. In fact, our society "discourages family change for the sake of a wife's career." (22)

Our culture expects that a man's career will be the priority, an expectation that was much stronger in the twentieth century—even routinely visible in family television programs during the 1950s. Although there are now recognizable exceptions to the cultural expectation that "the man's job has the priority," primarily because so many women are in the workforce, the underlying cultural value continues to be for men to assure the financial security of the family to the best of their abilities.

Women who are single parents may very well be the only income earner of the family. They then become place bound when factors such as child care provided by family members and security of their current job cannot be matched or improved by acquiring a higher-paying position with more benefits elsewhere. Provision of child care is an overwhelmingly beneficial factor.

Gretchen Gambel described an experience she and her family had when she had completed her Ph.D. in educational leadership and had a strong drive to apply for administrative positions. Her husband encouraged her to make application just to see what would happen. Their middle school–aged daughter even thought that it would be a good idea—*if* she could have a strong voice in "nixing" the places that her mother might consider.

Two months later, after submitting a number of applications and interviewing for several, Dr. Gambel was offered a high school principal position that she found to be an attractive opportunity. The high school was located in a rural school district about 180 miles away from where the family currently lived. Following family council, there was consensus that Gretchen should accept the officer. Her husband left his profession, and the three of them moved to the small town. Within a few months, her husband found work in his professional area, the daughter had "settled in," and Gretchen was relieved.

Interestingly, three years later, the same opportunity surfaced: Dr. Gambel was recruited to lead a school district in a mid-sized city about 160 miles away. Her daughter was reluctant. Her husband encouraged her because there was an opportunity to transfer to a similar position in that community through the company in which he was currently employed. Until now, Gretchen's husband had been bringing in the highest income. Gretchen's new estimated income increase would help cover college expenses for their daughter. Plus, Gretchen's status would increase considerably. These are details that can have negative effects on an unstable family. It gets worse.

The family again brought consensus to the move, with the daughter still hesitant. Gretchen moved in mid-June so that she could have a two-week training period—a transition—with the current superintendent. It was then learned by her husband that his transfer would not occur until January. The daughter moved to join her mother in August, and the family became a "weekend" family. In December, Gretchen's husband learned that his transfer would not occur until the fall of the next year. Eighteen months later, the transfer was complete; the family wrote in its family journal the stories of being a "weekend" family, and the three of them began to reunite with each other around the everyday details of life that they had missed during this transition. Here was a family that had decided to make it work—regardless of gender, potential income, and ego. Was it easy? Of course not! It was the individual members' value for equity of opportunity among family members that helped them succeed. Valuing and acting on equity of opportunity pays off in many ways.

Women's Nonsupport of Women

Cultural norms regarding sex-role behaviors are very strong. Those who choose to step outside cultural norms experience negative judgment and discrimination from members of the culture. Decades of years and overwhelmingly large numbers of men in the school superintendency every year reinforce sex-role expectations for men to be in CEO positions for public schools. Consequently, when the strong majority of the superintendent positions are filled by men, then simply observing who is "in charge" day after day, year after year, is a conditioning process. The effect is that men and women are accustomed and conditioned to working under the direction and leadership of men; they are not accustomed or conditioned to performing work that meets the expectations of a woman CEO. Although becoming accustomed to working for a woman CEO is something that women and men can do easily, changing those sex-role expectations comes with resistance at varying degrees and from a variety of people—some of whom are surprising and perplexing.

Changing sex-role expectations is one of the continuous challenges women leaders face. Not only are women working as school district leaders struggling to change the image of the public school CEO to include women, but also they have gender structuring and prejudice to face throughout their leadership work.

Subordinates and "The Woman"

Criswell & Betz (1995) report, "In the workplace, the attitudes that subordinates and superiors have toward women in administrative roles will have a direct effect on how women's job performance will be evaluated" (30). Subtle (and sometimes not so subtle) prejudice and gender discrimination can strongly influence the perceptions of both subordinates and superiors.

Women who are subordinates in an organization led by a woman CEO are likely to have been socialized completely by cultural norms for gender prior to their woman CEO's arrival. They will have conditioned prejudices favoring men as CEOs, as will men subordinates in the organization. Women's and men's work expectations for themselves will be gender structured. The slightest bit of discomfort or uncertainty about work expectations will influence how employees view their woman CEO. Many will be pleased that "a woman" is at the helm. Others will not be pleased because for them a change of gender in the leadership likely will mean a change in the norms of operations that they have been able to predict. So everyone remains on "wait and see" until the "woman" begins to lead.

Helena Cronton described her challenges and difficulties with women in the school district when she was employed as a superintendent of schools: "Beginning with the usual 'First Woman Employed as Superintendent' headline in the local newspaper, I was on alert." Dr. Cronton's entire central office administrative staff were men. Five of the eight elementary principals, all three middle school principals, and both high school principals were all men as well. One of the three middle school assistant principals was a woman; the rest were men.

It was the commentary that was challenging and discouraging to Helena. As she met with both the internal and external community members in groups of similar interests or similar jobs, she found that the questions were more about her personal experiences and her family than they were about her. When she attempted to return the conversation to the importance of students and solid educational programs, someone would ask her whether she favored reducing the number of administrators or not.

Dr. Cronton's director of maintenance referred to her as "the woman." Within the first month of making her rounds in the school district, she happened upon the maintenance director having a coffee break with a collection of maintenance staff members. She walked in and heard him say, "I don't know what we'll do with this woman! The woman wants to see our inventory, and we've never been asked to do that!" As she appeared in the room, the folks fell silent. She greeted them, visited awhile, had a cup of coffee with them, and then said, "Well, this woman has to keep on schedule. Have a great day. And thanks for working here! We need you."

Situations similar to this happened regularly. She heard faculty talk about "the woman" via her internal rumor mill. Her assistants told her in an administrative council meeting that employees were calling her "the woman." Most people used the label kindly and in a good-humored manner. Some did not. It began to grate on Dr. Cronton, but the only thing she could do to maintain strength was to gently and subtly refer to herself as "the woman" in casual conversation, with a grin on her face and a willingness to laugh.

During her third year in the school district, she met with the sixth-grade faculty who would be moving with their students into a new facility for the next school year. She set some expectations (alignment of curriculum with fifth and seventh grade; setting a timetable for developing skill; using best practices instructionally; creating ways to provide additional time to make use of volunteer tutors; outlining a module for teaching volunteers about effective tutoring). She also explained that there would be funding available for all of these responsibilities and suggested that the months of June and July would be good for getting these responsibilities completed—with pay.

The teachers began to respond negatively. They did not want to add all of this work to their responsibilities. Their contract did not state that they must do this. Just because she was a "workaholic," they were not going to be that. They had children at home to tend to. Ever since she arrived, unlike a man, she had failed to recognize that they had other lives in addition to teaching! Additionally, they said, "You need to know that we have already talked with the board of education about your earlier communications with us as well. They probably will be setting up a time to talk with all of us together." Helena was quite surprised, and she responded,

> Well, for now, these are your responsibilities. If you do not want to meet them, please let me know by the end of the month so that I can begin to develop alternatives for getting these responsibilities met. You will definitely need to use the curriculum that is developed and you will be expected to attend professional development provided to assist you in skill development related to best practices in the classroom. You are moving to a sixth-grade center where you will not have other grades around you. The situation calls not only for an opportunity to be increasingly creative and develop skills in assuring that all of your students succeed but also an opportunity to do some of the things you have expressed to me as helpful for student learning.

Dr. Cronton knew that her expectations did not differ from those of men CEOs which whom she networked. She also knew that leadership for "this woman" was increasing in difficulty.

"The Woman" and School Board Members

Similar experiences occur with school board members. The school board that hires the woman superintendent generally supports her leadership. They have a degree of ownership in the employment of the woman as their CEO by virtue of the selection process and their action to offer a contract. However, even then, school board members are subject to the cultural

conditioning each has experienced and as the woman superintendent begins to lead toward the goals they have established, they will have some underlying expectations of what that leadership should look like, and men will have been the ones to teach them what that leadership has looked like. In other words, board members are subject to cultural values, gender-structuring practices, and gender prejudice in ways that may be more subtle than they recognize. Previous chapters in this book have reported and documented the gatekeeping efforts of both school boards and the search firms they hire. The screen they set up is often gender structured and quite difficult to circumvent. Some women do, though, and generally it is because there are some women serving on the school board at the time and participating in the recruitment, interviewing, and selection process.

Criswell and Betz (1995) report interesting findings about school board members who participated in their study. Based on their research, they note: "Female board members consistently have had more favorable attitudes toward women administrators than have male board members" (31). However, in their study, which involved school board members from sixty-one school boards in Texas, Criswell and Betz found that

> (1) board members displayed a ". . . neutral attitude toward women in administration . . .", (2) there were indications that ". . . school board members still do not exhibit a positive attitude toward women in administration . . .", (3) that ". . . females are more supportive of women in leadership positions than are males . . ." and (4) that ". . . those who reside in a more urban area have more favorable attitudes toward women in administration than do those who reside in more rural settings." (32)

The first finding sums it up! If there is not positive support and not negative support, then neutrality is the position of the school board population in this study. Neutrality is not the kind of support that women must have when they enter and work in a position as superintendent of schools. The support must be positive—certainly from the school board members who were responsible for employing her. Initial support and celebration is critical to a superintendent's future success. The rest of the community may develop differing feelings as the superintendent has to deny requests for privilege or access, and citizens eventually will be able to pull from school board members less neutral comments about the leadership of the women superintendents in their school districts.

When school board members run for election on a routine basis, every superintendent is faced with the potential turnover of members of their boards. Annual turnover can be helpful if newly elected members are objective and helpful. Annual turnover of school board members can be disastrous if those with strong or hidden agendas are elected; usually the agenda is to "fire the superintendent." It is difficult for any superintendent to maintain solid support throughout her or his work. At times, the superintendent must take a stand on an issue because of the moral and ethical responsibility of serving children and providing for the "common good." That responsibility generally means that others may take a strong stand in opposition to a superintendent's decision.

Women's Nonsupport: The Principalship

"It's the small stuff that will get you!" So said Sherri Wakefield. She was referring to her years as a high school principal—the first woman high school principal. Sherri reported that from the first day teachers reported to work during Sherri's first year, the daily faculty room conversation centered around what faculty members called "The Daily Dig." Many faculty members had been somewhat aloof with Sherri when she first met with them. They seemed unsure of what Dr. Wakefield would bring with her, having never worked for a woman principal. They also noticed that Sherri dressed very well and even had her nails painted and makeup impeccably applied to her face. "The Daily Dig" became conversation around anything to do with Dr. Wakefield's appearance that could be transformed into a "fault."

This was a new practice for the faculty, one that was not part of previous faculty behavior. Sherri found out about "The Daily Dig" from an angry teacher who was also new to the faculty for her first year. The new teacher felt a moral responsibility to support her "leader." "It was hurtful to hear that, of course," Sherri said. "I felt as if I could not walk down a hallway or talk with anyone without someone purposefully satirizing or criticizing me or discussing my personal faults, which I thought weakened my leadership." She interpreted some of the satire or criticism as jealousy, primarily because women on the faculty initiated "The Daily Dig" and a man on the faculty who had applied for the position fostered and supported "The Daily Dig" practice. Those same people made sure "The

Daily Dig" made the rounds throughout the school. Sherri did not weaken, however. She recalled what a women's studies professor taught about the role of humor in strengthening leadership, and Sherri began "to look forward to 'The Daily Dig,'" finding some way to laugh at herself and to share some of that laughter with the faculty. The faculty quickly became aware of the fact that Dr. Wakefield knew what they were doing. Additionally, Sherri analyzed every detail of her appearance, became increasingly sensitive to the nature of the community culture, and made a conscious decision to dress and appear more "like them" while still remaining professional in appearance and demeanor.

Sexism and Sabotage

The classic case of women's nonsupport of women is visible in the history of England's Prime Minister Margaret Thatcher's failure to promote women for positions available in England's government during a time when there were a large number of qualified women waiting in the wings for the "open door"—their opportunity to begin to move into positions that would provide opportunity to influence government policy. Although two women during Prime Minister Thatcher's tenure had an opportunity to enter government leadership, Thatcher simply did not open doors for qualified women, nor did she go on record with a reason.

In general, people support that which is familiar or known to them. This is illustrated in the attitude expressed by citizens in an election for mayor where a woman and a man were the candidates. The man was the incumbent. The expression most commonly heard regarding the election was "It's better to support a known evil than an unknown evil!" Any reason will do when faced with the potential of having a woman leader for a boss.

Some label the problem as "sabotage" (Funk, 2004a). Sabotage generally occurs on two levels. First, for the subordinates who have been systematically culturalized to prefer male leadership (bosses), there is a jealousy factor that surfaces when a woman moves outside the cultural norms and assumes a position previously known as a "man's job"—particularly at the CEO level. Dr. Wakefield's experience reflected sabotage fitting this first instance.

Second, women who have achieved, like Margaret Thatcher, are pleased to have achieved but don't lead in ways that increase the equity of opportunity to lead for other women. Currently, approximately 14 percent of the nation's school superintendents are women who also are pleased to have acquired the position as a superintendent of schools. However, many of these women do not lead in ways that increase the opportunity for other women to lead in school districts.

Using the research of Gupton and Slick (1996), Benton (1980), Ginn (1989), Edson (1988), Shakeshaft (1995), and Matthews (1995), Funk (2004a) identified and analyzed categories of supportive and nonsupportive women. The four categories are the following:

(a) "activists" whose concerns are gender equity and the active support of women entering educational administration;

(b) "advocates" who support other women, belong to female advocacy organizations, and believe that women bring unique strengths to school administration;

(c) "isolates" who detach themselves from equity issues and do not believe that sex discrimination existed, was not worth worrying about, or was not even a problem;

(d) and "individualists" who believe that the individual, female or male, took precedence over the group and did not believe in supporting or promoting women or taking action to correct the sexual imbalance in school leadership. (6)

Women CEOs who are "isolates" believe that they were not "hit" with sexism, and few understand that they have achieved success because they have been socialized to behave the way sexist men expect a successful woman to behave. Women superintendents who are "individualists" do not advocate for women and do not pledge themselves to mentoring or socializing capable women to administration in preparation for a school principal or a school district superintendent position.

When the needs of other women aspiring to leadership positions are discussed with women CEOs who are "isolates" or "individualists," there is usually a nonresponse or a familiar excuse such as the following: "This job is incredibly busy. I don't know where I would find time for mentoring someone right now." Or "The best way for women who aspire to be a superintendent to learn is to find a successful male superintendent and ask him to be a mentor. That's what I did—and it worked!" Or "The easiest for me to mentor would be women in my school district because they are close. The only problem is that right now I do not see any superintendent leadership potential in the women currently working in my school district." Or finally, "Women can achieve what they want. They don't need to be mentored. They just need to go to the conferences that superintendents attend to learn what it is all about." Responses like the above clearly indicate that the woman CEO is unaware that she is behaving exactly the way her male mentors have conditioned her to behave—in ways that males find acceptable. It is not acceptable for a woman CEO to fail to promote equity for other women in accessing superintendent of schools positions.

Skrla and Benestante (1998) report that there is a persistent sexism that both men and women deny exists in the American culture. In fact, the denial of systemic sexism contributes to the problem of gender for women. The surprise is that women choose not to recognize it because of their deep cultural conditioning, or because they do not want to "lose" what they have by advocating for other women and being labeled a "feminist." The difference between gender and sexism is that gender cannot be changed except by surgery, and even that action is incomplete. Although it seems insurmountable, sexism must be eliminated from systems operations and outdated cultural norms. Most certainly, sexism must not be witnessed in women sabotaging other women's efforts to access a CEO position in male-dominated professions and occupations. Likewise, successful women CEOs must walk the talk in supporting social justice and not deny women the necessary support and advocacy that is required by men and women alike in order to be successful.

Paulo Freire (1970) identified a concept that has poignant relevance to women's nonsupport of other women in leadership positions: "horizontal violence." The term describes "the curious behavior of members of oppressed groups who lash out at their peers in response to oppression instead of attacking their oppressors" (Funk, 2004a, 2). This behavior occurs because of "powerlessness and impotence of oppressed that would be severely punished if they attacked the powerful individuals who actually control their lives."

Freire further identified the characteristics that lead these groups and individuals to punish others like themselves. Their reluctance or unwillingness to resist their oppressors, coupled with low self-esteem and self-deprecation, lead them to fear responsibilities or leadership because they might experience further oppression or, perhaps, retaliation

(Funk, 2004, 2). Women who experience these conditions can reach such levels of hesitancy to take a position (e.g., celebrating and supporting other women who are achieving) that they attack them in order to reduce the pain or discomfort of feeling devalued. They make comments that bring successful women to their own level of lack of self-confidence. Women in the United States must become clearer observers and inquirers so that they can recognize the sexism and "horizontal violence" that exist, and so that they can choose not to be a contributor to either factor.

Leading Organizational Change

In the first part of the twentieth century, men filled nearly all of the superintendent positions and they practiced authoritarian leadership. Educational systems supported that approach. Toward the end of the twentieth century, school and school district leaders had come to understand and practice both situational leadership (using a behavior or style that matched the circumstances in which they were providing leadership) and transactional leadership. Both still involved the CEOs in structuring all processes and making most of the decisions. Educational systems supported these approaches as well.

Perhaps the most difficult tasks for a superintendent have been those connected with leading a school district through organizational change. "Reforming Public Schools" has become a powerful theme accompanied by state and federal legislation that increased accountability of school leaders and teachers for assuring that students meet student achievement standards. Annual public reports of school district and school data are required in most states, informing local communities about how their schools are performing in meeting student achievement standards and other standards. Essentially, the accountability movement has placed the superintendent and principals in positions as change agents, a considerably more difficult and complex task than that required of more traditional leaders. Typically in an organization, about 10 to 20 percent of the workforce has strong interests in improving all that they do and those employees welcome learning, growth, and change and are top performers—frequently stepping forward to lead the processes needed for change. The leadership challenge becomes motivating the remainder of the workforce to embrace change efforts that at times are risky.

Leadership theory and practice that routinely are presented and discussed in preservice preparatory programs will provide principal and superintendent candidates with some knowledge and skill related to transactional and transformational leadership. Both represent a more comprehensive understanding of leadership practices that provide opportunity for some success in moving the organization through successful change. Lunenburg and Ornstein (2004) cite Bernard Bass (1997) in defining these two kinds of leadership practices.

> According to Bass, transactional leaders determine what subordinates need to do to achieve their own and organizational goals, classify those requirements, help subordinates become confident that they can reach their goals by expending the necessary efforts, and reward them according to their accomplishments. Transformational leaders, in contrast, motivate their subordinates to do more than they originally expected to do. They accomplish this in three ways: by raising followers' levels of consciousness about the importance and value of designated outcomes and ways of reaching them; by getting followers to transcend their own self-interest for the sake of the team, organization, or larger polity; and by raising followers' need levels to the higher order needs, such as self-actualization, or by expanding their portfolio of needs. (30-31)

The collaborative and shared decision-making styles of women leaders lend themselves to effective transformational leadership, which tends to be a more successful approach in this twenty-first-century era of "reform."

Part of the contextual challenge that women and men face when they must serve as change agents in education is the expectation that change be addressed immediately and that there are specific design, description, process, and results that must be put in place and achieved. If women are unable to use their preferred collaborative styles to achieve results—leadership styles that require more time and that tend to achieve more powerful results—but emulate men's leadership instead, they are perceived as authoritarians with directive behaviors and subordinate dissatisfaction with their leadership becomes open. In the same position, men can quickly move into a directive mode, explaining the reason, and most of the "troops" will fall in behind to follow the lead. The educational workforce simply has been so-cialized and conditioned to men behaving in a directive manner, but that's not what they expect women to do. Women face the dilemma again. The need requires a directive approach—which works for men but not for women. For women, there are actually two problems that together become a dilemma: their employees will not accept their directiveness, yet there may not be time to use a more collaborative, shared decision-making approach.

Data collected from women subjects in Fullan and Stiegelbauer's study (1991) identified some key themes that must not be overlooked when leading change related to school improvement. The factors most closely associated with achieving school improvement that results in im-proved student achievement included vision building, initiative taking and empowerment, staff development and resource assistance, restructuring, monitoring and problem coping, and evolutionary planning. The women professed that conversations must be filled with "positive messages" about the change, that change should be made incrementally with sensitivity toward reducing discomfort with the intended change, that a sound pro-gram must be what is implemented and the implementation should occur with flexibility of practice. Additionally, focus groups stressed the need to talk with all of the stakeholders who must make the change or who are di-rectly and indirectly affected by the change (Salsberry, 1998, 71).

Dr. Bonnie Seifers tells about her experience that required significant change over a fifteen-month period in her superintendency. She arrived on the job July 1 and shortly after received a letter from the commissioner of ed-ucation for the state informing her, as superintendent of schools, that the school district would be experiencing its first accreditation review using the newly adopted state standards for public schools and had fifteen months to prepare for the review. There were 243 new state standards for public schools in the state. When Dr. Seifers met with her administrative council to study the standards and identify those that needed to be addressed immedi-ately, she learned that the school district had evidence of meeting only thirty-seven of the standards. Immediately, Dr. Seifers became a change agent. Her leadership was strong over the next school year, and everyone had a share of the work to complete. Every employee in the school district felt the stress. Conversations routinely expressed doubt that they would "make it."

In October of the following year, the review team arrived and spent one full week in the school district reviewing evidence prepared for each standard and interviewing a random selection of employees. The final report: the school district barely met the bottom line for accreditation. Bonnie said, "I didn't know whether to laugh or to cry! We did not lose our accreditation—which was cause for celebration—but I lost a lot of support that I might otherwise have had, simply because I had to be a change agent and such a driver!"

Not always must significant change be made with such urgency as Dr. Soifers's school district experienced. However, change is continuous. The old maxim "You are either progressing or regressing; there is no standing still" helps illustrate the continuous nature of change. Research findings continually increase our learning, so there are always new pieces of information and insight and new strategies to guide the development of curriculum content, delivery of instruction for successful student learning, and school district operations. The use of collaborative and shared decision-making processes, which are strengths for women, are quite powerful in changing the direction of an organization. Change efforts will be successful only when all members of the workforce can participate in the discussions of how best to improve so that all students achieve more. Women are more likely than men to remember that the entire employee group—cooks, bus drivers, custodians, secretaries, maintenance personnel—can play a meaningful role in the educational development of students. In fact, ownership and commitment to the success of students can be enhanced by activities conducted within their job assignments by school district support staff. Leadership behaviors most directly associated with or related to school improvement and student achievement are those described as transformational—the common practices used by women.

Collaborative and shared decision-making processes should be extended to the school community. Engagement of the school community with the schools increases the power of results. Women's natural inclination to involve others, to practice inclusiveness of all stakeholders, offers a value-added opportunity to school districts. Gaining both internal and external community consensus brings all parts of the organization into sync and allows many opportunities to build on strengths. In fact, the typical orientation of women leaders is to be inclusive and to build on individual, organizational, and community-wide strengths. Decisions are more powerful and successful when the focus is on improving an organization or performance of people by building on strengths than when the focus is on removing the weaknesses of an organization and its people. Weaknesses disappear as strengths increase. There is great value in the leadership styles of women when working with expectations surrounding change for purposes of improvement. However, the dilemma for women remains—when involved in change or conflict, employees will state a preference for men as leaders because of the perception that they are stronger and give firm directions.

Power "With" or Power "Over": Another Dilemma

Yet another dilemma for women is that one of their strongest leadership tendencies is to provide leadership in organizational development that creates power "with" others—a collaborative approach. The literature on leadership at the superintendency level reports information and insight regarding men in leadership. The language of leadership in the literature of superintendents of schools provides mental pictures of power "over" as the leadership effect resulting from the way men make decisions, conduct performance evaluations (top-down) of personnel, select what will be improvement initiatives, and set the agenda for school district organizations. Men superintendents have been the major decision makers. Brunner's study (2000b) of twelve women superintendents captured the discomfort the women superintendents had with the term *power*. Brunner noted that the discomfort had to do with the way the term is defined as "control, command, domination over others" (84). Women do not assert power "over" others; their approach is to develop power "with" others. Relational leadership is preferred by women. Developing collaborative practices and sharing information, creative thinking, and problem resolution are desired by women as organizational processes through which the work of schooling is done. Working together to make decisions increases the "power of one," moving it to the "power of many."

Aiken and Tarule (1998) note the value of employing women's leadership as school leaders. In fact, they state that it is from women's leadership that transformational leadership was born:

> A number of writers from the field of women's leadership have provided evidence that soliciting input from others and willingly engaging in open communication and sharing of information creates new structures and definitions of power (Cantor, Baray, & Stoess, 1992; Goldberger, Tarule, Clinchy, & Belenky, 1996; Fennell, 1995; Regan & Brooks, 1995; Rosener,

> 1995). Certainly out of these experiences came what scholars are labeling
> transformational leadership. (160)

Using listening skills effectively, collaborating, and including stakeholders
in the decision making, women are more able to "transform" the culture.
Their change leadership allows those they lead to become empowered to
move forward in addressing change in ways that will work for them while
still acquiring the desired results. Farmer (1993) claims that "women use
power to empower others . . . [and] empowerment is the first attribute of
women's leadership" (53). Using power to empower others can have some
very positive results in challenging and difficult areas. Brunner (1997) reports, "Collaborative decision-making, although difficult, has proven to
facilitate school reforms that advance social justice with an emphasis on
academic achievement for every child" (9).

When asked whether power "over" or power "with" is most desirable,
most people—men and women—prefer to be independent from feeling
that others have power "over" them; being part of shared power is more attractive. Exceptions will be in times of turmoil when directive leadership
will be preferred. Women can be directive leaders when needed. They
would perceive those times as being related to urgency or emergency.

Earlier in this book an example of a faculty that was undergoing significant change was presented; the faculty became so frustrated with
studying and understanding all of the new expectations (called "best practices") that several spoke out and asked, "Why don't you just tell us what
you want? It would take much less time!" Practiced in being recipients of
power "over," this faculty was resigned to that "easier" way. Educational organizations are not polished yet in using processes for successful shared
decision making. The process seems long and tedious for those not skilled
or trained in examining data and going through processes to arrive at
good, collective decisions. However, there is a direct connection between
shared decision making and improved student performance. The early results following implementation of the Professional Learning Communities professional development model developed by Richard DuFour
(1998) provide evidence of the connection between teacher-teacher plus
teacher-administrator collaboration and improved student performance.

Having information that others want or can use creates power for
the holder of that information. When all have access to the information, the

power of the individual carrier might be reduced, but shared power is increased. Shared information helps establish a common language and bottom line for improvement efforts. Shared information creates common insight and is useful in informing decision making. Funk (1993) describes the workplace run by women as "'webs of inclusion' and not hierarchies and . . . a key factor in this inclusiveness is the sharing of information" (36). Sharing information and decision making, including others, building strength in involvement, and understanding are creating and using power "with" others—and that kind of leadership has solid advantages for school districts.

Reese (1993) completed a study of fifty Dallas Metroplex women school administrators, asking them, "How have your experiences as a woman—girl, wife, mother, sister, daughter—contributed to your leadership style?" Reese reported that

> responses to this question established that these women felt that their roles as women had made them be more affective leaders who were: nurturing, giving, adaptive, intuitive, flexible, peace-making, empathic, able to compromise, sensitive, humanistic, responsive to needs of others, better communicators and listeners, and more collaborative. (37)

Men have culturally deep support from school boards and faculty in positively biased ways and are more frequently the "winners" of the administrative positions, primarily because school board members see the potential for men taking a strong stand and successfully exerting power "over" others in times needing strong leadership. School board members often fail to see the actual leadership efforts and results of successful women superintendents, perhaps because those achievements are not obvious in terms of "winning" and "losing." Women superintendents will play the win-loss game if they must; their preference is "win-win," where all win. Hence, they build power "with" others, bringing all along on the journey toward achieving desired results for all. It's that "nurturing thing"—the cultural conditioning of women.

The Reason You're Hired Is the Reason You're Fired

Gupton and Slick (1996) present a number of statements supported by studies of female leadership:

A study released by Russell Reynolds Associates found that significantly more female executives display leadership potential than do their male counterparts. Several studies on principals' leadership qualities have found women to be even more effective than men as instructional leaders. Such findings run counter to the myth that leadership ability belongs primarily to the male gender. No longer is education or certification seen as the primary obstacle; instead, the main impediment to women's career advancement seems to be the unstated but understood requirements that aspiring candidates must look and act like those already in power. (xxix)

There is a potential dilemma that exists for school boards searching for a new superintendent—particularly if they have encountered research about women school district leaders and what they have to offer. Beginning with the 1990 school reform efforts across the country, school boards have begun to learn the value of strong instructional leadership. At first, strong instructional leadership was presented as essential for school leaders. However, recently, there is a growing recognition that superintendents of schools must not only be well-steeped in financial, operational, and political leadership, but they also must be equipped with skill in leading improvement in teaching for learning. This additional performance qualification has often meant that the way school board members have viewed the superintendent in operation is not the way a successful superintendent in operation might look. Some discomfort may attend the selection of a woman instead of a man to lead the school district. The superintendent might wear a skirt—and know a great deal about curriculum and teaching for learning.

Avila (1993) confirms Gupton and Slick's report. She remarks about a number of studies that have found women to have better knowledge of and insight to the teaching-learning processes, and Avilla states, "As schools focus more on the instructional leadership aspects of the administrator's job, women should be more promotable based on their instructional expertise" (48). One study in Avila's work, that of Grady and Bohling-Phillipi (1988), suggested that the amount of time spent on instructional work might be one of the reasons women have an edge on instructional leadership: "Women principals spend 38.4 percent of their time on instructional leadership activities and men spent 21.8 percent of their time on such duties" (48).

Tallerico and Burstyn (1996) investigated women's entrance into superintendencies and their ultimate departure from those positions. They reported that multiple factors contributed to the abandonment of the superintendency, but that four patterns characterized the "disenchantment" with the role: (a) deterioration of superintendent–school board relationships, (b) dysfunctional union-district relationships, (c) overemphasis on noninstructional issues, and (d) moral or ethical clashes with board members. There are clues in the above findings that suggest, at least in part, that women exit the superintendency because their dream of serving all children appears to be stymied by male societal bias and familiarity with previous practices in school districts. Both intervene in keeping the focus on the children—a focus that requires strong, instructional leadership.

Because school boards during the past decade were giving more attention to the possibility of a leader who can assure the increased achievement of students, there has been increased interest in considering women for employment as school superintendents. Between 1995 and 2000, studies reflect a greater than 3 percent increase, from 10 percent to nearly 14 percent, in the number of women serving as school superintendents. While this is considerable growth, the fact that less than 14 percent out of 100 percent serving in these CEO positions are women reflects the continued insignificance with which women's leadership is viewed.

Dr. Lois Franklin has an interesting story. She was a public school superintendent who was hired by a school board because she transformed a failing high school into a succeeding high school. That is, the dropout rate was reduced considerably, and student scores on state assessments demonstrated highly significant increases. Lois states,

> The honeymoon in my superintendency was wonderful! At least for the first two years. Now that I'm in my seventh year, I do think that the board is going to let me go . . . dismiss me. You know, a few are beginning to meet in secret. Now, I don't have hard facts; I only have hearsay of their meetings, but it all sounds and looks suspicious. I have accomplished what they brought me to this district to do, improve student achievement. It's been uphill all the way, staff resistance, limited staff participation on committees and failure to be involved in setting their own direction—the "Just tell me what to do!" syndrome. That certainly defeats the purpose. Anyway, I've kept true to my word to do this together. I found money to cover the expenses of what they said they needed, helped them learn how to analyze the data from the state about their students' performance, and so on. They have gained skills and ex-

periences that will stay with them after I'm gone. I'm sure that part of me stays on. It's frustrating to have a school board hire you for one purpose—to improve student achievement—then dismiss you because your relationships with some of the teachers are not good, implying that it affects *all* of the teachers. So because we have to go through considerable change to arrive at improved student achievement and that wore on some of the teachers, I have to pay for it by being dismissed.

The school board told Lois they were not renewing her contract because she was not able to control faculty attitudes about what they perceived to be their increased workload and that the school board needed to have a superintendent who could control those unworthy attitudes. Surely Lois would be able to recognize herself in the following:

> If the truth be told—I am guilty
> For if pride is a strength—I am strong
> And if trust is naïve—I am foolish
> And if leading means "care"—I belong.
>
> For if caring is key—I am golden
> And if love brings us light—I see clear.
> Yet I could not foresee myself knowing
> That the price I must pay would be dear.
>
> —Diana Bourisaw, 2004

Case Study: Women v. Women or the Tale of We All Lose

"I don't see how she got that job to begin with!" bellowed Cece after just hearing about a colleague's promotion. "I'm more qualified than she is." Regina replied, "Then why didn't you apply?" Cece slumped in her seat in the teacher's workroom and sighed. "I didn't know if I could do it. I guess I should have. I just can't believe she is going to be my boss now. I never thought it would end up this way. We've had our differences, you know."

Regina knew about their differences. In fact, everyone in the school knew. Now Marty Sawyer was the new assistant principal. Cece could not get over it. She and Marty had been together as teachers for years. While they disagreed on some things, they basically agreed that the welfare of the children and school was their primary concern. Cece did not apply because a man had always held that position, and she was sure that would be the case again. She did not want to fail. This time, however, things had changed and Marty was selected.

Cece would not let it go. She spent day after day dredging up Marty Sawyer's shortcomings and belittling her innovative ideas and school reform suggestions. It appeared that Cece was sabotaging Marty.

Marty decided to confront Cece about her negative behavior. She knew Cece had a downside, but she did not expect to see so much of it! Marty asked Cece to meet with her after school. Cece entered Marty's office angry and upset. Marty's former teaching colleague had become her number one opposition.

Chapter Questions

1. What concepts presented in chapter 8 can be identified in this situation?

2. Do you have any suggestions for Marty Sawyer in confronting Cece about her negativity?

3. How would you begin the conference with Cece if you were Marty Sawyer?

4. What suggestions do you have for Cece now that her behavior is "on record"?

CHAPTER 9
NEEDED SUPPORT

"The injustice that results from the division of labor between the sexes affects virtually all women in our society. . . . It is also destroying the family's potential to be the crucial first school where children develop a sense of fairness."

—Susan Moller Okin (1989)

From birth on, every human being needs support in order to have healthy survival, developmental growth, and opportunities for productivity and service to others and—certainly—to achieve goals and fulfill aspirations. Each of us reaches a point early in our lives where we understand that we need to become as self-sufficient as possible, developing our abilities to "go after it (the dream)" with our own energies and determination. We need to be able to "do it ourselves!" Recognizing this, however, does not belie the fact that there are goals that may not be achieved by certain segments of the human population because systemic barriers have emerged or have been fostered by those who are leading, those in power. Without assistance and support from others, the systemic barriers prevent some of the population from reaching their reasonable goals and injustice is the result.

As Brunner (2000a) notes:

Under representation of women in the position of superintendent of schools is well known. Depending on the year, between 88 percent and 99 percent of all school superintendents are men despite the prevalence of women in teaching positions (Blount, 1993; Glass 1992; Shakeshaft 1989). . . . Lack of role models, lack of support from networks and mentors, lack of experience in leadership positions in non-governmental institutions, and the greater amount of family demands for women are among the many factors thought to contribute to such under representation. (9–10)

The first eight chapters of this book present authentic situations, stories, and illustrations women have experienced coupled with the research findings of others describing the challenges women face in acquiring school and school district leadership positions, particularly positions as public schools' CEOs. Except for chapter 1, the stories were organized around the themes that emerged from the authors' research. The lessons learned will be clear; what to do to be more successful in acquiring principal and superintendent positions will be discussed in greater detail in chapters 9 and 10. It is difficult for women, as it is for men, to talk about their perceived failures. To all who have willingly provided their stories, we owe gratitude; the contributions assist in developing a clearer understanding of how women lead and the challenges that face them, specifically gender prejudice and gender structuring. Both are quite difficult to overcome. Nonetheless, leadership provided by well-prepared and thoughtful women must not be discarded—either by refusing them employment for reasons of gender prejudice and gender structuring (two factors generally denied as influencing candidacy choice) or by finding fault unreasonably in women principals' or superintendents' leadership because they lead differently (and often more successfully in terms of student and school outcomes). So . . . the following chapters should be helpful in identifying strategies that might work for women in acquiring and maintaining key leadership positions.

Gaining Support for Your Goals

Wisdom and experience inform women who are superintendent aspirants to pursue the support of sponsors, acquire and use mentors, and develop and participate in networks and networking. Because of the small number of women in the superintendency, women, in particular, need advocates—both in acquiring a position and in maintaining successful leadership in that position. Sponsors, mentors, and other advocates all identify and/or create opportunities for those for whom they advocate. Women superintendents, who have been successful not only in acquiring a superintendent position but also in maintaining and succeeding in that position, believe the support in their lives that came from mothers, fathers, grandparents, employers . . . and mentors was essential. These were the people who believed in them, who told them that they had the capacity and potential for doing anything they wanted. With support from these important people in their lives, they were more willing to "take on" the challenges that would be before them as women public schools superintendents.

For women who aspire to become public school superintendents, gender is the strongest barrier to acquiring and maintaining a position as a superintendent of schools. In addition to surmounting the gender barrier, even entry to school administration as an assistant principal or principal can be overwhelming. The jobs are complex and demanding, particularly at the secondary level. Making the large number of decisions a school principal must make is considerably different from making the large number of decisions a teacher must make. For school principals, the outreach of the decision is greater and the contact with those who are affected by the decision generally is more distant. Additionally, the number of people with whom the principal or assistant principal must make contact and develop relationships is considerably larger and probably more diverse in attitudes and beliefs, further challenging the competencies of these school leaders. The lack of sufficient training complicates the job responsibilities and duties and increases the stress level. School principals claim that the most stressful jobs for school principals are supervising personnel and adjusting to the social climate and culture of the organization. Both are challenging because of their complexities.

Preparatory programs offer a limited amount of learning and clinical experience to "prepare" graduate students for school leadership and, again, for school district leadership. A master's degree with specified course work in educational leadership is required for school principal licensure in most states. Completing that degree will require from thirty to thirty-six credit hours and, more frequently than not, there is not a research requirement. To offer credit for each of those hours, a professor must schedule twelve to fifteen "seat" hours for every hour of credit (referred to as a Carnegie unit). Master's level preparatory programs require a candidate for licensure as a school assistant principal or principal to be "in class" or "in clinical experiences" from a minimum of 360 hours to a maximum of 540 hours. To develop a knowledge base in leadership history, theory, research, and best practices; to develop a personal disposition that embraces standard-based professional practice; and to demonstrate standards-based competency in performance requires considerably more than 540 hours of graduate study. Consequently, school leaders in their first few years of work will feel stressed and, often, overwhelmed. Hence, support systems are needed—not only for school leadership but also for school district leadership, which is another story.

It usually is assumed that a number of years of experience at the school leadership level will adequately prepare administrators for their first superintendency. However, many who have been told by a school board president that they "are hired" as a school superintendent for the first time will agree that there is an accompanying, albeit temporary, shock. During the following weeks, the tension begins to mount as the newly selected superintendent begins the physical and emotional steps of "moving to" the superintendency. Like the move from teacher to school principal, the move from school principal to the superintendency places the administrator in "new territory." One reason the job seems so stressful is that the school district leader has no peers in the school district; she is alone. Yet, as superintendent of schools, she lives in a glass house where unlimited numbers of employees and citizens can judge what she does or does not do. The need for advocates at the superintendent level is great.

What is missing is effective socialization of school principal candidates and school superintendency candidates. Studying how to lead a school and lead a school district does not adequately prepare candidates for leadership at either level. This is particularly the case for women because the theory and research in preparatory program course work and their routine observation of school and school district leadership present leadership knowledge and understanding based on predominantly men's leadership in school systems. Increasing clinical experience in a preparatory program and acquisition to excellent support will come closer to producing women leaders who are more socialized to the positions they desire and, consequently, they can move into leadership positions and maintain them more successfully.

Sponsorship

Sponsorship is a proactive practice that involves serving as an advocate for someone in all appropriate arenas. The sponsor is a well-known person, an established woman or man who relates effectively to other leaders who have major decision-making responsibilities that include employment and promotion. Sponsors have their ears "tuned in" to opportunities that may surface for promoting someone. Sponsors make sure that those they support have their names included in discussions of candidates who have strengths and potential for serving well, if the opportunity were afforded to that person. Sponsors follow up on the progress of consideration being given to those they support. People listen to sponsors; they are influential.

Acquiring sponsorship takes time to develop and it has its rewards. In some ways, sponsorship might be considered an act of collecting professional obligations from protégés in return for promoting them to others who offer desired opportunities. More often than not, though, recognized citizens return to protégés the sponsorships that were provided for them when they were protégés. They are proud of protégé potential and accomplishment. Women who do not frequent this political area except with anxiety and, perhaps, some emotional trepidation must realize the politics of gaining sponsorships requires that protégés be top performers at their appropriate level of growth and development in the profession. Sponsoring a protégé must not reduce the credibility of a sponsor.

Women will find that acquiring sponsors—recognized citizens willing to advocate hiring them as school superintendents—will require more investment of their time than it requires for men, simply because it has not been a conditioned practice for women. This is a "go after," though, and hard work in developing sponsorship will provide a good return on your investment of time.

Begin by identifying those in your life who know you well and have been persons of some notable position. Your high school principal, minister, neighbor who serves on the city council, local businessman with whom you do business, friends who are school principals or school district superintendents, owner of the automobile agency where you purchased your car, and other potential acquaintances and friends are all prime candidates for serving as a sponsor for you. If you can develop an acquaintance with a legislator, a school board member or other board directors or officers, major women leaders in your community, and officers of professional associations, it will be of great value. Of particular help will be the League of Women Voters, American Association of University Women, and any businesswomen organizations. Meeting women through the Chamber of Commerce can also produce some potential sponsors that might have some clout. These folks might live in your hometown and be people you grew up knowing. Or they might be similar people whom you come to know in the community where you begin your teaching. Start having conversations with key people about your aspirations and the work you are doing. Bring them into your professional life in ways that help them recognize your work ethic, stable demeanor, rational thought, service and dedication to children, and contributions to your community. Find ways to be of service to them and you will be remembered.

Engage those you hope to have as sponsors in conversation to learn about them as well. When you apply for a position, let them know. If the position is available in a different community, let them know. They might have an acquaintance, a "critical contact," in the community where your opportunity exists. Also, if you have enough information about the position and the culture of the community in which the position exists, you can decide which of these folks will best add credibility and support to your application and include their names in your list of references, with their permission. If it is appropriate at the time you submit your application, be sure to have permission from your sponsor to list her/his name and address (for contact) and request from your sponsor(s) a letter of reference when you are ready to submit application for a position. Be sure to provide the name and address of the person who should receive the reference and a stamped, addressed envelope for your sponsor to use. Also, you can ask your sponsor if she or he would feel comfortable making a telephone call on your behalf to her or his acquaintance in the community where you are applying for a leadership position. It is always good to prepare your sponsor by providing advertised job descriptions, a copy of your resume, and what you think will be important for the searcher to know about you as a candidate for the position. Do not collect from your references a prewritten letter that you send. It will not carry as much weight as those that are sent confidentially. There is some inclination to believe that a candidate may have requested a number of letters to send and then sent only those she felt were praiseworthy of her performance. Of course, you'll hope that your sponsors will be praiseworthy of your leadership skills, but that will be something you'll just need to trust.

Develop relationships with and maintain professional dialogue with current principals and superintendents—both men and women superintendents. Remember that those with whom you attended classes in your preservice preparatory program might be peer sponsors as well, depending upon the level of influence they have in their current position. The possibilities are numerous. Because women are hesitant to ask for sponsorship, they do not routinely develop a number of "sponsors." Yet men who aspire to the superintendency do not stop recruiting sponsors. Recruitment of sponsors is an essential!

Antoine Belljar reported that the primary factor to his acquisition of a coveted suburban superintendency was sponsorship.

> Mr. Swafford was the owner of Ford Motor Company in the community where I applied for my first superintendent position. My second cousin, Jamone, attended college with Mr. Swafford and they became good friends. When Jamone told me that he knew the Ford dealer in the community where I was going to apply for the superintendency, I asked if he would take time to drive to that community with me to take Mr. Swafford for lunch. It was over lunch that Jamone helped influence the offer that Mr. Swafford made to have me come back the following week and he would take me around the community to introduce me to some of the "important people" who lived there. I accepted his offer—and the rest is history.
>
> Mr. Swafford was my first sponsor and several others in the community became other sponsors. There were absolutely no financial commitments, but considerably more powerful than that were the efforts on behalf of those who viewed themselves as my sponsors to be sure when the opportunity came that I met good friends and bosses of those sponsors, legislators, and other influential people who lived in the region. They made sure I became "known." I marveled at and learned from their behavior and, since then, have served as a sponsor for other new school administrators. It has had a rolling snowball effect. That is, the number of those in my support group and those I supported grew larger and larger. I'm sure that's why I have had an easier pathway to the coveted suburban superintendency I currently serve. I feel fortunate.

Sponsors, like mentors on-the-job, can provide excellent opportunities to be socialized regarding the position for which you are applying.

They are successful people who understand how to develop effective relationships and networks with other successful people. They understand politics within their professional area and have a degree of power in influencing others. They also may know specifically about the context of the leadership position for which you are applying and can be quite helpful in socializing you to that context.

Because women fear asking—likely a result of their cultural upbringing and conditioning—and often are not even aware of how beneficial the efforts to acquire sponsors are, their pathways to reaching a desired superintendency are not quite as smooth or open as Antoine's was. Women simply must step up to the plate and take some swings at professionally and carefully acquiring sponsors.

Mentors

The acquisition of sponsorship often has its roots in previously developed relationships with key individuals who were mentors. Frequently a mentor-protégé relationship begins with willingness of a successful superintendent in another school district or successful retired superintendent to mentor a novice. It also comes from the novice seeking support and involvement (information and advice) from someone known to have expertise, experience, and insight.

LaKinta Reed recalls how stunned she was when she was informed by the school board president that she was selected to serve as their school district's superintendent of schools. She reported that however surprising the message had been, it did not compare to what she learned the next week. The school board had arranged for her to receive copies of all pertinent information provided by the state or other agencies and sent to the current superintendent. One of the letters informed superintendents that for the next fiscal year, the state would be using a new formula for computing school district state funds receipts and a copy of the formula was enclosed. She said that she had not been informed and had not had an opportunity to practice applying the formula through simulations. It was complex and complicated.

The current superintendent was caught by surprise as well. He had not seen the new formula. The only piece of good fortune LaKinta had was that she had been notified of employment in March, which gave the current superintendent and her a few months to redo together the school district budget draft for the following fiscal year. Also, LaKinta had an opportunity to acquire from the state school board association a reference to a couple of current superintendents who were skilled and reputable in their financial work. She said, "You know, my mentors at the principal level were people skilled in understanding principal-level leadership functions. . . . So, I called the first superintendent on that list and was immediately invited to participate in small group meetings of school superintendents who were working on the financial challenge together."

LaKinta noted later in an interview that the superintendents in that small group became "sponsors of sorts" of her work. Two became mentors, spending a great deal of time over the telephone helping her with problem-resolution in other areas than finance as well as finance and with strategies for socializing herself to her school district's community's culture.

Bjork (2000b) reports that "mentoring has served as a powerful developer of human potential throughout the centuries. . . . Mentoring is a key component of induction programs" (156). Educational administrators frequently enter the educational administration profession through the encouragement of role models and mentors who then later become major "sponsors" of the protégé (Gardiner et al., 2000).

Having one or more mentors is essential. Each mentor has his or her own strengths and set of informative experiences. There is not a mentor, though, who can be expected to have strengths and experiences in all of the ways that a new superintendent may need. A superintendent aspirant can be a "top flier" with a resume that reflects graduating magna cum laude, can receive mentoring from a large number of family members who have served as school superintendents, or have other uncommon advantages. Even then, she is best served by adding one or more mentors to her contacts who are active and esteemed school superintendents not connected with some of her other advantages. It's a simple analogy that helps understand the essential importance of mentors. Almost everyone can quickly identify the one person in her youth who made a difference in her life because that person "believed in" her and, either directly or indirectly, communicated said belief to her on a repeated basis in addition to providing guidance and advice. Family members have a vested interest in your success. Mentors outside of the family have an interest primarily because you show some potential that they can work with and you are a person whom they can recommend. When you "believe in" someone, you provide information, insight, advocacy, and support to the welfare and success of that person. That is what a good mentor does.

Tallerico's study (2000) confirmed the value of mentors in the following report:

> Many candidates in this study sought and used multiple mentors. There are numerous lessons to be learned from this. Rather than relying exclusively on the relationship-building and career sponsorship that may occur naturally between you and some colleagues or superordinates, it is usually wise to seek and find mentors from others outside your immediate circle for specific purposes, such as assisting in the development of particular communication skills or, perhaps, gaining a greater familiarity with financial procedures. (132)

> Some candidates not only sought such assistance but expected and gently demanded it, particularly of administrators known to be key sources of referrals for superintendency vacancies. (133)

A potential advantage for a woman in being mentored by a male superintendent is developing an "in" with the "good ole boys" network. Research has indicated that superintendents believe the superintendency has been dominated by an "old boy" network of mentors and sponsors. In 1992, 56.5 percent of the superintendents reported the strong existence of an "old boy" network, and in 2000, 52.5 percent reported that this network exists (Glass et al., 2000). However, women must be forewarned that the "good ole boys" network in its weakest sense has some hazards. The idea can be perpetrated among the formal and informal members of the "good ole boys" network that women are influential only because of their sexuality (Brunner 2000a). It is unwise to associate with a "good ole boys" network if the "good ole boys" have the power to damage your dignity, intelligence, stature, and credibility. Avoid these unwise "opportunities."

There is often discomfort among men superintendents when they are together and when a woman superintendent is present. Men have their way of conversing informally (and sometimes formally) that differs from how women converse. Women are likely to hear an apology directed at them and, without waiting to see if it is accepted, men who are accustomed to a subculture of their own tell a "dirty" joke, often denigrating women. Women will not be included in the rumor or hearsay "grapevine" that men share regarding other superintendents, school board members, school districts, employees, and so forth. Both men and women will be better served if conversation within groups eliminates sexual innuendos and rumors/hearsay. Women can set the ground rules by initiating the conversation; changing the subject when some untoward discussion is initiated; making sure they can actively participate in discussing current athletic events, human interest events reported in the media, and creative ideas; congratulating fellow superintendents on achievements; and asking about family or other topics of interest, such as travel.

The value of good mentors is well documented. Reyes (2003) found that minority women who did not have mentors were still in the classroom as teachers one year after completing a master's degree and principal certification program at the University of Houston. In a longitudinal study of 142 female aspirants to the principalship, Edson (1988) found out that "of those who had mentors early in their careers, 42 percent became principals or beyond by the end of ten years, whereas only 17 percent who did not have mentors were able to advance" (42). Bell and Chase (1996) also emphasize the importance of understanding the broader social context of leaders' work: "They found that women superintendents' positive professional connections to white men held promise for being integrated into the power structures and support networks of educational administration" (129). However, they noted that choosing to affiliate with the men "can be risky" and found that "some women superintendents deliberately distance themselves from other women (to defeminize themselves) . . . because our culture defines 'professional' and 'woman' as contradictory identities" (130).

Hopkins-Thompson (2000) report that the standards movement, calls for school reform, and technological advances have increased the challenges for school leaders. She advocates that all aspiring principals and current principals work with mentors and seek coaching because of the advantages both bring them. As assistant principal, Hibert (2000) reports that from her mentor she has learned that leadership is about "serving others, having compassion, and practicing social justice" (16). Even though these may be lessons that also have been presented in the formal classroom of a school leader preparatory program, it is the actual work of the mentor supporting a school leader that helps most when preparatory programs are completed.

The insight and guidance that a mentor contributes will help the new leader become socialized to the way effective school leaders view their work and perform. In a survey of principal evaluation of their school leader preparatory program, 180 principals rated mentoring the most valuable experience during the course work phase of the preparatory program (McCabe et al., 2000). Bjork (2000b) states: "The absence of mentor relationships, role models, and networks is frequently cited in the literature as a primary reason why women and minorities do not go into the superintendency" (157).

Babcock and Laschever (2003) explain that where there exists a mentor, the relationship might be weak. When weak ties are with those who are acquaintances and who would be recognized if passing them on the street, it is not going to be a helpful mentoring experience for women. Strong ties come from close friendships in which considerable time is spent together. Their research supports the assertion that men can benefit from relatively weak ties but that women and other minorities benefit little.

The *2000 Study of the American School Superintendency* (Glass et al., 2000) reported, "Nearly all superintendents, men and women, consider themselves mentors, but more women [higher percent of those responding who were women] than men report serving as mentors. Since the 1992 study, overall, more superintendents are serving as mentors" (91). In the 2000 study, 77.9 percent of responding superintendents considered themselves to be mentors to those who had interest in pursuing a career as a superintendent. The 2000 findings reported by Glass, Bjork, and Brunner also included the following data: 58.5 percent indicated that in their own careers they had been mentored; 90.5 percent in large school districts reported that they had served as mentors; only 58 percent to 76 percent in small or very small school districts had served as mentors (157).

What women seeking mentors should know is that women superintendents, in general, have not mentored other women as readily as have men. The literature reflects an interesting dilemma related to mentoring. If women tend to lead differently than do men—and they do, in general and specifically—then, it is important for women aspiring to the school superintendent's position to understand from a woman's perspective what works and does not work for the woman superintendent in her school district leadership. What *does* effective leadership look like for a school district CEO who is a woman?

Regardless of the gender, mentoring relationships require the presence of certain factors in order to be successful. First and foremost, it is based on trust (Glass et al., 2000, 157). What mentor and protégé share with each other regarding the protégé's aspirations and/or performance must be maintained confidentially. Trust will be destroyed if there is not confiden tial treatment regarding problem resolution and coaching that directly addresses the professional leadership needs of the protégé. This is the case whether it is the mentor or the protégé who is the focus of discussions. There must be a sincere and genuine interest in learning—not judging. Judgment must be withheld if trust is to remain strong. Questions must be responded to in a timely manner. It's always best to develop the mentor-protégé relationship based on each other's strengths. Building from strengths creates the greatest gain in growth and understanding of how to move forward in leadership.

For women, identifying a willing mentor—and then developing a successful mentor-protégé relationship—does not necessarily occur with ease. Women aspiring to positions of school and school district leadership must remember that they are entering a male-dominated profession and that available mentoring may be conducted by men. Some discomfort with commitment to mentoring in a professional sense may exist because of the man-woman relationship. We simply have a difficult time moving outside our cultural norms, which seem to grow larger and more onerous when women are interested in leadership positions that historically have been filled by men. How spouses or significant others feel about the professional relationship must be considered. The key to success in acquiring a helpful mentor is to seek mentoring that occurs in professionally acceptable environments and within professional standards of ethics.

There are some tips to consider for acquiring an effective mentor. First, control your own behavior. You'll want to establish a "best of you" image as a competent leader. Avoid behavior that is demanding of attention, loud, pretentious, superficial, childish, coquettish, nonprofessional, or offensive. Because such a strong cultural expectation for women's behavior is different from the cultural expectation for men, women must behave as competent professionals without exception if they wish, ultimately, to be respected and to develop advocates: "All [candidates for the superintendency] were careful to avoid arrogance or immodesty" (Tallerico, 2000, 133). Conservative behavior is advised.

Second, identify men and women whom you would like to have as a mentor and who have influence and are viewed with esteem as school superintendents or as community leaders in the school district where you want to work or are working. Check state-level professional associations that serve school superintendents' interests and needs and identify as potential mentors the members of their executive committees and the school districts they currently serve. Their membership on the executive committees will imply that they have been recognized as a leader by other leaders among the state's school district superintendents and, consequently, may be influential on your behalf as an advocate, should a professional relationship be developed.

Third, under the supervision of a leader or a mentor, create opportunities to assume or be assigned a variety of administrative opportunities—even before you are appointed to an administrative position. Indicate interest in providing leadership or support for leadership in working on projects of interest and within the responsibilities of your school superintendent or of your mentor who is a superintendent. Write a grant for your school, your school district, or your community and, if awarded, implement it. Ask to serve on a steering committee for school improvement. Ask to share with school board members at school board meetings intermittent executive summaries of research relative to school or school district goals. Tallerico (2000) reported that

> members of historically underrepresented groups are being proactive about their own advancement in the existing systems of access to the school superintendency. . . . They create opportunities for themselves to acquire new administrative experiences. They solicit feedback on their performance so as to hone and expand existing strengths. They give serious attention to their growth as educational leaders, and they participate in professional development. They find mentors for different purposes and draw on others' expertise and connections. They nurture relationships—even ones that don't appear immediately beneficial but may provide powerful in the future. (135–136)

Fourth, join superintendent professional associations and attend their regional and state meetings where you will meet the superintendents whom you have learned are recognized and esteemed by their fellow superintendents. Introduce yourself to those on your "long list" of names and initiate conversations about leadership. Help each one understand your interest in gaining knowledge and understanding about the demands and challenges of the practitioner who is serving a school district as its superintendent. Ask for "pearls of wisdom" about superintendent leadership. Those who seem willing to mentor will begin to be apparent. Ask what they consider to be their strengths as superintendents. In doing so, you'll learn about job responsibilities they have and that knowledge can provide insight into how they might be able to help you. Ask them for advice regarding your interest, as a woman, in becoming a school superintendent and what they think is most important for you to do to access the position. Ask their opinions and insight regarding a number of leadership dilemmas. Being interested in learning and interested in discovering the other person's opinions and points of view is important. Potential mentors will remember that. Also, through the conversation, you will begin to know whether or not each person can help you and whether or not she or he will be a willing discussant and communicate interest in your potential for leadership.

Whenever possible mentors should be practitioners at the level of leadership you desire. They will have the keenest insight into what the job requires and how you should develop yourself further. Mentors have information and guidance that you need. Also, they may be willing to be a professional "sleuth" for you, garnering information that will be useful in making your application or participating in an interview at a specified school district. They may know personally the persons who will be conducting your interview. Their advocacy is invaluable. Evidence is clear that women who have mentors move into school district or school leadership positions sooner than those who are without mentors. One of the internal structural barriers to women accessing a CEO position, identified by the Glass Ceiling Commission, was the lack of mentoring.

Developing and Participating in Networks

Fundamental structures for sponsorship, mentors, and gatekeepers have historic roots in the field of public school administration (Ortiz and Marshall, 1988). Men have been successful in accessing all three to foster their own access to superintendent positions they desire. Women's experience is different, more challenging; the "patterns of stratification cannot be fully explained by individual circumstances or differential socialization" (Tallerico and Burstyn, 1996, 659). Because of gender disadvantage, it is increasingly important for women to pursue active participation in networks that will provide information, professional development, and, ultimately, advocacy.

Stating that, though, does not make the task of identifying and participating in helpful networks easy. Citing Mehra, Kilduff, and Brass (1988), Babcock and Laschever (2003) point out:

> Typically, men's "instrumental" networks and their "friendship" networks are predominantly male. Women's "instrumental" networks, in contrast, are usually made up of both men and women but their "friendship" networks tend to be predominantly female (Ibarra 1997 and 1992). As a result, women's ties to the men in their "instrumental" networks—frequently the more powerful member of the group—can be less strong and therefore less valuable. Compounding the problem, in workplace situations in which women are a minority, women are more likely to be marginal members of any informal friendship networks of which they do become members, a marginalization that appears to result "more from exclusionary pressures than from their preferences." (441)

Women who aspire to increasingly stronger and more influential leadership positions can find pathways to reaching that goal considerably strengthened when they establish strong and influential networks. However, as in any situation, care must be taken to avoid any exclusionary practice that would place a woman or minority "at odds" with their colleagues and peers or with those who have strong influence within other desirable networks. Also, women must participate in networks that avoid complaint sessions. They must search for opportunities to network with folks for purposes of (1) exploring "how to" address leadership needs, (2) responding to case studies for enlightenment and learning, and (3) problem solving around gender issues. Positive thinking is always the stronger route to follow.

An argument could certainly be made that in the case of women who aspire to be school and school district leaders, their efforts again must be extended beyond those of their male counterparts. For women, the challenge is to establish networks that are inclusive, especially being sensitive to including those who have been excluded from strong and influential networks. It is sometimes surprising to greet a previously disenfranchised person, who had been excluded from access to mentors and networks, and discover that she is a practicing superintendent of schools. Everyone is important. You never know when you will meet those with whom you had previous relationships; that's why good relationships are essential.

At the same time, women should foster opportunities to participate in stronger and more influential networks. But do not leave colleagues, peers, and friends behind. The adage that "It's not how many you know but who you know that will benefit you" is not true for women. They must know *both* the most influential people and a large number of people in order to develop and participate in the most helpful mentoring and in the most influential networking. Both must exist if women are to be successful in their access to a school principalship or school district superintendency and if they are to be successful in keeping that position. They must work continuously to expand their networks and through interaction and conversation allow their leadership skills to be evident. Babcock and Laschever (2003) report that for a man to "do a favor for a woman, he usually needs to know her well enough to feel completely confident in her abilities—his ties to her need to be strong" (152).

Janell Chung knew that she wanted to be completely involved in providing CEO leadership for a school district. However, she did not know whether or not she was making the right choices as she moved through her educational program. Was she picking and choosing the kinds of problem-based learning activities, projects, and clinical or field experiences in her classes that would best prepare her for school leadership and, ultimately, school district leadership? She knew that she had to develop the ability to demonstrate her growing competencies related to educational leadership standards—and at the superintendent level.

It had been difficult for her to enter administration as a school assistant principal to begin with. As she noted, "There simply was not a support system waiting for me!" Janell was able to develop a good relationship with the principal who was her supervisor, and he began mentoring her through the process. Many years later she would recall:

Bob was a jewel! He helped me understand how to recognize cultural values at work in our high school and how to develop strong relationships with the faculty who, like many high school faculties, was mostly intent on teaching the subject rather than the student. Without good relationships,

I recognized quickly that I would not be able to influence a change of focus to that of the student.

Ms. Chung commended her principal for providing so many opportunities for her to learn and grow under his tutelage. She soon was ready
to apply for a principal position that opened in the school district. Janell
reported that much to her surprise, she was hired and was assigned her
own school and faculty.

Within a three-year period, Janell became recognized as a skilled instructional leader and her influence as a principal continued to increase
with her faculty and her school patrons. It did not take long for her to set
that next goal at the superintendent level of service.

Deciding to move forward with education that would prepare Janell
to serve at the superintendent level, however, was a different story. Ms.
Chung expressed her frustration by identifying the barriers that surfaced
everywhere she turned. First was the selection of the most useful class activities to complete so that her competencies could be as developed as possible upon program completion. Second, trying to identify how to use
networking effectively was quite challenging. "How was I to know which
of the networks available through the Internet would serve me best?"
"Where are there face-to-face networks or support groups already in existence?" "I'm in classes where I am one of only three women. The men do
not seem at all interested in developing a support group that includes the
three of us. However, it is clear that they have their own exclusive networks and support groups." Many questions surfaced throughout Janell's
course work, and she judged that

> the impersonal nature of networks accessed through the Internet and the
> lack of opportunity or invitation for being included in existing face-to-
> face networks was downright depressing. Initially determined to not let
> anything get between me and my goal, it seemed that my determination
> to pursue my dream was disappearing!

What Janell Chung was experiencing was the lack of readily available
information about where school leadership networks existed. She also
needed to understand the purposes served by each network, how to develop
or locate an informal network that provided opportunity to discuss real issues and problems face-to-face, and how to identify if support and social-

ization to the context and milieu of the superintendent position were available. Each of these lacking network elements become increasingly important to a novice superintendent—or any other novice leader, for that matter.

Networking can occur anywhere. Women must make their opportunities if they have no other opportunities to access and participate in a network. A beginning superintendent, Dr. Ilene Rogers explained that her university adviser had encouraged her to identify some beginning superintendents in the area and invite them to meet monthly for purposes of discussing challenges and problems. She said:

> I followed his suggestion, and it was amazing to me how helpful that experience was. I was one of seven first-year superintendents working within a fifty-mile radius of each other. We all welcomed the opportunity to meet. Our monthly meetings were conducted in an interesting way, meeting the parameters each of us had suggested for our meetings. Each of us came with a problem. We drew straws to identify who would begin our discussion. To be sure that all of our problems could be addressed with the scheduled hour of our meeting, the format set as agreed upon. First, the person with the short straw presented the first problem. Then, moving to the right around the circle, each of the other six presented things to think about in trying to solve the problem or alternatives that can be considered before deciding the problem. Each of us presented whatever came to our minds right up front. After everyone in the circle had given their thoughts, the person to the left of whomever presented the problem then presented his or her problem and we went around the circle again giving our thoughts. If there was time remaining after we all had presented our problem and thoughts, then the conversation was "open" to discuss further any of the problems and ideas that had been shared. By the end of the first year, we were all in a "network" that has lasted throughout our careers so far.

This superintendent, now in her thirteenth year, noted that the seven who began their first superintendencies the same year continued to be a team and to experience measured success. Three served on the state superintendents' professional organization's executive board, and all seven were recognized across the state as strong school superintendents.

In the early 1980s, under the leadership of Dr. Gale Bartow, president of the American Association of School Administrators (AASA), a minority liaison was added to the staff for purposes of serving the leadership needs of women superintendents and women who aspire to the superintendency. She was employed to pull together a planning committee and develop and sponsor a national project to encourage more women and minorities to prepare for the superintendency. Project AWARE (Assisting Women to Advance through Resources and Encouragement) emerged from planning committee work, and state branches of AASA were encouraged to develop and sponsor a Project AWARE organization in their states.

Approximately twenty-three Project AWARE chapters were established, some that were new "stand-alones" and some that were added to existing state-level organizations or associations with similar purpose. Project AWARE and like organizations or associations provided a substantial opportunity to make greater gains in diversity within CEO leadership for public schools and provided substantial opportunity for women to network with each other. Many other state organizations have developed networking opportunities and these continue to exist to this day. Some are sponsored by their state-level AASA associations. Many are independent.

As an illustration of how Project AWARE chapters developed and operate, Missouri Project AWARE organized in 1983 with support from the University of Missouri–Columbia and the Missouri Department of Elementary and Secondary Education (DESE). The chapter applied to DESE's Leadership Academy for LEAD (Leadership in Educational Administration Development) grant funds to acquire initial resources for existence of the chapter. Over the next fifteen years, the organization sponsored statewide and regional conferences for women aspiring to and actually contracted in school and school district leadership. The chapter provided consultant support for local "networks" to organize and provided some mentoring. Missouri Project AWARE changed its name to The Network for Women in School Administration, produced newsletters, and established a Regional Network for Women in Leadership Center at Saint Louis University. The local groups continue to operate in Kansas City, Columbia-Jefferson City, and St. Louis. Information about women leadership groups that exist can be acquired through the state AASA associations.

Many states have organized groups of women who are (or aspire to be) school district or school leaders and who meet routinely for purposes of sharing information, sharing insight and strategies for problem resolution, and developing relationships and support for each other. These informal groups also share information about current job openings and future openings. Members and guests have the opportunity to inquire of group members about the school district openings that they are considering. It is surprising how much insight can be gained from these group members. Even in informal groups, women focus on problems that women, in particular, face and the milieu in which women work. More formal organizations routinely meet to discuss goals of the organization, which generally include advocating for women in school administration.

Women who are serious about their future aspirations should make sure that they participate in organized networks. The networks provide opportunities to establish connections with other women and, less frequently, with men in or connected to the superintendency. It's an opportunity to become socialized to leadership functions and challenges, develop good judgment regarding challenges women will or do face, and identify successful strategies, approaches, and steps to be taken to enhance leadership qualities and market one's strengths.

The Internet has created access to some networks that specifically address topics and needs of interest to women. Professional organizations often offer topic-specific "networks" that are available to anyone who demonstrates interest in participating. For example, the Association for Supervision and Curriculum Development (ASCD) offers a Women's Leadership Network. It is initially accessible through ASCD via the Internet. Once you join the network, communications come electronically through e-mail addresses. The Women's Leadership Network maintains a good bibliography of readings related to women in leadership. In addition to joining networks of interest, women should take the necessary steps to identify networks where influential and esteemed school superintendents are and seek ways to be included.

Without formal network participation, women can professionally develop themselves through reading current research and literature. Indirect "mentoring" occurs through exposure to researchers' and leaders' publications of lessons learned and successful strategies employed in leadership. Advancing Women in Leadership (www.advancingwomen.com) offers literature published by other women about school district and school leadership topics. In the absence of sponsors or mentors, these readings can provide some socialization to the superintendent and principal positions for aspiring leaders and novice leaders.

Two of the more valuable advantages of networking through the state-level organizations are accessibility and a focus on women in leadership.

State-sponsored organizations advocating for women in school leadership positions have provided opportunities for women to address cultural barriers and openly work to remove—or at least work through—those barriers. The job is not easy. Beekley (1999) notes,

> All of these women understood the value of networking and appeared successful in gaining acceptance from their peers. However, the women had to work at it, understand that there were some barriers that would not be overcome, and had to accept the "benefit" the heightened visibility of the "red shoes" brought. All of the women acknowledged the lack of role models, a support system (with the exception of their husbands), and close friends among other superintendents. (173)

Symes and Sharpe (2005) note that 60 percent to 80 percent of all jobs are found by way of networking. Their advice to women is to network extensively. When you interact with those who are in positions to which you aspire or those who may become your employers, always be honest; don't misrepresent yourself. Put together lists of people who can help you and "work" the list. Set up appointments with people on your network list to explore more about the leadership position you hope to acquire. Send thank you notes immediately after all appointments or meetings. If you note anything positive printed about them, clip out the article and send it to them. In other words, court them in hopes of acquiring some helpful insight and potential mentoring.

Superintendent search firms are powerful gatekeepers. Gatekeepers "rely heavily on networks of friends, professional associates, and associations to develop a field of candidates to present to boards of education for consideration" (Kamler and Shakeshaft, 1999, 51). She is a wise woman who courts search firm personnel, keeping them informed of her leadership experience and accomplishments. Keeping in mind that superintendent search firms have their own networks and rely extensively on them, becoming acquainted with members of those networks is also wise.

Networking during the Superintendency

Public education is a people business. A school administrator generally does not succeed, regardless of gender, unless she or he can develop strong interpersonal relations with others. Strong relationships must exist with the internal school community; the employees of the school district will be the first "judges" of the level of respect to be given to their school district superintendent—based on first impression and then on interpersonal relationships. In addition, there are many others with whom the superintendent must establish good interpersonal relations. Maintaining participation in one or more networks established prior to attaining a superintendent position is wise, particularly if the networks provide opportunities for interaction related to current needs of leading successfully as a superintendent of schools. Also, stay alert to other networking opportunities with groups that are influential at local, regional, state, and even national levels. Through interaction with influential individuals and groups in the network, superintendents can keep current with information that relates to their jobs, gaining early understanding and insight to potential issues that will help them bring their boards of education through necessary change more successfully.

The advantages of networking are clear; particularly for the novice, networking is essential. Through networks, the novice can become acquainted with school superintendents who can provide knowledge and insight for them in their efforts to maintain positive and supportive board of education relationships as well as succeeding in other contexts in which the novice works. A novice superintendent can learn from the "stories" associated with being a school superintendent that pass throughout the network, other superintendent's styles and practices in leading, and advice regarding leadership within the various functions and responsibilities of a school superintendent. Additionally, the opportunity then exists to begin to develop professional relationships with those serving as school superintendents, perhaps gaining mentoring and sponsorship. Telephone calls seeking insight, advice, direction, and advocacy become more natural and easy experiences because the beginning of a professional relationship exists.

Findings published in the *1992 Study of the American School Superintendency* reported that networks, specifically those referred to as "old boy/old girl" networks, helped superintendents. Brunner reports in the *2000 Study of the American School Superintendency* that 76.9 percent of the women superintendents responding to the study "benefited from the influence of these networks" (Glass et al., 87):

> If networking works as it's supposed to work, and if a mentor and protégé are successful, beginning administrators will develop and strengthen

their emotional intelligence and improve their style and relational skills, whether they are school principals or school district superintendents. Additionally, the reserves of emotional intelligence will broaden and deepen to better serve the principal and school superintendent as she spends her years serving her school district in the increasingly complex context that presents itself to school and school district leaders in this century.

One of the best opportunities to expand the depth and breadth of emotional intelligence (style and people skills) is to interact routinely with willing school superintendents for purposes of becoming well socialized to the context, challenges, and responsibilities of a school superintendent. Women school leadership aspirants and practitioners should seek out both women and men with whom to network, simply because they need to learn from multiple perspectives and have diverse sponsorships when it comes time to submit an application for a school principal or school district superintendent position. It is important to have men as sponsors; however, it is also important to recognize that large groups with strong male memberships have been unreliable for helping women (Shakeshaft, 1989).

Women superintendents also should step forward to mentor other women who aspire to serve in a school leadership or school district leadership position. As Evans (2003b) admonishes:

> There is one message I want to highlight above all: Women are in this together—whether we want to be or not. So you might as well join with enthusiasm. Those of us who don't help each other, hurt each other. Everyone else sees you as part of this team. It's time you start seeing yourself that way. Once you embrace the idea that you and the women around you are going to make it together and that you don't have to be a lone wolf, you will discover new ways to network and form teams. (187)

The message in this chapter is summed up in Shakeshaft's (1989) words:

> Family and work support, although crucial, need to be supplemented with a large system of contacts so that women can both learn about job availability and about how other women handle similar administrative situations. There needs to be a system that can compete with the Old Boys' Club. A common vehicle for providing women with both contacts and information is a network. (136–137)

Case Study: Sex and the Superintendent: A Woman's Challenge

Dr. Carla Block began her new job as Withering Heights Public Schools superintendent last July. Her predecessor was dismissed due to "misappropriation of funds"—or so she thought. The headlines in the local newspaper had read, "A Million Dollars Missing in School Coffers." Following her predecessor's dismissal and the advertising of the superintendent vacancy, Dr. Block applied for the vacancy and was interviewed and hired. In her interview, Dr. Block convinced the school board that she welcomed the challenge of returning fiscal integrity to this beleaguered school district.

Dr. Block began her work by assembling a task force to address the issues that resulted in the missing money. The task force worked closely with the school district external auditor, Jerry Jones, to review recommendations and to develop policies and procedures for school board approval. She knew this process would take months. While Carla Block tried to ensure the task force as much independence as a corporate audit committee, she did want to hold them accountable. So, each month, she and Mr. Jones met for lunch at a restaurant just outside school district boundaries and close to Mr. Jones's office.

Mr. Jones and his firm had held a contract with the school district for annual auditor services for the past ten years, and he knew the school district history. During lunch one day in a brief and casual way, Mr. Jones told Dr. Block that her predecessor had been involved in several affairs with several current and former employees and that the school district had a history of ignoring such behavior. According to Mr. Jones, the real reason for Dr. Block's predecessor's departure was "his indiscretions," not his poor fiscal management. Also, Mr. Jones casually mentioned that a current assistant superintendent was rumored to be "fooling around" with his secretary. Dr. Block mentally filed this information, then turned her attention to the school district's fiscal accounts and monitoring efforts. She had little time to be concerned with hearsay and rumors.

One month later, Carla Block received a visit from the school board president, Mr. Wayman. Mr. Wayman had received a call accusing Carla of conducting a romantic affair during the workday while on the school district payroll. Mr. Wayman explained that the school district had a history of such behavior, and he was not going to tolerate this sort of thing—particularly from a woman. The school board had met, he said, and decided to have their school district attorney investigate. He also announced that the attorney was in the school board conference room now, interviewing the assistant superintendent. Upon making that statement, Mr. Wayman departed.

Dr. Block sat at her desk in silence. She was stunned, shocked, insulted, and humiliated—all at the same time. Questions rushed through her mind: Who was the person she allegedly was having the affair with? Who was setting her up? Who made the telephone call? Why had the school board president turned on her so abruptly? Was Mr. Jones trying to warn her? Was everything he said true? If so, with whom was the assistant superintendent having an affair? The allegations had already damaged her, her work, and the school district. Carla Block pondered what to do next.

Chapter Questions

1. Using what you have learned in chapter 9, identify what Dr. Block could have done early in her work as the school district superintendent to establish independence from hearsay and rumor mongering.

2. How will Dr. Block discover the origins of hearsay and allegations?

3. At what point does Dr. Block need to contact her own attorney?

4. If you had been Dr. Block, what would you have done from the beginning of your superintendency up to and following where the case study ends?

5. What role will the media play and would you accommodate their interests in acquiring information about the allegations? Defend your answer.

CHAPTER 10

SO ... ARE THERE SOLUTIONS? LESSONS LEARNED?

In public opinion surveys, women consistently rank their own *inequality*, at work and at home, among their most urgent concerns.

—Susan Faludi (1991)

Regardless of known barriers and cultural attitudes, the background, stories, principles, and analysis surrounding the topic of discarded leadership and introduced in the first eight chapters of this book present a highly complex set of interactions among and between sociocultural values, prejudices, political and religious ideologies, and intentional and unintentional gender structuring. The evidence challenges and, at times, threatens those seeking equity in educational leadership at the CEO level. Nonetheless, intensive and extensive study and experience provide a number of strategies women may use to acquire school district and school leadership positions in the twenty-first century. Chapter 9 offers some essential strategies—ones that are particularly important throughout the experience from gaining educational development to service as a school district CEO. The following sections in this chapter identify additional strategies.

Go Get It, Girl: Leadership Acquisition

Women entering a gender-prejudiced and gender-structured leadership environment to attain a leadership position in a school district or school must be strategic and political. Land mines, placed by men and women who are subconsciously uncomfortable with the idea that a woman might be the CEO, will be present. To be competitive in acquiring a leadership position, women must be aware of the potential land mines in the beginning and throughout their careers. Expect surprises, but maintain your focus on your goal and stay positive. You are building and maintaining your professional reputation.

It's also important for women to remember they contribute most, to their gender and minorities who also are challenged by prejudice and systemic structuring, when they perform admirably in their leadership positions, look for and capitalize on opportunities to employ other women and minorities, and keep the importance of equity and social justice at the top of their "Wanted" list. With that said, the following is suggested to help women deal with some of the issues they may face as they pursue a principal or superintendent position and then work to keep that position.

Self-Development

All endeavors to lead require continuous self-development and determination to grow and perform in ways that are expected by the culture in which service is rendered and, ultimately, in ways that are exemplary. Exemplary performance is evidenced in leadership that goes beyond expectation, modeling clear and unyielding ethics, solid and acceptable reasoning, excellent communication, numerous solid relationships, and a driven purpose of serving the educational needs of all children in the public school system. Of course, there are many other routine characteristics and behaviors that are expected on a daily and predictable basis. The following sections provide suggestions for both personal and professional self-development.

Personal Development

The smallest of personal choices can create an image that will not match that commonly expected of a school principal or a school district superintendent. This can be detrimental to you when interviewing for a leadership position, as well as when serving in that leadership position. Two areas particularly require attention in terms of the habits of successful school district and school leaders. First, identify the nature of the culture in which you will be working, and assess what image you need to present to "fit" that culture. This does not under any circumstances intend to negate one's individuality and right to express self. The intent is simply to alert you to the importance of being ready and adjusting for a professional fit with the culture to increase the likelihood that you will be judged as appropriate and acceptable as the school principal or school district superintendent. Once you are viewed as part of the culture—and it takes longer than one year—you will have opportunity and support for leading in ways that produce gains for your school district. There may even be an opportunity in the future of your leadership, given a sound community acceptance and respect, to have a significant influence on improving (changing) the culture. It is the hope of the authors that by melding with the culture you can make more powerful contributions to achieving equity for all.

Women must be controlled in what they wear and how they act if they wish to diminish or remove the barrier of gender prejudice that is likely to exist. Interestingly enough, they can usually afford to be feminine in dress, but not overly so. They also can be more masculine in dress, but not overly so. Ruffles and heavy perfume do not smack of CEO behavior to school boards. Neither do nonfitting suit pants or smoking a cigar at a ball game. Heavy or even moderate perfume will create a problem for some asthmatics with whom you work. Out-of-the-ordinary hairstyles might provide good conversation pieces, but your knowledge, skill, evidence of the right disposition, and ability to perform by providing influential answers to questions will need to be substantially better than others if you have an "unusual" hairstyle; the hairstyle will be a detractor. The same goes for makeup that is heavily applied and for body piercings, except for some innocent holes in your ears for earrings. School district and school leaders are not thought of by most of the American culture as "faddish." Rather, the public generally prefers that you will be clean, organized, and conservative in appearance.

Earlier literature informed women that except for their gender, they can reduce the appearance of unsettling differences from men by dressing in dark colors; dressing simply; wearing plain, two-piece suits, low heels, a clean-cut haircut, softly colored fingernails; and—if something must be carried—carrying a small, clean/polished, soft/leather briefcase or bag with a shoulder strap for keeping hands free and for storing a few important papers about the school district as well as essentials for maintaining hair, soft makeup, glasses, and so forth.

Particularly helpful is looking fit and healthy. Exercise on a routine basis will be a plus in positively affecting your appearance, your look of health, your ability to think quickly and clearly, and your ability to perform better when you are working in the leadership position. You don't have to be thin, but looking fresh and well exercised does help. You can participate in conversations about health, exercise, and nutrition, all of which will communicate to others that you have value for yourself and that you will be modeling the importance of keeping fit. Because women work longer hours than men in the superintendency, both exercise and nutrition become increasingly important to physical and emotional status.

Be able to discuss areas of interest that men typically have—business activities, the political scene, sports events—and discuss each carefully, without bias, demonstrating objectivity as well as a credible level of knowledge about the topics. If you cannot contribute to the discussion, ask sensible questions periodically to demonstrate interest in the conversation. Most school board members are men. Most school superintendents are men. Most community leaders are men. Men will be a significant number of the population with whom you need to be skilled in discussing subjects of interest to them. This skill precedes the development of strong sponsorships and strong interpersonal relationships with community members during your leadership service.

Additionally, successful women leaders might have an interest in recipes and creative cooking, but they will be more interested in successful leadership and achievements for their students and staff. The one topic in common that everyone has is successfully educating children. Help others construct their perceptions of what your shared purposes will be regarding the educational development of the children in the school community, doing this through how you present yourself and the nature of your conversations.

Another very important trait to demonstrate is a sense of humor. It's difficult to be humorous when it's not an innate part of your nature. However, it is easy to avoid taking yourself too seriously—and that you must do. You also need a sense of humor about yourself. Laugh readily—a *real* laugh. Artificial laughter is easily detected. You'll be expected to be genuine and sincere, so don't violate your image with an artificial laugh.

Initially, it's mostly reputation and image. During the interview, it's all about knowledge, disposition, examples of performance, and "connecting" to those who interview—the relational piece.

Above all, learn patience and practice persistence. Both result in a return on your investments.

Preparatory Programs

Chapter 3 presented some of the effects that a school administrator preparatory program can have in theoretically, philosophically, historically, and pragmatically offering knowledge and skill development to its graduate students. While a strong clinical component to the preparatory program certainly can produce effective beginning leaders, the program cannot produce highly effective school and school district leaders just by offering and having students complete the required classes. The commitment to enter school and school district leadership requires dedication to learn all that can be learned while enrolled in a preparatory program— whether you agree with what you are hearing from a professor or not. Your ability to function as a strong leader will be at stake for you; if you short-change your opportunity to learn everything from whomever is your instructor, you will be the one to suffer the loss.

There are familiar reports about graduate students enrolled in certification course work commenting, "The professor is boring," or "I'm not learning anything in this class," or "What are we supposed to be learning?" or "This is common sense." By the time students have completed an undergraduate program, they are expected to have reached an understanding about what good learning requires, that they are in charge of their own learning and that all learning has value. Graduate student comments about professors and classes actually tell more about the graduate students than they do about the professors or classes. The knowledge base and experience of the professor offer value to a student of leadership, if the learner earnestly wants to learn. Those who constantly challenge themselves—with new ideas, to make sense out of what may seem senseless or irrelevant and to ask questions to probe the knowledge of the instructor and of fellow class members—are often the greatest beneficiaries of any preparatory program. They also are the ones who complete their readings in advance, take good notes, identify and request more insight about concepts that they do not understand, work ahead to complete assignments, and accept the work and assignments as designed (rather than negotiating to remove an assignment or complaining that an excessive class workload interferes with full-time professional demands and family activities). Creating a positive attitude toward class work, others in the class, the instructor, the opportunity to be in the preparatory program, and the energy it will take to complete quality work creates your success, contributes to your reputation, and conditions you for CEO work as a superintendent. To do less is to deny your full development, given the time and the context. Unfailingly, some of our strongest leaders are folks who were not able to attend the finest, most expensive, or most demanding preparatory programs, yet they demonstrate outstanding preparation and effective performance because they dedicated themselves to doing so. Likewise, unfailingly, those who fail to apply themselves are school and school district leaders who do not make a contribution to the educational opportunities of all children in their school district. Children do not deserve leadership like that. Your work ethic must be very strong.

While working through the preparatory program, women must be sensitive to the stereotypes that undergird social prejudice. Women must refrain from reinforcing stereotypes. In the course of your preparatory program, avoid talking about personal selves, do not avoid analyzing situations or making decisions from an organizational and objective point of view, and do not gossip or repeat rumors and hearsay. These are all bad habits that can create trouble for you when you are a school or school district leader.

Developing and maintaining a positive attitude is a challenge. However, it is what will give you strength in challenging times. A positive attitude will inspire others to stay with the important tasks. A positive attitude will contribute positively to your reputation at the college/university where you are completing your preparatory program. A positive attitude will help you earn the support of professors to prepare and send supportive and strong recommendations on your behalf. Having a positive attitude does not mean that you are a Pollyanna. Rather, it demonstrates your belief in yourself and others, your self-confidence, and your ability to make good decisions on behalf of those you serve.

For school district and school leaders, course objectives in thirty-eight states in the country are developed around being able to demonstrate the knowledge and skill, dispositions, and performance described in the School Leadership Standards (Interstate School Leaders Licensure Consortium,

1996), which are likely to be the objectives of your preparatory program course work. At the college/university level, those standards are translated into Standards for Advanced Programs in Educational Leadership and specific performance factors are spelled out for school principals and school leaders. Your learning goals must be tied to developing your leadership knowledge and skills to the extent that you can provide evidence of meeting every one of those standards. Then, with some good socialization to the leadership positions, you will be ready to provide (and continually improve) your leadership as a superintendent of schools or a school principal.

Women in superintendent and principal positions, joined with women who are participating in a superintendent or principal leadership preparatory program, need to strongly lobby preparatory programs to provide more clinical opportunities. In particular, those clinical opportunities for women need to be opportunities to learn how women lead as well as how men lead. Studies of women superintendents can be integrated into class readings as well as problem-based learning projects. On-site learning activities under the leadership of school superintendents, whether women or men, provide graduate students opportunities to interact with school district leaders other than those in their own school districts. On-site learning assignments also provide them opportunities to participate in authentic school district work and to build relationships with school district leaders and school leaders. On-site activities must reduce the amount of observation that has been traditional in preparatory programs and increase the amount of involvement in issue discussions, product development, and other leadership experiences within a school district where graduate students can make contributions. These opportunities assist preparatory programs in socializing their graduate students to real leadership experiences. Being "on site" opens up an opportunity to start networking with those in leadership positions. Sponsors and mentors often evolve from on-site participation and interaction.

Professional Experience

Although the following suggestions are not absolute in terms of what an aspiring leader should consider, they are generally important for women who aspire to administrative positions. Remember: in general, men are hired on their potential and women are hired on their actual leadership skills. All other professional characteristics being equal among competitors for a principal or superintendent position, the broader and deeper your experience, the more attractive you are to those who interview you. You certainly are not required to have followed the typical career path for school leaders. However, teaching long enough to fully understand how to develop effective curricula and deliver effective instruction using the best practices is essential in the twenty-first century when leaders at all levels are expected to have strong instructional leadership skills. The insight you will have as a school or school district leader and your instructional coaching skills will serve you well.

You also should acquire experience participating in and chairing a number of committees, task forces, and other administrative activities that reflect your leadership skills, particularly those that make decisions collaboratively and use consensus-gaining skills in bringing the group to general agreement. These experiences will provide substance for you to use in your interviews. Volunteer to take on some of these opportunities and assignments. Other examples include conducting summer school programs, organizing an after-school tutoring program for students in need, developing a parent outreach program for your school, and organizing teachers to offer an activity that serves the educational development of children. In all of these examples, there can be evidence of your service as a transformational or transcendental leader, two important ways of leading. Also, there can be evidence of how you brought people together, how you organized, how you developed consensus, and how you achieved measurable results.

Find ways in which to contribute to community activities and participate in one or more activities that will open up opportunities for you to demonstrate leadership within the larger community. The evidence of your work can include leadership activities such as organizing to achieve a goal set by the leadership or congregation of your church, attending city council meetings and keeping school personnel informed of decisions made that may impact the future of the school district, and organizing your neighborhood to participate in a Clean Earth Day involving those in the neighborhood each year. Those experiences on your résumé all spell out the breadth of your interest and your natural leadership proclivities.

How to Not Take Things Personally

During the times when you are developing yourself, pursuing opportunities to access CEO positions, and serving children and the community as a CEO, there will be plenty of opportunity to practice how to not take things personally so that you truly can become a leader who does not take things personally. It's a survival tool for you. As the leader who occupies the chair "where the buck stops," others will follow their habits of observing, second-guessing, and criticizing any decisions that do not completely match their beliefs about what should be done or that establish an expectation for them to change in ways they don't want to change. This happens much faster for women than for men. There is a human tendency to take the criticism, barbs, and negative commentary personally—and if they are intense and continue, the tendency is to become quite angry and return retorts or behave punitively. Letters to the editor may take you to task. Parents may express open disapproval of how the schools "treated" their children. Football teams may experience losing seasons. Any number of things can find folks criticizing the leadership of the superintendent of schools. Particularly confounding is the development of rumors about what "the superintendent said" that will distort or purposefully misrepresent a conversation you might have had with someone.

What you must remember is that you cannot control anyone except yourself. When folks have something negative to say, it reflects more about them than it does about you. The words come from them, as do the intonations and the implied attitudes. At best, what others say about you informs you about their attitudes, beliefs, and frustrations. They own what they say, how they behave, and how they treat others. You own what you say, how you behave, and how you treat others. If you allow negative commentary to affect your behavior and limit your decisions to do what is right for the students and their education, you have chosen to allow others to control you. You must be strong as an individual and recognize your own value. Of course, criticism can be helpful—if it is objective and if it suggests that your actions improve by not overlooking some important action that you simply did not think about. What is more helpful is not taking what others say and do personally. You must be strong enough to hear criticism, analyze its source and what you might do to help reduce the frustration that is communicated, and be supportive wherever possible of your work, your job, others who work for and with you, and—above all— what all of the children in the school district deserve educationally.

Key leaders sometimes allow themselves to become so affected by the criticism aimed at them by a group of people that they cease to be able to act and to make the right decisions. They cannot go to sleep at night because anger grows and worries appear. You must be able to understand that you control only yourself. Students are relying on your advocacy and your service, making decisions on behalf of the common good. To rectify problems created by criticism, it often can help to involve the critics in decision making—but only after respectful and dignifying parameters are established for their interaction and participation in decision making—and only if the decisions result in recommendations that serve the common good for all children.

Sociocultural Checks

Make a checklist using Edgar Schein's "Ten Categories of Culture," religious and political ideologies, and kinds of power with indicators represented in the items on the checklist. If you are employed as superintendent, it will serve you even better if at that time you began setting up a table with the X axis across the top listing each of Schein's ten categories for defining culture and the Y axis down the side listing each sociocultural, religious ideology, political ideology, community power structure, gender prejudice, and gender-structuring characteristic you have read about in this book plus other characteristics you may know about. Then, as you collect more information, you can fill in the cells across and down with descriptors of the school district community you will be serving.

Studying the data collection from that effort will assist you in thinking about and deciding how to work with issues, change, communication, decision making, and any other school district task or function. If you currently are a superintendent, complete the evidence collection and analysis and reflect on your leadership to consider any changes you might make to experience a better fit with the school district's community that you serve. Remember that any decision you make can raise your perceived status in the community—or influence your dismissal. Be sure you know your community well.

Strategies that you can use early on in your superintendency include asking your school board members to complete a profile of the community and include descriptors from the substance presented in chapters 2 through 4. You might also consider asking community leaders to complete the same activity. From that you can conduct interviews with key communicators to identify the history of the school district and what they believe citizens want for and from their schools. Again, you will be able to use some of the indicators from chapters 2 through 4 in your interviews. Focus groups can confirm the important indicators describing the school community's socioculture.

When you are first interviewing for the superintendency, try to locate educators who have lived in or served the community and interview them about the school community culture and what they believe the community wants from its schools. Visit with state teacher association executives and state school boards association executives to find out what they know about the community. Check publicly available data on state department of education's websites and state government's websites to identify student performance and community population data. Access to income profiles by occupation or family factors (single parent, etc.) for your school district will provide a good idea of what might be a reasonable stretch for your salary, should you be offered the position as superintendent of schools. The 2000 Census Report has a broad and deep collection of data you can use for analysis of the school community. Often the data are reported by county in each state but even then, unless there is something unusual, the school district in that county will generally reflect those data.

When you arrive at the "selected candidate" stage and begin negotiations with the school board related to your salary and benefits, you want to have asked for and received a history of the school district's end-of-year budget report, noting the trends and balances. In addition to having some insight to the social, cultural, religious, and political preferences of the community, the fiscal balances will tell you whether you can ask to be paid what you are worth or whether you are going to agree to work in that school district even though the salary and benefits are not what you would like them to be. However you begin, it will be difficult to negotiate jumps in your salary and benefits later. Both authors of this book knew the same woman superintendent who was so eager to enter a superintendent position that she settled for what the school district offered her and then lamented much later at how often she had suggested that her salary be placed at a commensurate level with other school superintendents serving school districts the size of hers—and how every time the school board felt that the community would not approve. The sixth year of her service to that school district was a landmark—she was the first superintendent in that school district whose salary crossed the $50,000 a year mark!

Building and Maintaining Support Systems

Chapter 9 presented considerable detail about developing support systems. Simply put, women who have sought and developed mentors and sponsors who will be strong advocates for them, and who have connected with and participated in several networks, have an advantage in accessing and keeping a leadership position. It's a matter of identifying those who have knowledge, insights, and contacts and initiating professional dialogue with them. The professional conversations provide an opportunity for those already influential persons and leaders to develop a professional acquaintance with you, and to offer insight and suggestions for your leadership. An intermittent professional conversation can develop that will provide opportunity for mentoring via telephone conversations or when attending professional meetings. In most cases, there will be an opportunity to ask those influential leaders directly if they will mentor you.

Remember that the number of women who can be mentors is considerably smaller than men in superintendencies. Also, remember that women superintendents tend to work more hours each week than do men. Their collaborative and transformational leadership requires more hours than unilateral or hierarchal decision making. Consequently, access to women superintendents as mentors will be limited. This is lamentable because there is value in being socialized to the way women lead school districts; however, it also is understandable.

Of course, mentoring from a school superintendent or a school principal is not the only kind you can acquire. Community leaders, retired public school employees, state education workers, colleagues also working to obtain a superintendent or principal position, and people in communities who are deeply respected by the local citizenry can all be good mentors. Your need will be to collect ideas, information, and strategies to use to make successful decisions, interact appropriately with numbers of people with vested interest, identify the best pathways to bring about organizational development, find experts to assist with legal issues, identify local community interests in financing schools, develop partnerships with reliable partners, and understand the social-psychological relationships between and among the citizens in the school community at large.

Ruderman and Ohlott (2002) advise:

Do your research and know as much as you can before making a direct approach, so you can avoid establishing a tie with someone who cannot in fact help you and whose presence in your life may preclude more useful relationships. One woman told us that she asked a number of people in her division to identify the senior manager who might be most open to providing a mentoring relationship for her. She wanted someone who was friendly, approachable, and easy to talk to. After she found such a person and became his protégée, she discovered that he was really in a tangential role and did not hold much influence in the broader reaches of the organization. (68)

Family and friends provide very important support. There are many times for school district leaders when they need that support. For married women desiring to work as school superintendents, it is nearly impossible to do so without the support of their spouses and children. Stress is ready to assert itself at any number of points in superintendent work and when the most important relationships women want to maintain begin to show signs of dissatisfaction with the time required for work, it can have an undesirable effect. The conditions of the job as superintendent need to be forthrightly discussed with family members and reasonable family agreements must be made in advance and kept. Without that, the immediate family support system may dissolve at the very time it is needed by the superintendent. Superintendents' spouses and children find it very difficult to have a private family life. The superintendency is a very public position for most school districts. Larger metropolitan or urban school districts may be the exception because the size of the school district and community prevents the superintendent from being able to be visible everywhere. However, more visibility than desired occurs when a major issue arises with the superintendent in any size school district.

Dr. Victor's experience illustrates the importance of a family support system. Following many years of service to a school district, a small segment of the community decided quietly to "go after her" and replace her with a man. Eventually, she was dismissed with a 4-3 board member vote, and when she arrived home after the executive session, her husband heard the report—detail by detail—and simply hugged her, laughing, and said, "I'm so glad! You did not deserve that stress! It's their loss and your gain!"

Friends can assist very effectively by listening. Most friends do just that. Developing and maintaining relationships outside of work has multiple benefits in addition to having empathetic listeners who can provide insights. They also share strategies, make sure support is provided where needed, make public statements in support of the superintendent, and squelch inaccurate rumors and hearsay about the superintendent. Friends also can encourage the superintendent to relax and to recreate by planning relaxing evenings together and routine exercise together. Early in a superintendency, Mary Jane McDonough remarked that 5:30 A.M. comes early, but she was not going to miss a jog with her friends. It was uplifting and helped her start her day right every day.

Communication Savvy

Effective communication is an essential—and tough to achieve. Regardless of excellent efforts on the part of school district personnel, school district accreditation reviews or program evaluations nearly always recommend that communication within the organization be improved. Because sending and receiving messages to each other passes through numerous complex "screens" and "lenses," the complexity of establishing good communication among and with others is highly challenging. Even the simplest of tasks—sending school board meeting minutes—can be a confounding variable in the "eyes of the beholder." In fact, it is generally problems with communication and the relationships developed through communication that trip up bright, skilled, knowledgeable, and otherwise successful superintendents. Sometimes, the unanticipated meaning that folks draw from the simplest of unintended miscommunications creates more challenge for the superintendent than is easily managed and can keep a superintendent from her dream of achieving successful leadership as a superintendent or principal.

To prepare and to develop yourself as an effective and successful leader, you must keep in mind the simple as well as the more complex challenges. A small thing is your appearance, which makes a statement about you in the first fifteen seconds of your entrance into a room—whether for an interview, obtaining an application, attending a reception or seminar, or for other purposes. Your communication and presentation of self send messages to those who watch and listen to you. Assuming that you have taken care of your personal appearance, work diligently on communication.

It is helpful to understand communication from direction and balance factors—particularly when considering how to communicate with and receive communication from employees and residents of the school district. Grunig and Hunt (1984) identify a two-factor and two-directional communication model to assist with understanding the flow and balance of communications with the public; use of the model can be most helpful for school superintendents. The two factors are direction (flow of information) and symmetry (balance). One-way asymmetrical communication is frequently called press agentry and is used for positive publicity such as newsletters, informational brochures for potential school district residents, and any other information about "your schools" that would contribute to pride in the school district. The communication flow is from the school district to the school community population, with an intended benefit to the school district. For years, one-way asymmetrical communication has been the primary approach taken. This level of communication sends information out and does little to engage the public in communication. However, information dissemination is important. How to disseminate the information is the challenge. A minority of the parents read communications from the school or school district that are sent home with their children or mailed to them. Of course, the larger population of nonparents generally does not receive school newsletters.

One-way symmetrical communication is more neutral in its dissemination of information. One-way symmetrical communication moves from the school district to school community residents, again benefiting the school district. Instead of a report of all positive information, the report would include improvement needs as well. A good example is the annual report card that many school districts are required to publish for local school district residents. The annual report card reports strengths and concerns regarding student achievement data and other measures by which states evaluate schools. Whether required or not, it is always a good idea to provide a performance report to the community supporting its schools with taxes and other contributions. Annual school district report cards allow taxpayers to learn where goals are being met and where needs for improvement exist.

Two-way asymmetrical communication involves communication not only from the school district to the community but also from the school community to the school district. The superintendent provides vehicles to collect input from employees, students, and community residents. The information is used by administrators for planning and designing recommendations and future actions. If potential change in operations, funding, or accountability can be foreseen in the future of the school district, a wise superintendent establishes insightful questions around what may be coming and collects residents' opinions, beliefs, and attitudes regarding issues created by potential changes or potential future requirements. For example, if the school community is likely to be held accountable for meeting standards that have been developed by the state (legislature or state departments of education), a smart superintendent will carefully identify the pivotal questions to elicit public opinion; collect that opinion through surveys, focus groups, public forums, or neighborhood coffees; and then use the information to guide how to develop and implement whatever comes out from state officials. This helps the superintendent frame the school district work in ways that are acceptable to community stakeholders and residents.

Two-way symmetrical communication is challenging to accomplish, and yet it is the most effective kind of communication if managed well. For decades, male-dominated leadership has used position authority to establish decision-making processes that allow formal leaders to highly influence decisions, even making them unilaterally as the "authority." Because of an increasing interest of community stakeholders to have a voice in school district and school decision making, superintendents who give time and attention to designing effective, routine, two-way symmetrical communication will experience benefits. Two-way symmetrical communication provides real opportunity for school employees, community stakeholders, and residents to participate in decision making on big issues. By way of illustration, consider Dr. Charts's successful leadership in organizing key communicators in the school district community to discuss the potential of closing some elementary schools as a cost-reduction measure for schools in need of continual and costly maintenance.

Dr. Eleanor Charts gave several months of time to systematically interview key communicators and stakeholders in order to identify members of the school community who had credibility. She developed a list of forty-three citizens who had credibility in the community. Each citizen received an invitation to serve on a school district Schools and Fiscal Accountability Task Force, which would work over an eighteen-month period to study costly schools in the school district, identify options for school board consideration in reducing costs, and bring forth a set of legitimate consensus options worthy of the school board's considerations. The task force members elected their own co-chairs who led the effort to set agendas, identify information needed, and develop strategies to keep communication flowing with the school community.

At the first meeting of the task force, Dr. Charts presented school district data related to the decision-making tasks the group would be facing. Then, prior to each monthly meeting, Dr. Charts provided research-based articles that were objective, based in fact, thought-provoking, and filled with ideas for resolving issues. Each meeting began by asking several task force members to help summarize the key points and discuss whether any of these points might be applicable to this work. Within a short period of time, task force members were current in their knowledge about options that might be workable, and they began to invite school district officials to meet with them to discuss answers to questions they had raised. The meetings were open to the public, highly publicized, and summarized and discussed in the local newspaper. Initially, task force members experienced heightened public interest, and sometimes heated warnings not to close schools. About ten months into the process, it seemed that serious consideration for closing a few schools was going to be the only real option. Dr. Charts facilitated discussions that led to the task force's understanding that the primary option for fiscal accountability was closing schools, and she turned the group's attention to designing a phased process for taking action. Within the eighteen-month period, the task force reported to the school board, summarized their work, recommended that five elementary schools be closed, presented a phased plan for closing them, and identified where the student population would then be served. By this time, there were few issues remaining. Dr. Charts had facilitated the process most effectively, an excellent example of two-way symmetrical communication. Because their nature is to collaborate and nurture, women need to fully understand how best to use each kind of communication to involve employees, stakeholders, and other school community residents.

Listening

You've heard this for years, but here it is again: you must *listen* carefully, actively, and effectively. It's the most important behavior you can practice if you want to be a successful leader. Study what active listeners do. If you are in a group discussing an issue and you consistently comment following the tail end of another person's concern or idea, you are not listening effectively. Most likely, you are listening to the beginning of the idea and, within split seconds, identifying what you want to add or present before the idea is completely expressed, thereby missing the total message. You need thought time. You need to demonstrate that you value and listen to others who are participating in the discussion. You need to let the discussant know that you are listening by establishing good eye contact, asking questions that dignify the person's knowledge and understanding of what she or he is talking about, and being facially expressive in ways that are appropriate to what is being said. Practice in front of a mirror. Create hypothetical conversations and watch yourself respond to those conversations to be sure that oral and body language indicate that you are truly listening.

In addition to getting the message and information right, there are many advantages to listening. Once you have established with others that you are a good listener, you will soon learn how to control the discussion where needed by using appropriate inquiry processes. Leading part or all of the conversations through use of an inquiry method will serve you very well as a school or school district leader. Using the above tips for your work in your current job will be quite helpful as well. You are creating a context—and that context includes you—the person whom interviewers will be evaluating regarding whether or not they want to hire you. If you do not listen well, you will not be able to disguise that weakness in an interview process.

Listening also has great advantage to a school district leader who wishes to develop and maintain public support for the schools and school district. People feel dignified when you listen earnestly and completely. The more you listen and the more you learn about the culture, the more successful you can become as a leader. This does not mean that you fail to take positions—just do so judiciously. Firm and purposeful communication is very important—but your leadership will not be as successful as needed if listening clearly is not your priority. The best advice that veteran superintendents provide to novices is that they should listen, listen, listen. A former superintendent routinely advised those who hope to be successful superintendents how to work with angry people who arrive in the office to complain. She said that when an angry or complaining parent or patron arrived in the office, she or he was invited into her office and invited to take a seat at a round table that was in the corner of the office. The guest also was invited to have a cup of coffee or some water. The nature of the round table's placement did not allow the parties to place the table between them; rather they sat at angles facing each other. There was a blank writing pad and pen in the middle of the table.

The superintendent would begin by saying, "Why don't you tell me what you would like for me to hear? I hope you'll understand that I will be taking notes. What you have to say is important to me, and I want to be sure I remember it all." Then she would listen. Periodically she might ask questions for clarification, and she wrote down all of the points the patron(s) made. When the patron(s) had finished, she asked, "What would you like for me to do?" If the patron made a suggestion and she could honor it, she simply stated, "I can do that" and made a date for reporting back to the patron. If the patron made a suggestion that she could not honor because of policy or law or counterproductive consequences, she would inform the patron that she would not be able to honor that request and explain why. Then she would offer an alternative that involved her attention and those specifically involved in the complaint in discussion and problem resolution. Before the patron left, she would read back the points she had recorded and ask for any corrections to her notes that needed to be made. She also would tell the patron(s) by when she would contact them to let them know the "next steps" if that was what needed to occur.

She reported, "Ninety-eight percent of the time, the patron simply wanted me to hear the complaint, trusting that I would resolve the problem. The other two percent of the time, we would work to agree to disagree and I would enter into my notes for my secretary to place on my calendar a telephone contact with the patron in a few days to ask if everything else is going OK." Listening resolved 98 percent of the concerns. Even then, for the other 2 percent, careful listening helped reduce the anger or calm the concern a bit.

Because information is so important to your success, you need school board support for listening and learning as a priority during your first year. Invite school board members to mentor you through processes, developing a depth and breadth of knowledge about the school culture and school community culture so that this knowledge will assist you in successfully leading important change efforts in the future. While you are listening and learning, you can collect information that will help you identify where administrative reorganization or realignment of roles and responsibilities needs to occur.

Speaking

Speaking is of equal importance. To help the culture reduce prejudice toward you as a woman leader, you will have to "speak the language." In public schools, that language is standard English. Work on speaking in complete sentences, speaking without jargon (a difficult task for those of us who are jargon users), using active verbs, and speaking without personal reference (this takes a lot of work) except for when there is not an option to speak without personal reference.

Speak from what you know from good research (however, avoid the phrase "research states . . ."), expertise that has developed from your experience, and values that will be important to the members of that school district community's cultural core values. Under questioning, do not guess at answers. If you do not know for sure, state that you do not know and state it as a matter of fact (no dismay in your voice) followed by, "I would be interested in knowing that." Then ask an appropriate question about what you were asked, if there is one that makes good sense at the time. If the question has an answer that you as the superintendent are expected to know, state directly that you will find out and deliver the information to the questioner.

The language that you speak may also need to include some dialects or a foreign language used widely by varying sectors of the school community. This does not necessitate that you learn a foreign language; it may necessitate that you learn colloquial or dialectical conversational language—or at least phrases of it—enough to convey your earnestness in being able to communicate with those who do not use standard English. However, standard English will be expected of a professional most of the time.

Your vocal tone and volume must be strong and controlled. You need to be sure to be expressive with an effort to convey dynamic and strong belief in core values for serving all children very well. Your communication efforts should include honoring the work of the school district employees and those connected to the school district in governance roles. Women tend to speak in softer voices; if you do, you'll need to work on volume.

Speaking firmly about your convictions is important. Of course, you'll need to do considerable homework about the school district in order to know if your convictions match the values, needs, and interests of the school district where you plan to interview. Practice answering questions in front of a full-length mirror, pretending that you are at a table around which sit ten interviewers. Work on establishing eye contact and maintaining an open and receptive expression.

Say what you mean and mean what you say. Patrons and employees will be listening carefully to what you say in the interview; you will be employed based on what you have convinced them of—that you meet the job description and are ready for the leadership and its challenges.

There are a few maxims that accompany the communication of successful leaders. One is keeping your word so that your word will be considered "good." You must build credibility if you hope to serve the school district well. Seitel (1998) credits Sharpe with identifying five processes that a person needs to use in order to be effective in communicating and developing meaningful relationships. Those processes and results are the following: (1) If you want to be described as credible, you must be honest in your communication; (2) if you want to have people feeling confident about you and their school district, then your communication must demonstrate openness and consistency of actions; (3) if you hope to experience reciprocity and good will, your words and actions must be perceived as fair; (4) if you want to avoid alienation of employees, students, stakeholders, and other community residents, then you must provide routine opportunities for continuous two-way communication; and (5) if you hope to build social harmony between and among the school district community members and groups, then you must complete environmental research and communicate the results of your research, including results of evaluations of educational programs and school district operations and results of school district work on a routine basis.

Another wise maxim is to communicate your interest in learning all about the school district as an organization and the community as a context for educating children. Tell the citizenry that you want to listen to them and that you hope they will let you know their interests. Make no major changes the first year of your superintendency. To do this will require negotiation with the school board because they will be eager for you to "begin leading" as soon as your job begins.

To collect the information, set up a series of interviews before you enter your contracted superintendency and/or immediately after you begin your work in the school district. The interviews should be conversations with important school district patrons, community leaders, and employees—people other people listen to, people who are influential with others—at all levels of school district operations. Learn how they view their school district, ideas they have for improvement, and what they would like to see in your leadership. These informal, one-on-one conversations very early in your tenure reap great benefits for you, as well as for others in the school district. Repeat the effort intermittently throughout the years of service, perhaps organizing folks in like-interest or differentiated-interest focus groups to gain insight about their perceptions of their schools and school district and to seek ideas and suggestions for continued improvement. This visibility with your public does have its rewards—building public support, collecting ideas, creating relationships, and maybe even influencing extension of your superintendent contract.

Speak objectively, thoughtfully. Use dynamics when needed but don't deliver them in high speed. There are many who will pose loaded questions to you when the opportunity arises. Learn to identify the loaded questions and develop skills in rephrasing the questions and responding with illustrations of your point.

Whenever possible, demonstrate a sense of humor. It has such a leveling effect during times of stress or tension. If you are not easily a humorous person, if punch lines for jokes that you tell fall flat, if what you think you have said humorously usually gets no response, then do not try to be a joke teller or a comedian. However, you can learn how to tell stories that have a humorous bent and you certainly can develop an easiness in not taking yourself too seriously, creating laughter around something you were thinking or had done—as long as the laughter is tasteful and not offensive.

Writing

A great amount of written communication and written record is expected and produced by schools and school districts. The leader must lead the way in communicating—and doing so effectively. Another maxim helps to guide the care with which a leader communicates in writing:

"Don't put anything in writing that you don't want to see on a billboard in a highly trafficked area of your school community." Of course, there are confidential written records in which personally identifiable information must be maintained confidentially—meaning that only authorized persons can have access to that information. It is easy for women who are ready conversationalists to write too much detail in their communications. Be objective. Be straightforward. Be as brief as possible and still get the message communicated. Advice on letter writing and memo writing is to try to keep the message confined to one page. This takes practice, of course.

It is important that you take great care when writing e-mail messages. All e-mail messages exist in perpetuity. Baner, Koberlein, and Reichart (2005) found that knowledge about appropriate use of e-mail is essential for educators to learn. The researchers created an "E-mail Etiquette" professional development activity to teach educators how to communicate through e-mail without violating the legal confidentiality rights of students and school personnel. Also, it is important to be careful with how you write and what you say. Providing information via e-mail creates vulnerability for the sender since e-mail can be accessed from cyberspace and become public. Additionally, poorly written e-mails that educators compose can expose the writers' improper use of sentence structure and language, suggesting that they may not be as literate as they should be—particularly as educators and as school leaders and school district CEOs. Because technology plays such an important role in electronic communications, one who aspires to or serves in a leadership position must take care to be legal, ethical, and professional in all written communications.

Reading

Ironically, the primary focus in elementary school is to teach children to read; yet, the higher up the organizational ladder an educator is, the busier it seems and the easier it is to produce, guide, meet, plan, and so forth—but not read. Not only is professional reading important so that you can avoid being dated in your knowledge and understanding of new learning, new evidence, and new approaches, but also staying current is required for decision makers who are making decisions that affect so many.

Recreational reading is a must—if for no other reason than leaving behind the rigors of the day and escaping into a different occupation of one's mind. Keep a high-interest piece of fiction or nonfiction by your bedside and read twenty pages before going to sleep. Recreational reading provides opportunity to converse about literature, themes, historical examples, whether character development was realistic or not, and so on with citizens who might be more comfortable talking with you about recreational reading than about school district topics. It's a good way to develop relationships.

It really goes without saying that professional reading is essential. Obviously, it is so important that even though it "goes without saying," we are saying it here. It does not take long to become dated in what you know and understand. Strong and successful leaders stay current regarding educational and leadership research and best practices in leading, teaching, and learning.

Conflict Resolution

Interacting with others in groups can be satisfying when problems are resolved or when creative thinking is needed. At times, though, when groups are organized to discuss issues that have differing points of view, a controversial atmosphere may be created, calling for the leader to use effective conflict resolution skills. It will be important for aspiring leaders to be professionally developed in planning and using conflict resolution activities and tools. Some conflict contributes positively to group interaction and decision making. Because conflict can get "out of hand," however, it is wise for group leaders to have skills in using the conflict effectively and in redirecting the group to problem resolution or identifying group recommendations for addressing any issues that exist.

A Few More Important Details

It is especially important that women do not repeat rumors and hearsay because the age-old stereotype of women is that they are gossips. Both rumors and hearsay can be damning. It is essential that school leaders do not demonstrate anything except the most objective, knowledgeable, and professional behavior and attitude. Remember that the leader's job is to value every student and all contributions to the welfare and educational growth of each student. Negative or critical behavior and rumoring or hearsay practices will deny you credibility with the school district employees and the school community.

Women have reported being embarrassed during interviews because their throats were dry, a cough or "tickle" developed in their throats that could not be controlled, a nose became drippy or running because of air conditioning in the room. Take cough drops and tissues with you when you are scheduled for an interview or even for a speech. You will find both very helpful if you are interviewed throughout the day or are interviewed by a small or large group of stakeholders for a lengthy time and discover that you have a dry throat or nonstop cough developing. At times, different agents are in the air that will cause you to sneeze. You'll wish you had a handkerchief or some tissue when that happens.

Also, when men interview, they have the advantage of several pockets and do not carry anything in their hands—unless there are copies of a résumé that they might want to distribute or there is a handout of the interview schedule that the board president has provided. Women need to find a way to operate without handbags. Hide them in your car when you arrive and securely lock the car. If you must carry something, keep it very small and as out of sight as is possible. Handbags can easily become professional detractors. If anything is in your hands, make sure it is a leather-bound notepad that will have a pocket for school district information or extra copies of your résumé and a pen to record notes.

School Board–Superintendent Relations

In our country, lay school boards provide the governance for local public school districts. Members are elected by registered voters in the community and often it will be the first time a community member will have won an election—often elevating the importance and sometimes lending itself to misinterpreting responsibilities of power for the winner(s) in a school board election. For the most part, though, school board members—called directors—have a commitment to doing what will help the education of a community's youth. Each novice director will begin just like a novice entering any position—with a need for learning and development so that decisions can be more informed.

School boards also act as gatekeepers in the process of selecting superintendents of schools. They will be inclined to seek out the familiar and write job descriptions for the spectacular. Communication with school board members must be consistent and predictable, and this is probably your most important task. Common tips to assist you when you enter the superintendency follow.

(1) Be sure you have successfully negotiated your contract for salary and benefits with the school board. Do not trust the system or even the school board that hired you. You must take care of your own welfare in this regard. Also, be sure the contract clearly spells out how and when you will have a performance evaluation completed by the school board and what the performance criteria will be. At the same time, you might consider as part of your contract including a description of the roles and responsibilities of the superintendent and of the school board. Some school boards may see this as adversarial, but if they are receptive, move forward in contracting these conditions.

(2) Communicate with school board members every week, sending a weekly newsletter to keep them updated on events being held and issues being addressed in their schools. When you do this, keep in mind that legally this communication must be available to the public, if requested. Consequently, the communication must be written carefully and all confidentialities must be protected. It is advisable that you also conduct a weekly (or more often) telephone call with each school board member individually. Be sure, however, that all school board members have the same information. It will be important that you are not viewed as giving preferential treatment to one school board member over another. The *only* exception to this is if the school board as a board (not individually) agrees that the appropriate protocol will be for the superintendent to communicate with the board president and the other members agree to rely on the board president to communicate individually with each of them.

(3) Provide weekly school district–related material for both required and recreational reading. The required reading will consist of articles, data, reports, and other information that will help them prepare for study session and board meeting discussions. Recreational reading will consist of additional educational literature that is entirely supplementary or that is

a piece of research that could surface in the future with predicted trends about changes coming "down the pike."

(4) Spend time over lunch with each school board member as an individual every quarter to explore issues each has, further develop the relationship, learn interests and needs, and share stories that unite common interests. This time together has nice rewards in terms of solidifying relationships.

(5) Publicly recognize the extensive contributions of the school board to the education of all children and to the educational community. Serving as a director and performing the responsibilities of governance requires commitment and time, and, at times, a school board member's family or work are sacrificed. Make sure each school board member knows her or his value and the appreciation you have for his or her loyalty and dedication. Take every opportunity to nominate the board for exemplary work. In fact, set the stage wherever possible for school board work that is exemplary and that meets the qualities required for nomination for recognition.

(6) Provide school board members routine professional development regarding governance, roles and responsibilities, understanding the budget and school law, and working effectively with the constituency they serve both in the community and in the school district. Be a participant and learner in that professional development along with the school board. Should there be problems that seem to be developing between school board members or between one or more directors and you, the superintendent, try to resolve those right away and, if the school board is agreeable, bring in an expert who can conduct professional development related to effective team operations and team building. Intraboard conflicts occur with as much frequency as board-superintendent conflicts. Regardless of the nature of the conflict, if everyone is willing, team-building experiences can pay off in improved governance and leadership. Without reducing the intraboard or board-superintendent conflict, conditions and relationships grow worse.

CHAPTER 10

Strategic and Political Leadership

Formulate a plan for interviewing, for discussing conditions of employment, and for developing and executing your contract and know that plan well before going in to interview for a superintendent vacancy. You can always modify the plan, based on what you learn after you have developed all of the desired parts of the plan and after you have met the school board, discussed the expectations for the position, and identified their goals for the superintendent of schools. Keep in mind throughout your contacts that you must be politically wise. You must not give up the ranch, so to speak.

Dr. Louanna Figston recalls her introduction to politics two decades ago. Her school board president, who was a woman, met Dr. Figston on the post office steps and visited with her about going to the capital to meet with the local congressman for purposes of encouraging him to lead his fellow congressmen, convincing them that a change in proposed legislation needed to be made. The legislation to be debated by the house of representatives proposed eliminating funded health services available through the schools for children who qualified. Representative Horace had already telephoned Dr. Figston to see if she would provide leadership among superintendents of schools to drop career ladder funding in order to continue funding of children's health service. Dr. Figston said that she was so upset with the proposal that she could not agree to take that step. It was robbing Peter to pay Paul. She told her school board president that she simply refused to play politics with children, that she would write to the congressman, but that she would not travel to the capital to be embroiled in a legislative struggle that penalized children however you looked at it. And she repeated, "I simply will not play politics with children!" Her patient school board president recognized that she had a lot to learn.

Do not leave yourself vulnerable by refusing to be political. Build relationships. Anticipate what is coming and start your lobbying efforts early. Lay the groundwork for later requests of support from the school board. Build coalitions advocating for improving services to children.

Your contract is the beginning of your strategic and political work. States generally designate a limit for the number of years a person can be contracted to serve as a superintendent of schools. Do not sign a contract that covers less than the maximum number of years allowed. Change efforts will require at least five years, and you'll leave the school district workforce at a disadvantage if you work less than three years. Your goal should be to hold the position for much longer.

A strategic step you can use to influence longer service to the school district is to request what is called a "golden handcuffs" contract. A "golden handcuffs" contract calls for the school board to set aside a sizable sum in an investment program under the school district's and superintendent's names. The invested funds earn annual interest, which is added to the principal for the account. The superintendent agrees to stay a designated amount of years, usually longer than the largest number of years she can be contracted as designated by law. If she chooses to depart the superintendency before those years have passed, the funds stay with the school district. If the school board dismisses her prior to the completion of the agreed-upon years, the superintendent is paid those funds and the interest earned. School boards frequently include in the contract that the funds stay with the school district if the dismissal is for reasons of legal or moral violations committed by the superintendent. A "golden handcuffs" contract is actually a separate agreement between the superintendent and the school board; it can be an addendum to the employment contract.

Dr. Sharon Summers had a golden handcuffs contract in which she agreed to serve the school district ten years, even though her superintendent employment contract initially was for three years, the longest her state allowed by law. She and the school board also signed a three-year contract for her superintendent of schools services. Each year, after serving the first year of her three-year contract, Dr. Summers and the school board would declare the current contract null and void and the school board would offer her a new three-year contract. In the spring of her fifth year, the school board voted to dismiss her. She left with payment in the amount of the remaining two years' salary and the investment, which at that time equaled approximately $150,000.

Planning strategically and using political savvy helped to assure that Dr. Summers was protected with her salary and benefits. It must be noted here that there is a risk in declaring the current contract null and void and then having the school board present the next contract for three years. The risk, of course, is that there is a brief period between the null-and-void three-year contract and board action on the promised "new" three-year contract. There could be a conspiring school board that acquires your agreement to follow this process and then, after declaring the current three-year contract null and void, chooses not to offer the new three-year contract, which means that you would not be able to collect on whatever remains of your three-year contract for superintendent services. Also, know state law regarding length of contract for public school superintendents and learn whether or not it is legal for the school board to simply add on another year and take action on rewriting the contract, thereby keeping the superintendent on a "continual" three-year (or however many are allowed) contract.

Remember that while you work through this process, you must be ever cognizant of the values, expectations, and norms of the community so that you and the school board do not agree to something that will become a big problem for you with the community. Strong and effective school boards will be able to influence others regarding the rationale of offering a contract that pleases all of you; you simply might be working with a school board that neither is strong nor effective.

Intermittently, doing a reliability check on school board support of your work is good practice. Each year, the potential is for this lay board to change significantly in terms of ideological structure, political leanings, vested interests, and so forth. You need to be ready to change with them, being careful to learn all you can about their leanings and interests and maintaining frequent contact with each one individually to keep a relationship strong.

Facing Dismissal

At times, a superintendent will know that her relationship with the school board and/or the school district is eroding and she may be unable to control the erosion. At other times, a superintendent can be surprised with dismissal, as many of the case studies and stories throughout chapters 1 through 9 have illustrated. Either way, the process is painful and debilitating for the superintendent.

Be prepared, personally and professionally. Know what your leadership accomplished for children. Know that you have worked loyally and diligently on behalf of the children in the school district. You simply are going to have decisions to make periodically that are counter to what an individual or individuals want. One of the analogies that is used to explain the situation you are in, if facing dismissal, is that for every decision you must make on behalf of all children, there are some people with long memories who will be upset with the decision and will not be able to forget it. If you were to pick up a rock and put it in your pocket for each of those times someone is upset, when your pocket becomes too heavy to carry all of those rocks, your dismissal may be imminent. It may be time to leave. However, do not choose to resign if you have a "golden handcuffs" contract. You will want to be dismissed so that you can depart from the school district with full remuneration. It may take another year or so to acquire the next job and you will appreciate having the income from your investment. When you resign, you give up your contract and all agreements. Consequently, the investment goes back to the school district and you are left without financial support.

It is most helpful at these times to have a sturdy and supportive contract and to remember that you cannot control what others say and decide to do. You can control only what you say and decide to do. Face whatever decision is made with personal firmness, belief in yourself, dignity, and grace. Know that you have given your service in good faith. Do not take personally what others say unless, of course, it is true and you have committed malpractice. If the latter is true, you need to acquire a personal attorney. The school district attorney with whom you probably have an excellent relationship cannot help you; the school district attorney must represent the school board. You also would need a personal attorney if the school board has decided to dismiss you without full remuneration. The procedures are not pleasant; however, if you have documented inappropriate behaviors of school board members that have led to your dismissal, such as routinely meeting in private homes after school board meetings to discuss your performance—a violation of the sunshine law—you will find the evidence legally supportive on your behalf.

Whatever the situation, add up your accomplishments, pack up your books, take a brief break, and then apply for another school district leadership position. Unless you have violated the law or stepped outside of expected moral or ethical behavior, there will be a number of school districts that will consider your application seriously. You will have had experience, faced tough challenges, and managed a dismissal with great dignity. Men have frequently advised other men not to worry about dismissal because their next job will be a better job. Whether that is true or not for women is not yet clear. The more women go after their interests to continue service to school children through their work as school district CEOs, the stronger they become as leaders. The children benefit. And that's the point of your work.

Maintaining a Leadership Position

Social justice is served, in part, if women can maintain a superintendent or school principal position to such an extent that there are sufficient numbers of them serving in these positions over a period of time. It will help culturalize communities to women CEOs, creating a greater comfort level and confidence with women in leadership. This is not an easy task. It's not an easy task for any gender, any race. School district leadership and school leadership have been transformed during the past twenty years from management roles to leadership and public accountability for successful schools and improved student achievement. The nature of a superintendent's work has changed to greater emphasis on public relations and leadership related to the curriculum, instruction, and assessment programs for students. Leaders also face cross fire in nearly all of the work they do.

However, that is not to say that one should avoid seeking and acquiring those positions. This country needs good school district and school leadership. Our children need good leadership working earnestly on their behalf. Someone will have to provide the leadership; those someones should be the folks who have prepared rigorously for that leadership and who are willing and dedicated to the service of others. Public schools are the only institution that welcomes all youth to their classrooms. Fully employable high school graduates "up the quality" of life in many ways, not the least of which is contributing to the country's social and economic systems. A worker who can earn a salary that purchases essentials and also have some discretionary money does not depend on assistance or subsistence programs. In fact, that worker contributes to the health of the economy. The local, state, and national educational policies assist children with skill and knowledge development to provide them with a quality life and, in doing so, provide the social order with maintenance of a stable, successful, and healthy democracy. Women understand this well and can provide the leadership for developing children to be productive and successful, contributing to both the social and economic order in which we live.

When women go after their dreams of becoming school superintendents and actualize the dreams, making them reality, they then have a powerful opportunity to touch the lives of children who have dreams and influence the transformation of those dreams into realities.

BIBLIOGRAPHY

Aiken, J. A., and Tarule, Jill M. (1998). The centerpiece in women's leadership: Perspectives from the field. In Funk, C., Pankake, A., and Reese, M. (Eds.). *Women as school executives: Realizing the vision*. Commerce: Texas A&M University Press.

Avila, L. (1993). Why women are ready for educational leadership positions. In Brown, C., and Ivy, B. J. (Eds.). *Women as school executives: A powerful paradigm*. Huntsville, TX: Sam Houston Press.

Babcock, L., and Laschever, S. (2003). *Women don't ask: Negotiation and the gender divide*. Princeton, NJ: Princeton University Press.

Baner, M., Koberlein, J., and Reichart, T. (2005). Legal, ethical, and professional implications of effective e-mail for educational administration and staff. Doctoral Research Project, Saint Louis University. Dissertation Abstracts International. Publication in progress.

The Baptist Faith Message. (2000, June 14). Southern Baptist Church Report. Retrieved May 7, 2005, from http://www.sbc.net/bfm/default.asp.

Barth, R. (2001, February). Teacher leader. *Phi Delta Kappan 82*(6), 443.

Bass, B. M. (1997). *A new paradigm of leadership: An inquiry into transformational leadership*. Mahweh, NJ: Laurence Erlbaum. Cited in Lunenburg, F. C., and Ornstein, A. C. (2004). *Educational administration: Concepts and practices*. Belmont, CA: Wadsworth/Thomson Learning, 30–31.

Beekley, C. (1999). Dancing in red shoes. In Brunner, C. C. (Ed.). *Sacred dreams: Women and the superintendency*. Albany: State University of New York Press.

Bell, C., and Chase, S. (1993). The underrepresentation of women in school leadership. In C. Marshall (Ed.). The new politics of race and gender: The 1992 yearbook of the politics of education association. Washington, DC: Falmer Press.

———. (1996). The gendered characteristics of women superintendents' professional relationships. In Arnold, K., Noble, K., and Subotnick, R. (Eds.).

Remarkable women: Perspectives on female talent development. Cresskill, NJ: Hampton Press.

Bell, C. S. (1988). Organizational influences on women's experience in the super-intendency. *Peabody Journal of Education 65*(4), 31–59.

Benton, S. (1980). Women administrators for the 1980s: A new breed. *Journal of the National Association of Women Deans, Administrators, and Counselors, 43*(4), 18–23.

Bjork, L. (2000a). Introduction: Women in the superintendency—Advances in research and theory. *Educational Administration Quarterly 36*(1), 5–17.

———. (2000b). Professional preparation and training. Cited in Glass, T., Bjork, L., and Brunner, C. C. *The study of the American school superintendency: A look at the superintendent of education in the new millennium.* Arlington, VA: American Association of School Administrators.

Bjork, L. G., Bell, R. J., and Gurley, D. K. (2002, April 2). School board politics and superintendent roles. A paper presented at the American Educational Research Association 2002 Annual Meeting, New Orleans, Louisiana.

Blount, J. (1998). *Destined to rule the schools: Women and the superintendency, 1873–1995.* Albany: State University of New York Press.

Bolman, L. G., and Deal, T. E. (2003). *Reframing organizations: Artistry, choice, and leadership.* 3rd edition. San Francisco: Jossey-Bass.

Break the Glass Ceiling Foundation. Statistics: Women. Retrieved January 11, 2005, from http://www.breaktheglassceiling.com/statistics-women.htm.

Brunner, B. (2004). Timeline of affirmative action milestones. Retrieved on August 29, 2004, from http://www.infoplease.com/spot/affirmativetimeline1.html, page 6.

Brunner, C. C. (1997). Exercising power. *The School Administrator 54*(6), 6–10.

———. (1999a). Do it anyway: Gaining access. In Brunner, C. C. (Ed.). *Sacred dreams: Women and the superintendency.* Albany: State University of New York Press.

———. (Ed.). (1999b). *Sacred dreams: Women and the superintendency.* Albany: State University of New York Press.

———. (1999c). Women's ways of succeeding in administration. *ERS Spectrum 15*(4), 25–31.

———. (2000a). *Principles of power: Women superintendents and the riddle of the heart.* Albany: State University of New York Press.

———. (2000b). Unsettled moments in settled discourse: Women superintendents' experiences of inequality. *Educational Administration Quarterly 36*(1), 76–116.

Brunner, C. C., Grogan, M., and Prince, C. (2003a). Leadership on the Line—For women. In Sobehart, H. C. (Ed.). *Women Administrators Conference 2003 Monograph.* Pittsburgh, PA: Duquesne University School of Education Institute and the American Association of School Administrators.

———. (2003b). The American Association of School Administrators' national study of women superintendents and central office administrators: Early findings. A paper presented at the Annual Meeting of the American Educational Research Association, Chicago.

Butler, D., and Geis, F. (1990). Nonverbal affect responses to male and female leaders: Implications for leadership evaluations. *Journal of Personality and Social Psychology 58*(1), 48–59.

Carli, L. L. (2001). Gender and social influence. *Journal of Social Issues 57*(4), 725–741. Cited in Lips, H. M. (2003). *A new psychology of women: Gender culture, and ethnicity.* Boston: McGraw Hill.

Carter, G. R., and Cunningham, W. G. (1997). *The American school superintendent: Leading in an age of pressure.* San Francisco: Jossey-Bass.

Catalyst. (2004a, June 24). Statistical overview of women and diversity in the workplace. Retrieved August 8, 2004, from http://www.catalystwomen.org.

———. (2004b, June 28). Women's earnings and income. Retrieved August 28, 2004, from http://www.catalystwomen.org.

Chapman, C. H. (1997). *On becoming a superintendent: Challenges of school district leadership.* Upper Saddle River, NJ: Prentice-Hall.

College Board. (2005). Advanced placement report to the nation. Retrieved April 27, 2004, from http://www.collegeboard.com/pro.downloads/about/news_info/ap2005/ap_report_nation.pdf.

Craig, R. M., and Hardy, J. T. (1996, October). Should I be a superintendent? A feminine perspective. *American Secondary Education 6*, 17–22.

Criswell, M., and Betz, L. (1995). Attitudes toward women administrators among school board members: A current perspective. In Irby, B. J., and Brown, G. (Eds.). *Women as school executives: Voices and visions.* Huntsville, TX: Sam Houston State University.

Czaja, M., and Herman, M. (1997, December 20). Excessive school district superintendent turnover: An explorative study in Texas. *International Electronic Journal for Leadership in Learning 6.*

Dana, J. (2006). Differentiating dismissal factors for women and men public school superintendents. Manuscript in progress.

DuFour, R. (1998). *Professional learning communities at work: Best practices for enhancing student achievement.* Bloomington, IN: National Educational Service.

Dunlap, D. M., and Schmuck, P. A. (1995). *Women leading in education.* Albany: State University of New York Press.

Eagly, A. H., Makhigini, M. G., and Klonsky, B. K. (1992). Gender and the evaluation of leaders: A meta-analysis. *Psychological Bulletin 111*(1), 3–22.

Eakle, S. (1995). Going where few women have gone. *Thrust for Educational Leadership 24*(6), 16–21. Cited in Craig, R. M., and Hardy, J. T. (1996, October).

Should I be a superintendent? A feminine perspective. *American Secondary Education 6*, 17–22.

Edson, S. K. (1988). *Pushing the limits, the female administrative aspirant.* Albany: State University of New York Press.

———. (1995). Ten years later: Too little, too late? In Dunlap, D. M., and Schmuck, P. A. (Eds.). *Women leading in education.* Albany: State University of New York Press.

Estes, C. P. (1992). *Women who run with the wolves: Myths and stories of the wild women archetype.* New York: Ballantine Books.

Evans, G. (2000). *Play like a man, win like a woman: What men know about success that women need to learn.* New York: Broadway Books.

———. (2003a). She wins, we win: Remarks from a keynote presentation. In Sobehart, H. C. (Ed.). *Leadership on the Line: Standing Up for Public Education.* AASA Women Administrators Conference 2003 Monograph. Pittsburgh, PA: Duquesne University School of Education Leadership Institute and American Association of School Administrators.

———. (2003b). *She wins, you win: The most important rule every businesswoman needs to know.* New York: Gotham Books.

Faludi, S. (1991). *Backlash: The undeclared war against American women.* New York: Crown Publishers.

Farkas, S., Johnson, J., and Folina, T. (2000). A sense of calling: Who teaches and why? Retrieved August 30, 2004, from http://www.publicagenda.org.

Farmer, E. (1993). Paying our rent. In Brown, G., and Irby, B. J. (Eds.). *Women as school executives: A powerful paradigm.* Huntsville, TX: Sam Houston Press.

Federal Glass Ceiling Commission. (1995, November). *A Solid Investment— Making Full Use of the Nation's Human Capital. A Report.* Washington, DC: U.S. Department of Labor.

Fowler, F. C. (2004). *Policy studies for educational leaders: An introduction.* Upper Saddle River, NJ: Merrill Prentice Hall.

Friere, P. (1970). *Pedagogy of the oppressed.* New York: Seabury Press. Cited in Funk, C. (2004, Winter). Female leaders in educational administration: Sabotage within our own ranks. *Advancing Women Leadership Journal.* Retrieved on March 2, 2005, from http://www.advancingwomen.com/awl/winter2004/Funk.html.

Fullan, M. G., and Stiegelbauer, S. (1991). *The new meaning of educational change.* New York: Teachers College Press. Cited in Salsberry, T. C. (1998). Speaking of change. In Funk, C., Pankake, A., and Reese, M. (Eds.). (1998). *Women as school executives: Realizing the vision.* Commerce, TX: Texas A&M University.

Funk, C. (1993). Leadership in school administration: The female advantage. In Brown, G., and Irby, B. J. (Eds.). *Women as school executives: A powerful paradigm.* Huntsville, TX: Sam Houston Press.

———. (2004a, Winter). Female leaders in educational administration: Sabotage within our own ranks. *Advancing Women Leadership Journal.* Retrieved on March 2, 2005, from http://www.advancingwomen.com/awl/winter2004/Funk.html.

———. (2004b, Spring). Outstanding female superintendents: Profiles to leadership. *Advancing Women in Leadership Journal.* Retrieved August 16, 2004, from http://www.advancingwomen.com/awl/spring2004.

Gardiner, M. E., Enomoto, E., and Grogan, M. (2000). *Coloring outside the lines.* Albany: State University of New York.

Gardner, J. (2000). The nature of leadership. In *The Jossey-Bass Reader on Educational Leadership.* San Francisco: Jossey-Bass.

Geis, M. (1987). The language of politics. Cited in Tannen, D. (1990). *You just don't understand: Women and men in conversation.* New York: Ballantine Books.

Gideon Bibles in the Schools. (2001, June/July). *Freedom Writer.* Retrieved October 23, 2004, from http://www.buildingequality.us/ifas/fw/9107.bibles.html.

Gilligan, C. (1982). *In a different voice: Psychological theory and women's development.* Cambridge, MA: Harvard University Press.

Ginn, L. W. (1989). A quick look at the past, present and future of women in public school administration. *Research in Education.* RIE Document Reproduction, No. ED 3310 498.

Glass, T. E. (1992). *The 1992 study of the American school superintendency: America's educational leaders in a time of reform.* Arlington, VA: American Association of School Administrators.

———. (2000, June). Where are all the women superintendents? *The School Administrator Web Edition,* 1–8. Retrieved September 13, 2004, from http://www.aasa.org/publications/sa/2000_06/glass.htm.

Glass, T. E., Bjork, L., and Brunner, C. C. (2000). *The study of the American school superintendency 2000: A look at the superintendent of education in the new millennium.* Arlington, VA: American Association of School Administrators.

Glasser, W. (1998). *Choice theory: A new psychology of personal freedom.* Chatsworth, CA: The William Glasser Institute.

Goldberg, M. (2001, June). Leadership in education: Five commonalties. *Phi Delta Kappan 82*(10), 757–761.

Grady, M., and Bohling-Phillipi, V. (1988). Now that we have all those women graduate students, how should we train them? *NFEAS Journal 5*(1), 85–90. Cited in Avila, L. (1993). Why women are ready for educational leadership positions. In Brown, C., and Ivy, B. J. (Eds.). *Women as school executives: A powerful paradigm.* Huntsville, TX: Sam Houston Press.

Grady, M. L. (1992) Women in educational administration: Certified but not employed. *Educational Considerations, 20*(1), 33–36.

Grady, M. L., LaCost, B. Y., Wendel, F. C., and Krumm, B. L. (1998). A pernicious problem: The absence of women from administrative roles. In Funk, C., Pankake, A., and Reese, M. (Eds.). *Women as school executives: Realizing the vision*. Commerce: Texas A&M University–Commerce Press.

Grogan, M. (1996). *Voices of women aspiring to the superintendency*. Albany: State University of New York Press.

Growe, R., and Montgomery, R. (2002). Women and the leadership paradigm: Bridging the gender gap. *National Forum Journal*. Retrieved June 20, 2002, from http://www.nationalforum.com.

Grunig, J. E., and Hunt, T. (1984). *Managing public relations*. New York: Rinehart and Winston.

Gupton, S. L., and Slick, G. A. (1996). *Highly successful women administrators: The inside stories of how they got there*. Thousand Oaks, CA: Corwin Press.

Gutek, G. L. (1991). *An historical introduction to American education*. Prospect Heights, IL: Waveland Press.

Hall, S. (1833). Lectures to school-masters on teaching. Cited in Gutek, G. L. (1991). *An historical introduction to American education*. Prospect Heights, IL: Waveland Press.

Harris, S., Lowery, S., and Arnold, M. (2002, Winter). When women educators are commuters in a commuter marriage. *Advancing Women in Leadership Journal*. Retrieved January 15, 2005, from http://www.advancingwomen.com/awl/winter2002/index.html.

Helgeson, S. (1990). *The female advantage: Women's ways of leadership*. New York: Doubleday.

Hess, F. M. (2002). *School boards at the dawn of the 21st century: Conditions and challenges of district governance. A report*. Arlington, VA: National School Boards Association.

Hibert, K. M. (2000). Mentoring leadership. *Phi Delta Kappan 82*(1), 16–18.

Hodgkinson, H., and Montenegro, X. (1999). *The U.S. school superintendent: The invisible CEO*. Washington, DC: Institute for Educational Leadership.

Hopkins-Thompson, P. A. (2000). Colleagues helping colleagues: Mentoring and coaching. *NASSP Bulletin 84*(617), 29–36.

Houston, P. (2001, February). Superintendents for the 21st century: It's not just a job, it's a calling. *Phi Delta Kappan 82*(6), 428–433.

Hoy, W. K., and Miskel, C. G. (2005). *Educational administration: Theory, research, and practice*. Boston, MA: McGraw Hill.

Hudson, J., and Rea, D. (1998, Summer). Advancing women in leadership: teacher's perceptions of women in the principalship a current perspective. *Advancing Women in Leadership Journal*. Retrieved October 20, 2004, from http://www.advancingwomen.com/awl/summer1998/index.html.

Interstate School Leaders Licensure Consortium. (1996). *Standards for school leaders*. Washington, DC: Council of Chief State School Officers.

Jacobs, J. (2002, Winter). Can you be an effective principal when you don't smoke, swing a club, or ride a Harley? *Advancing Women in Leadership Journal*. Retrieved January 15, 2005, from http://www.advancingwomen.com/awl/winter2002/index.html.

Kamler, E., and Shakeshaft, C. (1999). Career paths of women superintendents. In Brunner, C. C. (Ed.). *Sacred dreams: Women and the superintendency*. Albany: State University of New York Press.

Keller, B. (1999, November 10). Across the nation: Leadership: A special report. Woman superintendents: Few and far between. *Education Week 19*(11), 1.

Lichtenberg, R. (2004). Double standards. Retrieved September 23, 2004, from http://www.womensmedia.com/business-meyerson/double/standards.htm.

Lindle, J. C. (1990). Coping in the superintendency: Gender-related perspectives. A paper presented at the University Council of Educational Administration Convention, Pittsburgh, Pennsylvania. Cited in Pavan, B. N. (1999). The first years: What should a female superintendent know beforehand? In Brunner, C. C. (Ed.). *Sacred dreams*. Albany: State University of New York Press.

Lips, H. M. (2000). College students' visions of power and possibility as mediated by gender. *Psychology of Women Quarterly 24* (1), 37–41. Cited in Lips, H. M. (2003). A new psychology of women: Gender, culture, and ethnicity. Boston, MA: McGraw Hill, p. 179.

———. (2003). *A new psychology of women*. Boston, MA: McGraw Hill.

Lott, B. (1985). The devaluation of women's competence. *Journal of Social Issues 41*(4), 43–60. Cited in Lips, H. M. (2003). *A new psychology of women*. Boston, MA: McGraw Hill.

Lunenburg, F. C., and Ornstein, A. C. (2004). *Educational administration: Concepts and practices*. Belmont, CA: Wadsworth/Thomson Learning.

Lynch, K. K. (1990, August). Women in school administration: Overcoming the barriers to advancement. *Women's Educational Equity Act Digest No. 2*. Newton, MA: U.S. Department of Education. ERIC Document ED 360753.

Matthews, E. N. (1995). Women in educational administration: Views of equity. In Dunlap, D. M., and Schmuck, P. A. (Eds.). *Women leading in education*. Albany: State University of New York Press, 247–265.

McCabe, D., Ricciardi, D., and Jamison, M. (2000). Listening to principals as customers: Administrators evaluate practice-based preparation. *Planning and Changing 31*(3–4), 206–225.

Mehra, A., Kilduff, M., and Brass, D. J. (1998). At the margins: A distinctiveness approach to the social identity and social networks of underrepresented groups. *Academy of Management Journal 41*(4), 441–452.

Members of the U.S. Senate. Retrieved May 1, 2005, from http://www.email yoursenator.com/senators.html.

Meyerson, D., and Fletcher, J. (2000). A modest manifesto for shattering the glass ceiling. *Harvard Business Review (78)*1, 125–136.

Miller, S. (2002). Teacher leadership for effective schools. A report prepared for the Oregon Education Association, July 2002. Retrieved on April 11, 2004, from http://www.ous.edu/aca/SAELP/OEA_ldrshp.

Morrison, A. (1992). New solutions to the same old glass ceiling. *Women in Management Review 7*(4), 15–19.

Mountford, M. (2004). Motives of power of school board members: Implications for the school board-superintendent relationships. *Educational Administration Quarterly 40*(5), 704–741.

National Commission on Excellence in Education. (1983, April). *A nation at risk: The imperative for educational reform*. Washington, DC: United States Department of Education.

National Women's History Project. (1997–2002). Timeline of legal history of women in the United States. Retrieved March 22, 2005, from http://www .legacy98.org/timeline.html.

Office of the Clerk. (2005). House of Representatives of the United States. Retrieved May 1, 2005, from http://clerk.house.gov/members/olmbr.html.

Okin, S. M. (1989). *Justice, gender and the family*. New York: Basic Books.

Orenstein, P. (1994). *School girls, young women, self esteem and the confidence gap*. New York: Bantam Doubleday Dell Publishing.

Ortiz, A. M., and Marshall, C. (1988). Women in educational administration: A project of AERA. Cited in Bogan, N. J. (Ed.). *Handbook of research on educational administration*. New York: Longman.

Pardini, P. (1999, February). "When termination's in the air." School Administrator Web Edition. Retrieved March 19, 2005, from http://www.aasa.org/ publications/sa/1999_02/pardini.htm.

Pavan, B. N. (1999). The first years: What should a female superintendent know beforehand? In Brunner, C. C. (Ed.). *Sacred dreams: Women and the superintendency*. Albany: State University of New York Press.

Public Agenda. (2005, September). Poverty rate rises for fourth straight year. Retrieved September 23, 2005, from http://www.publicagenda.org/headlines/ headlines2.

Reed, J. (1999). Running against hurricane "W," scrambling for dollars. Elizabeth Dole was raised to be in control. Now she's trying to keep smiling in a storm. *Newsweek 134*(2), 28. Cited in Lips, H. M. (2003). *A new psychology of women*. Boston, MA: McGraw Hill.

Reese, M. (1993) Rethinking the paradigm: The potential effect on aspiring women administrators. In Brown, G., and Irby, B. J. (Eds.). *Women as school executives: A powerful paradigm*. Huntsville, TX: Sam Houston University Press.

Reskin, B. F. (1998). Bringing the men back in: Sex differentiation and the devaluation of women's work. Cited in Myers, K. A., Anderson, C. D., and Risman, B. J. (Eds.). Feminist foundations: Toward transforming sociology. *Gender and Society Readers 3*, 278–298.

Reyes, A. (2003). The relationship of mentoring to job placement in school administration. *NASSP Bulletin 87*(635), 45–64.

Reynolds, C. (2002). Changing gender scripts and moral dilemmas for women and men in education, 1940–1970. *Women and school leadership. International perspectives*. Albany: University of New York Press, 29–48.

Ringel, J., Gates, S., Chaung, C., Brown, A., and Ghosh-Dastidar, B. (2004). *Career paths of school administrators in Illinois: Insight from an analysis of state data*. Santa Monica, CA: Wallace Foundation, Rand.

Ruderman, M. N., and Ohlott, P. J. (2002). *Standing at the crossroads: Next steps for high achieving women*. San Francisco: Jossey-Bass.

Rudman, L. A. (1998). Self-promotion as a risk factor for women. The costs and benefits of counter-stereotypical impression management. *Journal of Personality and Social Psychology 74*, 629–645. Cited in Lips, H. M. (2003). *A new psychology of women*. Boston, MA: McGraw Hill.

Salsberry, T. C. (1998). Speaking of change. In Funk, C., Pankake, A., and Reese, M. (Eds.). *Women as school executives: Realizing the vision*. Commerce: Texas A&M University Press, 68–72.

Sanders, J. (2002). Something is missing from teacher education: Attention to two genders. *Phi Delta Kappan 84*(3), 241–244.

Schein, E. H. (1992). *Organizational culture and leadership*. 2nd edition. San Francisco: Jossey-Bass.

Schmuck, P. A. (1999). Foreword. In Brunner, C. C. (Ed.). *Sacred dreams: Women and the superintendency*. Albany: State University of New York Press.

Schmuck, P. A., Hollingsworth, S., and Lock, R. (2002). Women administrators and the point of exit: Collision between the person and the institution. Cited in Reynolds, C. *Women and school leadership: International perspectives*. Albany, NY: State University of New York Press, 93–110.

Seitel, F. P. (1998) *The practice of public relations*. 6th edition. New York: Macmillan.

Shakeshaft, C. (1995). Foreword. In Dunlap, D. M., and Schmuck, P. A. (Eds.). *Women leading in education*. Albany: State University of New York Press, xi–xiv.

———. (1989). *Women in educational administration*. Newberry Park, CA: Sage Publications.

———. (2000). Foreword. In Brunner, C. C. *Principles of power: Women superintendents and the riddle of the heart*. Albany: State University of New York.

Short, B. (2004, June 24). New catalyst study finds female executives just as likely as male colleagues to aspire to CEO jobs. Retrieved August 8, 2004, from http://www.catalystwomen.org.

Skrla, L., Reyes, P., and Joseph-Scheurich, J. (2000, February). Sexism, silence and solutions: Women superintendents speak up and speak out. *Educational Administration Quarterly 36*(1): 44–75.

Skrla, L. B. (2000a). Mourning silence: Women superintendents (and a researcher) rethink speaking up and speaking out. *Qualitative Studies in Education 13*(6), 611–628.

———. (2000b). The social construction of gender in the superintendency. *Journal of Educational Policy 15*(3), 293–316.

Skrla, L. B., and Benestante, J. J. (1998). On being terminally female: Denial of sexism in educational administration is no protection against its effects. In Funk, C., Pankake, A., and Reese, M. (Eds.). *Women as school executives: Realizing the vision*. Commerce: Texas A&M University.

Symes, B., and Sharpe, C. (2005, April 21). Networking 101. A presentation at the Saint Louis University Fifth Annual U.S. Bank Women in Leadership Spring Conference, St. Louis, Missouri.

Tallerico, M. (2000). *Accessing the superintendency*. Thousand Oaks, CA: Corwin Press.

Tallerico, M., and Burstyn., J. N. (1996). Retaining women in the superintendency: The location matters. *Educational Administration Quarterly 32*(Supplement), 642–664.

———. (2004, December). Women and the superintendency: Insights from theory and history. *Educational Administration Quarterly 40*(5), 633–662.

Tallerico, M., and Tingley, S. (2001, November). The leadership mismatch: An alternative view. *The School Administrator Web Edition*. Retrieved February 24, 2005, from http://www.aasa.org/publication/sa/2001_11/Tallerico.htm.

Tannen, D. (1990). *You just don't understand: Women and men in conversation*. New York: Ballantine Books.

U.S. Senate. (2005). Senators of the 109th Congress. Retrieved May 1, 2005, from http://www.senate.gov/general/contact_information/senators_cfm.cfm.

Usdan, M. (2001, April). Leadership for student learning: Redefining the teacher as leader. Project prepared for the Institute of Educational Leadership. Retrieved April 11, 2004, from http://www.iel.org.

Watkins, R. M., Herrin, M., and McDonald, L. (1998). The juxtaposition of career and family: A dilemma for professional women. *Journal of Advancing Women*. Retrieved May 26, 2005, from http://www.advancingwomen.com/balancing/career_family_dilemma.html.

Webster's New Universal Unabridged Dictionary. (1996). New York: Barnes and Noble.

Westerhaus, T. (2004, February 1). A killing and a crowning: A story of two superintendents facing similar forces but needing vastly different outcomes. *The School Administrator Web Edition*. Retrieved January 10, 2005, from http://www.aasa.org.

Women deserve equal pay for equal work. (2004, November 22). *News Leader*. Springfield, MO: News Leader.

Woody, B. W., and Weiss, C. (1994). *Barriers to work place advancement: The experience of the white female work force. A report.* The Glass Ceiling Commission. Washington, DC: U.S. Department of Labor, 1–13.

Wynne, J. (2001, November). Teachers as leaders in educational reform. *ERIC Digest*. Washington, D.C.: U.S. Department of Education.

Zafarullah, H. (2000). Through the brick wall and glass ceiling: Women in the civil service in Bangladesh. *Gender, Work, and Organization* 7(3), 197–209. In Lips, H. M. (2003). *A new psychology of women.* Boston, MA: McGraw Hill.